Ireland's National Theaters

Sanford Sternlicht, *Series Editor*

Denis Gwynn as "Fionn" in the St. Enda's production of *The Coming of Fionn* (1909). *Courtesy of Pearse Museum, Dublin*

IRELAND'S
National Theaters

Political Performance and the Origins
of the Irish Dramatic Movement

Mary Trotter

Syracuse University Press

First Edition 2001
01 02 03 04 05 06   6 5 4 3 2 1

The paper used in this publication meets the minimum requirements of
American National Standard for Information Sciences—Permanence of
Paper for Printed Library Materials, ANSI Z39.48–1984.∞™

Library of Congress Cataloging-in-Publication Data
Trotter, Mary.
Ireland's national theaters : political performance and the origins of the Irish dramatic
movement / Mary Trotter.
p. cm.—(Irish studies)
Includes bibliographical references and index.
ISBN 0-8156-2888-9 (alk. paper)—ISBN 0-8156-2889-7 (pbk. : alk. paper)
1. Theater—Political aspects—Ireland—History—20th century. 2. Theater—Political
aspects—Ireland—History—19th century. 3. Irish drama—20th century—History and
criticism. 4. Irish drama—19th century—History and criticism. I. Title. II. Irish studies
(Syracuse, N.Y.)
PN2601.T76 2001
792'.09417'09034—dc21   00-046218

Manufactured in the United States of America

To Tom and Gania Trotter,
from their kid

Mary Trotter is an assistant professor of English at Indiana University–Purdue University at Indianapolis. She has presented her research nationally and has published several articles and book chapters on an array of Irish theater subjects, including the Field Day Theatre Company, contemporary Northern Irish women playwrights, and the riots surrounding *The Playboy of the Western World*.

Contents

Acknowledgments

JUST AS CREATING a national theater movement is a collaborative act, so is the process of writing a book, and I wish to mention my gratitude to key contributors to the writing of this work. William B. Worthen mentored this project from its inception, and I am grateful for both his shrewd guidance and his constant optimism and excitement about all my projects. Christine Froula's excellent editorial analysis taught me much about both this book and writing and research generally. T. William Heyck helped me make sense of the ornate politics of the nationalist movement and helped me comprehend Irish theater in a clearer historical context.

The above scholars and friends mentored this project most closely, but I also owe a debt to other teachers. Particularly, Tracy C. Davis taught me the delicious rigors of historical research, and Elizabeth Cullingford exposed me for the first time to contemporary Irish critical discourse. I still strive to adapt to my own projects the discipline and grace inherent in their work. And the influence of other teachers— especially Sandra Richards, Margaret Thompson Drewal, Ronald Schuchard, and James W. Flannery—informs all of my work.

Colleagues in the field have generously contributed their time and advice. Stephen Watt always provided inspiring *craic* concerning my research. Janelle G. Reinelt's conversation, her editing of some of my other projects, and her personal and professional encouragement were elemental to seeing this book come to fruition. Likewise, Margot Gayle Backus, John P. Harrington, Charlotte Headrick, Madonne Miner,

Marilynn Richtaryk, and Sanford Sternlicht, among many, provided important advice about the book.

The archival work for this project was facilitated tremendously by the generous economic assistance of the Center for Humanities at Northwestern University, the Graduate School at Northwestern University, the American Society for Theatre Research, and a Gloria Lyerla Research Grant from Texas Tech University. Once I got to the archives, librarians and archivists—especially Russel Maylone of the Deering Special Collections at Northwestern University, Turlough Breathneach at the Pearse Museum in Dublin, and Maire Kennedy at the Dublin Public Library—answered my queries with patient and thorough care. I also wish to thank Elizabeth Myers and Amy Farranto of Syracuse University Press for supporting the publication of this manuscript.

Parts of the third chapter are adapted from "Women's Work: *Inghinidhe na hEireann* and the Irish Dramatic Movement," in *Crucibles of Crisis: Performing Social Change,* edited by Janelle Reinelt (1996). Also, a version of my discussion of the *Playboy of the Western World* riots appeared in *Theatre Survey* 39, no. 2 (1998). Grateful thanks to University of Michigan Press and Georgetown University Press, respectively, for permission to reprint some of the ideas that originally appeared in their publications.

Finally, thanks to friends and colleagues at Texas Tech University, Northwestern University, and the University of Texas at Austin for providing friendship as well as intellectual and emotional support throughout the conceiving, writing, and revising of this book. My sisters, Ruth Trotter and Tania Batson, and my brother-in-law, Greg Batson, were always as close as a telephone and ready to provide a sense of perspective and a good laugh. Most of all, I wish to thank my parents, F. Thomas Trotter and Gania Trotter, for their unconditional love, support, and encouragement. I dedicate this project to them.

Introduction

National Formations, Theatrical Formations

CREATORS OF A NATION do not exactly identify a community out of which to build their state so much as they imagine one, establishing a sense of commonality among a people that overrides the ideological and cultural differences within the national group.[1] In Ireland's case, cultural nationalists sought this national common ground by resurrecting and rewriting a body of national myths, thus promoting an ideology of common heritage, tradition, and belief. Every Irish person—a fisherman in Connemara, a clerk in Waterford, an estate owner in Galway, a mother in Cork, an intellectual in Dublin, a casual worker in Killarney, a factory worker in Belfast—needed to feel some sense of common ground, a shared past, and an interrelated future.

The promotion of Irish culture through performance was an important vehicle for asserting a sense of Irish identity among nationalist groups at the turn of the twentieth century.[2] Although Ireland had been officially a part of the United Kingdom in an uneasy relationship since 1800,[3] England's authority over its western neighbor continued

---

1. See Anderson 1991 and Hobsbawm 1992.

2. For discussions on the relevance of creating a cultural myth to solidify the idea of the nation, see Hobsbawm 1991, 9–13.

3. The Irish people had little if any say in the government of Ireland until the establishment of the Irish Parliament (Grattan's Parliament) in 1788. That governing body

to foster anticolonial sentiment and protest among Irish nationalists. The task for the Irish nationalist in the face of this economic and cultural oppression was to set herself or himself culturally apart from both British identity and the British caricature of Irish personality. Yet the idea of Irish culture—much less the plans for building an independent Ireland—differed greatly among nationalist groups. To speak of cultural identity in turn-of-the-century Ireland, therefore, is to speak of a range of Irish—and English—national identities, tempered by individual class, gender, and religious positions. Nationalist artists were integral parts of this cultural discourse and political protest, for their work performed two important functions for the Irish cause. Their retellings of Irish history, myths, and folktales developed counterhegemonic representations of Ireland and also attempted to create what Eric Hobsbawm (1991) terms an "invented tradition" of common cultural history for Irish persons of different class and religious backgrounds. Political theater in turn-of-the-century Ireland became (as it continues to be) an important site for these negotiations between nationalist ideologies and the people these ideologies claimed to represent: ideas about forming the Irish state were practiced in performance.

The idea that theater plays a role in nation formation is not unique to Ireland. In *Melodramatic Formations, American Theatre and Society, 1820–1870* (1992), Bruce A. McConachie illustrates the vital ways in which aesthetics and politics as well as audience and performance adapted reciprocally over time during that particularly fecund period in American culture. He bases his historical and critical inquiries on an adaptation of Tony Bennett's notion of the reading formation: "an attempt to think of context as a set of discursive and intertextual determinations, operating on material and institutional supports, which bear in upon a text not just externally, from the outside in, but internally, shaping it—in the historically concrete forms in which it is available as a text-to-be-read—from the inside out" (Bennett qtd. in McConachie 1992,

dissolved with the establishment of the Act of Union in 1800, giving the Irish representation in the British Parliament, but not home rule.

xi-xii). This contextual process is even more obvious in performance practice, in which, as McConachie puts it,

> Audiences shape performances over time, encouraging or discouraging elements of dramatic style, certain character types, and various acting conventions. At the same time, similar performances are shaping the audience, driving away some spectators from the theatre and pulling in others eager to be entertained and persuaded in ways particular to these productions. In effect, groups of spectators and theatre performers produce each other from the inside out as artists-to-be-experienced and audiences-to-be-entertained in a given historical period. The result is what may be termed a theatrical formation, the mutual elaboration over time of historically specific audience groups and theatre practitioners participating in certain shared patterns of dramatic and theatrical action. (1992, xi-xii)

The more self-conscious the theater is in its role in identity production, the more defined the audience's politics, the more apparent this reciprocal relationship. A national (or nationalist) theater and its audience clearly are aware of each one's role in making ideological meaning—in its particular theatrical formation. What makes the Irish case especially exciting in the context of national formation and theatrical formation is the heterogeneity of politics and aesthetics in the germinal years of the Irish dramatic movement. Several Irish theaters of resistance fought against the political, cultural, and theatrical hegemonies of the British Empire in Ireland during the turn of the century, but exactly what they were fighting for (besides Irish autonomy) and how they were to fight for it (besides through performance) differed from group to group.

Irish nationalist organizations developed theater companies to create a sense of cultural identity among the Irish people outside the colonial definition of Ireland already well established on the English stage. The Gaelic League performed short folk plays in Irish and tableaux on Irish mythic themes. Inghinidhe na hEireann (the Daughters of Erin) performed *ceilithe* and tableaux celebrating Ireland's great women heroes. The boys at Padraic Pearse's school performed heroic dramas on the school grounds. Occasionally, professional theaters joined in the discourse by performing their own versions of Irish nationalism, as when the Queen's Royal Theatre produced patriotic, sentimental dramas about Ireland's revolutionary history. The establishment of the Abbey Theatre in the midst of these nationalist performance activities and the interest it aroused point to Ireland's commitment to cultural legitimation through theater. Yet the theater in all its forms provided more than a means of resisting English domination; it provided an important field on which nationalist groups—each with its own ideas of what made up Irish nationhood—vied for political legitimacy. This energetic and vital theater scene has all but disappeared from most accounts of the Irish dramatic movement in favor of a narrative that focuses on the Irish Literary Theatre (1899–1901) and the company that became the National Theatre Society, Ltd.—that is, the Abbey Theatre (1903-present). The Irish Literary Theatre and the Abbey Theatre occupy exclusive places in Irish theater history for several reasons. One of the clearer reasons is the stature of their chief personnel: W. B. Yeats, Lady Augusta Gregory, George Moore, and Edward Martyn in the Irish Literary Theatre; Yeats, Gregory, and J. M. Synge at the Abbey. All had significant literary reputations during and after their tenure as workers for the Irish Literary Theatre or the Abbey, and their literary credentials gave their project a degree of intellectual respectability not afforded the projects of amateur playwrights, making their work more visible to audiences, critics, and, later, historians.

Unlike other theater groups, in which artistic and administrative authority is spread across a wide swath of personnel, the directors of these two theaters retained high visibility and complete authority over their companies. They wrote and produced most of the plays, and their money and influence controlled the persons they hired as actors. Because only a few individuals made significant decisions in these companies, they developed and maintained relatively straightforward, unified aesthetic and political agendas that are much easier to trace than those of less hierarchically structured performance groups.

Further, through their extensive publicity work, the Irish Literary Theatre and the Abbey directors made it even easier to follow the progress of their companies. Yeats tirelessly worked to keep the Irish

Literary Theatre and later the Abbey in the nationalist and artistic eyes of Ireland and the world through essays and editorials in the press and through his theater journals *Beltaine, Samhain,* and *The Arrow.* Both the nationalist community and the international art world responded with spirited interest to the philosophical and practical issues surrounding both the Irish Literary Theatre and the Abbey in reviews, essays, and letters, although from different perspectives and with different agendas. And beyond the public discourse, those involved in the Irish Literary Theatre wrote profusely about the project privately and, aware that they were involved in a history-making enterprise, often saved their writing. Adrian Frazier comments, "Those at the Abbey knew, even as they planned, that they were nation-building, that what they made was history; as a result, they recorded every day in the light of the age and kept very nearly every scrip of the multitudinous record" (1990, xxi). This activity left a broad paper trail for contemporary critics and audiences and, later, for theater historians. The care with which members of the Irish Literary Theatre and the Abbey wrote about their work is indeed fortunate, but also deceptive. In his lifetime, Yeats collected his essays on the theater in anthologies of his work. Lady Gregory published *Our Irish Theatre,* celebrating her version of the movement. George Moore's satiric look at the movement, *Hail and Farewell,* inspired not only a revenging drama from Edward Martyn in 1914 but added another record of the Irish literary renaissance that (inadvertently) focused the eyes of Irish theater historians on Yeats and his circle.

Most of the autobiographies, essays, reports, and interviews of Abbey and Irish Literary Theatre members are full of fascinating anecdotes and information, yet they are also glaringly subjective, as writers consciously and unconsciously rewrote their history in order to secure their place in the larger narrative of the movement or to smooth out rough spots in their own personal narratives. As the identity and goals of the two theaters and of their members changed, so they often rewrote their past in keeping with their current situation. George Moore's recollections of the Irish Literary Theatre, for example, read like satire instead of history, as Moore recounts the naïve idealism of the other directors in the face of his urbane knowledge of the European theater world. Although offering a largely fictional portrait of himself and the company, he characterizes in bold relief the attitudes, insecurities, and conflicts among the directors in those first years.[4] The emphasis these two companies placed on writing *about* their theaters reflects the importance they placed on writing *in* the theater. They focused primarily on developing dramatic texts—often to the detriment of issues of theatrical production.[5] Other nationalist theater groups worked with hastily written and formulaic dramas, and focused their energies on creating a theatrical moment of political efficacy. For the Irish Literary Theatre, performance was important, but mainly as a means of developing, promoting, and publishing a strong body of Irish dramatic literature.

But even for those who insist that the Abbey legacy of texts overshadows the less-polished, though more politically urgent, works of their contemporaries, the assumption that Irish nationalist theater received its main impetus from the Irish Literary Theatre and the Abbey creates several problems. It occludes political and aesthetic theater developments that were equally or more popular on the contemporaneous Dublin scene, thus hiding the density of cultural and political negotiations that occurred among various groups. It obscures the influences all the theaters had on one another as they competed for nationalist audiences or as theater practitioners and audience members participated in more than one theater. It maintains a bias of high over

4. Fictionalized autobiographies often more clearly reveal the biases of their authors, making them indeed relevant historical documents, and the form has been deftly employed by many Irish writers, including Sean O'Casey, Flann O'Brien, and Brendan Behan. Especially in situations in which a conscious awareness of history or myth making occurs, fictionalized accounts can provide insight into the attitude and mood of the times. See the example of Anonymous, *Primary Colors* (1996), an allegorical satire of the 1992 Clinton campaign. For critical analyses of the use of biography among Irish writers, see Kenneally 1989, 111–31.

5. Of course, performance was a vital issue in both theaters. The Fays' acting innovations and Yeats's symbolist ideas influenced notions about stage design that revolutionized Irish performance practice and would even influence other modern theater movements, such as the Little Theatre movement in the United States.

low art forms, a privileging of the literary quality of the text over the political efficacy of the performance. Finally, it examines what Irish drama gleaned from European theater movements, but overlooks the relevance of indigenous developments in performance and playwriting. Such an analysis denies or refigures the work of other individuals and groups in the development of the "Abbey Theatre aesthetic": Yeats learned from Alice Milligan of the Gaelic League as well as from Antoine of the Théâtre Libre.

The enormous volume of texts surrounding the Irish Literary Theatre, the Abbey Theatre, and their famous directors makes it difficult to discern the slippery borders between the image of these companies as icons of the Irish dramatic movement and their actual work in turn-of-the-century Dublin. But some historians have helped debunk the mythic assumptions and juicy gossip surrounding these theaters by constructing their arguments out of a shrewd analysis of contemporaneous documents—by eschewing or reframing evidence colored by its author's bias or focus. Adrian Frazier's *Behind the Scenes: Yeats, Horniman, and the Struggle for the Abbey Theatre* (1990) includes a chapter on the Irish Literary Theatre that reclaims the emotion and energy poured into both sides of the arguments regarding Yeats's play *The Countess Cathleen,* thus placing it within the larger historical, cultural, and religious arguments the play reflected for its audiences. Anne Saddlemyer's meticulously annotated selection of the letters of the Abbey Theatre directors, *Theatre Business* (1982), provides insight into that theater's active competition to be considered the developer of the true Irish aesthetic. Roy F. Foster's (1998) comprehensive biography of Yeats elegantly weaves the Abbey's theater practice into not only Yeats's other personal and artistic activities, but the activities of other performance groups. Such research does not serve to defame the Irish Literary Theatre or the Abbey Theatre and their directors, however. Rather, it complicates the myopic viewpoint that these companies emerged out of nothing but the minds of their directors—a notion generated to a large extent by the self-representations of the personalities involved.

My goal here is to reevaluate the traditional view of the creation of modern Irish drama at the turn of the twentieth century by interrogating how the representations of Irish culture by several nationalist groups contributed to the establishment of both Ireland's dramatic aesthetic and its national identity. Such an inquiry recovers the work of many forgotten or ignored actors, playwrights, and theater practitioners in the early Irish dramatic movement. It breaks up the traditional, linear narrative of the origin of the Irish dramatic movement by contextualizing the work of the Irish Literary Theatre and the Abbey in the creative nationalist milieu of Dublin performance. By looking at a broader range of nationalist performance practices, it also reevaluates the function of nationalist theater as a counterhegemonic tool in Ireland's colonial situation, an aspect of the Irish dramatic movement in its first decades that has not been sufficiently examined.

Each chapter presents a historical analysis of a particular theatrical representation of Irish nationhood and of the organization or institution from which that representation emerged. Along with this historical research, I point out how the dramatic and performance techniques of each theater reflect the intersection of the political and aesthetic goals of that theater. My research involves examining contemporaneous texts from and accounts of the nationalist activities and dramatic performances of each of these groups. I rely on interpretations of performances in primary accounts as well as in English and Irish newspapers and journals to derive a sense of audience response to the productions and of the larger influence of the theater on nationalist thought. I also reevaluate more recent history and criticism of Irish nationalist political movements and postcolonial critiques of Irish literature, seeking a more comprehensive strategy for interpreting the function of political theater in turn-of-the-century Ireland.

Chapter 1 examines the Irish Literary Theatre in the context of contemporaneous Dublin debates regarding the role of drama in the Celtic Revival and the performance activity of other nationalist groups, such as the Gaelic League. Chapter 2 examines the popular nationalist discourse of the Queen's Royal Theatre. The popular melodramas at this commercial house elucidated tensions between Irish resistance to English stereotypes and the potential for subversive, politicized readings of the melodramatic form. In chapter 3, the discussion moves into issues of both street and theatrical performance, of both politics and gender. It examines how Inghinidhe na hEireann (the Daughters of Erin) produced a space for women in the nationalist public sphere and, with the efforts of W. G. Fay, effectively trained the first group of Irish nationalist actors. These actors formed the core of the theater group that is the subject of chapter 4, the Irish National Theatre Society, better known as the Abbey Theatre. In this chapter, we see the Irish National Theatre Society change from a democratic, nationalist endeavor into an increasingly hierarchical, professional theater company. The establishment of the Abbey Theatre building, further, raises questions about the company as both an ideological and physical site for nationalist discourse and its viability as a national theater. Finally, chapter 5 explores the rhetoric of martyrdom and redemption enacted in the plays of Padraic Pearse, as performed by the students at his nationalist schools, St. Enda's School for Boys and St. Ita's School for Girls. This discussion also interrogates how the plays served as ideological training grounds for his followers, reflecting the mystic nationalism that led to the bloody drama of Easter week 1916.

This inquiry is designed to broaden the historical and critical understanding of political performance in the first decades of the Irish dramatic movement. But in order to do that, I found it necessary to limit my discussion in particular ways. Nationalist performance activity could be found throughout Ireland, with important movements in Belfast, Cork, and other communities, but this project deals almost exclusively with Dublin performance practice. Dublin was unique in the number, intensity, and diversity of political performance events going on there, as nationalist groups shared the same actors, playwrights, and spaces to perform their ideas of the Irish nation. By analyzing this one community, I was able to track more clearly the direct influences of groups and individuals on one another.

Each chapter covers a group that reflects an important aspect of the conflicts and collaborations of the diverse nationalist milieu of turn-of-the-century Ireland. Other companies—such as the National Players Society, the Theatre of Ireland, and the Independent Dramatic Company—provided their own contributions to the movement. I discuss them in this book, but not in the detail they ultimately deserve, and I hope mentioning them here will promote further interest in their work. The Gaelic League's performance work merits its own book: its activity was a constant, nationwide presence throughout the Celtic Revival. I have chosen to represent the Gaelic League in a way that reflects its omnipresent role in the theater movement: every chapter comments on concurrent activity in the Gaelic League or on that society's influence on each company's practice.

Each chapter describes a national theater in that the work of each theater was designed on some level to be a site for representing and building the Irish nation. But the performances on those stages were inevitably fragments of Ireland's cultural picture in the complex work of imagining the nation. When the Abbey celebrated its subsidy in 1904 from the British and politically unsympathetic Annie Horniman and claimed for itself the title "national theater," it likewise claimed the dominant position in political and theatrical discourse as arbitrator of national dramatic standards in the Irish nationalist movement. The Abbey was indeed a vital part of the Irish dramatic movement, and its work was constantly observed, critiqued, interrogated, praised, and condemned throughout the first decades of this century. But so was the work of other groups. The Abbey claimed the laurel of Ireland's representative national house too soon.

In December 1898, Lady Augusta Gregory—philanthropist, Irish-language enthusiast, and folklore collector—held a party at Coole for the county workhouse children. Among the events that day was a Punch and Judy show performed in Irish (Dunleavy and Dunleavy 1991, 216). The children laughed to recognize the Irish turns of phrase they heard in their own homes—to be entertained at an Anglo-Irish big house in the language that had been shunned from Ireland's national schools since the 1830s. The adults might have been aware that one of the bastions of English children's entertainment—the Punch and Judy show, a performance trope imported from the continent centuries before—was being reappropriated for the use and pleasure of an Irish audience.

The puppeteers were the Gaelic Leaguer Norma Borthwick and Douglas Hyde, the president of the organization devoted to the "de-Anglicisation" of Ireland and later the first president of the Republic of Ireland. This anecdotal performance, one of thousands in the first decade of the Celtic Revival, encapsulates some of the most prescient issues of nationalist performance. The political power of performing Irish language and culture, the dilemma over how to adapt English or European theatrical models, the ways the political convictions of the performers, producers, and audience members shaped or were shaped by the event—all come into play in thinking about this children's entertainment.

In 1906, when Hyde was lecturing in San Francisco, a reporter reminded him of this Irish Punch and Judy show, saying that Lady Gregory had claimed that it was "the beginning of modern Irish drama."[6] Hyde laughed but insisted that the credit for the Irish dramatic movement belonged to another collaborator of Lady Gregory, William Butler Yeats. Both comments were clearly light-hearted compliments among three old friends. A year before this puppet show, Gregory had been actively involved in starting the Irish Literary Theatre. Hyde recognized Yeats's contribution to Irish dramatic literature and the international attention Yeats garnered for the Irish dramatic movement, but he was also intimately aware of dramatic efforts by groups such as his own Gaelic League throughout the 1890s and of Lady Gregory's important work as a playwright and producer. Both comments—Gregory's overstatement of her friend's production as an originating event and Hyde's erasure of the relevance of other kinds of nationalist performance in favor of a Yeats-centered version of Irish theater history—occlude the actual significance or even the existence of a diversity of Irish nationalist performance events that thrived during this period of the Celtic Revival.

This book seeks to recover such moments of political performance—to remember the collaborations and confrontations among indi-

6. "Dr. Douglas Hyde and the Irish National Theatre," *San Francisco Bulletin*, 18 February 1906, Abbey Theatre Papers, ms. 19, 845.

viduals, groups, and ideologies in creating the Irish dramatic movement. Examining such moments reveals a richer, more complex history
of the first years of the Irish dramatic movement, for just as Ireland's
idea of the nation was—and is—multivalent, so was—and is—its theater practice.

Ireland's National Theaters

I

"Ancient Idealism" on a Modern Stage
The Irish Literary Theatre

The aim and object of the Irish Literary Theatre was to embody and
perpetuate Irish feeling, genius and modes of thought. The Irish Literary Theatre was one, an important one, but still only one of the many
agencies which were [in 1900] at work in trying to create a new Ireland, proceeding upon national lines.

—"The Irish Literary Theatre,"
Irish Daily Independent, 22 February 1900

IN 1897, WILLIAM BUTLER YEATS, Lady Augusta Gregory,
George Moore, and Edward Martyn created a new theater company on
the already active landscape of Irish nationalist performance. They
poured enormous time, energy, and passion into establishing the Irish
Literary Theatre, a society devoted to creating a body of Irish drama
that would combine Ireland's rich cultural legacy with the latest European theatrical methods. Yeats hoped the company could "do in Dublin
something of what has been done in London and Paris" (Yeats 1975,
170): invent a theater for an elite few interested in moving beyond the
tropes of the commercial stage. In their three seasons, Yeats, Gregory,
and Martyn generated performances of seven plays; a journal related to
the theater; hundreds of letters, essays, and pamphlets written by the
founders and by others concerning their project; and international attention to the Irish literary revival.

By 1901, the directors had had enough. "Here are we," Yeats wrote

Lady Gregory after a particularly painful rehearsal, "a lot of intelligent people who might have been doing some sort of decent work that leaves the soul free . . . going through all sorts of trouble and annoyance for a mob that knows neither literature nor art" (qtd. in Gregory 1913, 28–29). They terminated the Irish Literary Theatre, but each of them continued to work for the Irish dramatic movement through the channels of other nationalist groups.

Despite the company's short life and the prevalence of nationalist performance practice throughout turn-of-the-century Dublin, the Irish Literary Theatre receives almost exclusive attention in accounts of this period in Irish theater history. Its connections to the Abbey Theatre or to the European avant-garde are usually acknowledged, but its relationship to other Irish theatrical practices—including those Irish nationalists Yeats referred to as "the mob"—have been ignored. Such an understanding of the Irish dramatic movement—one that focuses on literary over nonliterary dramas—favors tightly structured over loosely structured groups, critiques the European influences of the dramas rather than their grassroots Irish influences, and misrepresents the fecund energy of nationalist performance practice in this exciting period of Irish history.

Until recently, both theater history and dramatic criticism have emphasized text over performance, leaders over workers, and high aesthetics over low culture in their evaluations of theater and drama. The Irish Literary Theatre plays into the hands of such traditional methodologies. Its plays were published before or immediately after production, whereas most nationalist dramas of this period have disappeared or, often written in Irish, are not accessible to an English-speaking audience. Irish Literary Theatre productions were written about in major newspapers and art journals in the United States and England, such as the *London Times* and the *Dome,* whereas other productions received international acknowledgment only in small-circulation, nationalist papers. And in the Irish Literary Theatre's plethora of easily accessible documents, its directors credited the nationalist movement for their *political* inspiration, but claimed that their *artistic* influence was mostly European or intellectual. Yes, they bowed to the influence of the

Dublin-based National Irish Literary Society, but gave credit for their theatrical inspiration to such projects as J. T. Grein's Independent Theatre Club, the national theater of Norway, the Théâtre Libre, and the plays of Maeterlinck and Ibsen.

Those influences are clearly present in the Irish Literary Theatre productions and management structure, but the company was also lifted by the tide of nationalist performance on stages and streets throughout Ireland. The Irish Literary Theatre productions that ended up being most significant to the movement were those with which the directors steered their boat into that current of energetic art. In this chapter, I explore this facet of the Irish Literary Theatre by discussing its relationship to other developments in nationalism and performance in turn-of-the century Ireland. The Irish Literary Theatre, as Yeats hoped, was indeed like "something of what has been done in Paris or London," but it was also something of what had been done in Dublin. It was an *Irish* theater, ultimately shaped by the sensibilities of the Dublin nationalist as well those of the London aesthete or the Parisian *bohème*.

The Irish Literary Theatre may have had the most intellectually sophisticated standards of nationalist performance groups at the turn of the century, but it was only one of several groups using performance for nationalist ends. The largest contributor to nationalist theater practice was the Gaelic League, which sponsored *feisianna* (festivals) and *ceílithe* (dances) throughout Ireland, creating local forums for the development and practice of Irish art.

Early work toward the cultural revival, such as the establishment of the Gaelic Athletic Association, translations and adaptations of Irish sagas and myths, and the rising interest in Irish folklore, reached a critical mass in 1892, with Hyde's lecture "The Necessity for De-Anglicizing Ireland." In that speech, Hyde called for the perpetuation of Irish language, culture, and ideals as a national, anticolonial goal against English oppression. A year later, the cultural organization the Gaelic League was formed and quickly gained hold across the country, even opening branches in Irish diasporic communities in England, the United States, Australia, and Brazil.

The Gaelic League was remarkably successful at uniting Irish from diverse backgrounds for the cause of renewing Irish culture. Even in the nationalist movement, the Irish people were divided along many political and cultural lines: Catholic Irish versus Anglo-Irish; urban versus rural folk; Irish speakers versus English speakers; those who sought a purely Irish nationalism versus those who sought a cosmopolitan Ireland with close ties to Europe. Issues of class and gender further complicated the nationalist picture.

Through its ubiquitous influence in the nationalist movement by the turn of the century, the Gaelic League provided one of the few venues in Irish culture where these diverse groups could interact. With varying degrees of success, Gaelic League branches created a nonpartisan, common ground for Irish regardless of their class, religion, or gender backgrounds. Stephen Gwynn describes "a tall young [working class] Kerry man, who certainly looked little enough like a schoolmaster," teaching a Gaelic League Irish class to an enthusiastic group of pupils from diverse backgrounds (1903, 88–89). The Gaelic League even withstood attacks from conservative elements of the church angered that men and women attended the same classes. Sean O'Casey noted a sadder side to class integration when he recalled better-off Gaelic Leaguers in the elite Dublin suburbs "wincing at workmen like himself who frequented their meetings" (Kiberd 1995, 149). Individual differences certainly created tensions within Gaelic League branches, and plenty of its members were seeking a social outlet or a possible rise in their social status as well as a return to Irish ways. Particular branches attracted particular kinds of people, imposing a kind of self-segregation among various groups within the Gaelic League. But the fact that so many Irish persons with such a range of experiences shared this organization at any level foregrounds how influential the Gaelic League was in the formation of national identity.

The Gaelic League performed the politics of Irishness by holding festivals and contests throughout the country that included singing Irish songs, dancing Irish dances, reciting nationalist poems and speeches, and even performing dramas in Irish; and they made such activity central to their agenda. The May 1900 annual report of the Central Branch of the Gaelic League (only one of several in the city of Dublin) reported that the group held weekly meetings with guest speakers; set up nine weekly classes in Irish language and history; arranged monthly music concerts that filled the hall at the Gresham Hotel; sponsored the Leinster Feis in January; and helped fill the Round Room of the Rotunda at the annual *oireachtas* (festival) in May (Moonan 1900, 215). As the Central Branch report stated it, "It [was] impossible to exaggerate the influence of these [performance] gatherings in creating an interest in the movement and in dissipating the idea that the language movement was merely a pedantic effort" (Moonan 1900, 215).

But the conscious performance of Irishness did not end at the boundaries of the stages at Gaelic League events. Rather, membership compelled many people to perform their cultural identity in particular ways as part of their everyday activity. By purchasing only Irish goods, wearing only Irish-made and Irish-styled clothing and jewelry, playing Irish games, dancing Irish dances, singing Irish songs, or speaking the Irish language, Gaelic Leaguers embodied their ideology in easily readable ways. The pervasiveness of this form of political action is reflected in the economic impact of the Gaelic League among Dublin retailers. Shopkeepers learned the advantage of advertising that their goods were Irish made, and nationalist papers were full of messages from merchants touting the Irishness of their products.

At a time when even understanding the Irish language was considered a sign of backwardness by much of the Irish population, Irish-speaking Gaelic Leaguers wore a small medal on their lapel announcing to other Gaelic Leaguers and to the world their knowledge of and pride in their national tongue. Young women wore hats with ribbons bearing slogans in Irish. These tokens may seem to be pale expressions of anti-imperialism, but to use the Irish language was to refuse to acknowledge the English language—and consequently English authority—in Ireland. When the Gaelic League went so far as to challenge the use of English in governmental activities—for example, by addressing letters for the post in Irish or registering Irish names on horse carts—it created heated national debates that reached as far as London's Parliament.[1]

In the wake of this heightened sense of the performance of national identity, performances of Irish plays and *tableaux vivants* at *ceílithe* and *feisianna* became common practice among amateur nationalist groups. To enact an idealized image of the Irish nation on the stage was to embody a representation of the Irish counter to the negative images found in English discourse and to the oppression or colonialization Irish nationalists asserted was their everyday experience in the United Kingdom. It was a vital part of imagining an independent Irish nation.

Popular dramas on nationalist themes were also being produced throughout Ireland by commercial companies. In his autobiography, W. G. Fay recounts working as an "advance man" for a theatrical troupe performing the work of Dion Boucicault, Hugh O'Grady, and other Irish dramatists, along with some English perennials such as *East Lynne,* throughout Ireland. The Queen's Royal Theatre, Dublin, performed patriotic Irish melodramas to wide popular acclaim.

By the first Irish Literary Theatre production in 1899, theatrical performance as a political activity was firmly enough entrenched in nationalist circles for audiences to have developed particular modes for interpreting and understanding nationalist theater. These audiences inevitably valued the earnestness of the politics of a nationalist play over the quality of its aesthetics. Part-time playwrights and amateur actors strove to address the immediate urgency of Ireland's colonial subjection rather than to create an "immortal" work of art. These early nationalist plays functioned like church pageants or "founder's day dramas" in that the performances generated a sense of community in the group: the intimate bond between audience and actors

---

1. By attempting to require the postal system to accept letters addressed in Irish, the Gaelic League effectively challenged the British Empire to acknowledge the right of the Irish to use Gaelic to the extent that an item mailed anywhere in the empire addressed in Irish would have to be translated and sent. The postal debate was discussed in Parliament. See Dunleavy and Dunleavy 1991, 229–43.

in these grassroots performances evoked the popular spirit of the movement.

Occasionally the amateur nature of these productions stirred up some complaint. In a 1903 *Leader,* a critic complained that Gaelic League events never began on time and did not end until eleven or eleven thirty at night. "Concert Committees," he added, "shouldn't choose Mr. (or Miss) So-and-so because it will be such a compliment and he (or she) has done such good work for the branch. . . . A few good artists, singers and instrumentalists should be procured, even if they have to be paid for" ("Gaelic League Concerts," *Leader* 20 September 1903, 5). More common, however, was the excitement over the performance of art that edified Irish culture, regardless of the quality of the performers. And when leaders of a branch performed on the stage, they strengthened the sense of the event as a communal, political activity. When "Mr. (or Miss) So-and-so" did their nationalist "turn" at a Gaelic League event, fellow Gaelic Leaguers in the audience identified him or her as both a nationalist performer onstage and a hard worker for the nationalist movement offstage. To hire and pay a nonmember was as absurd for Gaelic Leaguers as paying an atheist to serve as a church acolyte. Enthusiasm and commitment, more than talent, were the criteria for Gaelic League performance, and Dublin audiences were used to interpreting political theater according to that standard by the dawn of the Irish Literary Theatre.

The Irish Literary Theatre points to a revolution in Irish nationalist performance practice that was more than aesthetic. Because the Gaelic League was a democratic organization, its bureaucratic structure was designed to get as many individuals involved as possible, thus promoting grassroots nation building. The Irish Literary Theatre, however, was clearly the work of a few individuals who were either Anglo-Irish or "landed" intellectuals. Although each member of the Irish Literary Theatre—especially Yeats and Gregory—had been involved in more populist nationalist activity, their theater emphasized its connections with European theater practices and with the literary elements of the Irish cultural revival, not with its debt to popular nationalist performance practice.

The Irish Literary Theatre emerged out of conversations and commitments made in 1897 in two neighboring "big houses" in the West of Ireland—Lady Gregory's Coole Park and Edward Martyn's Tulira Castle. William Butler Yeats had already spent several summers at Coole with Lady Gregory,[2] who had become both patron and collaborator of sorts for the young but already prominent poet. Born the fourth of eight children on a nearby estate, Gregory was married at twenty-three to Sir William Gregory, a former governor of Ceylon thirty-nine years her senior. Although she never relinquished the economic and social advantages granted a wife of a British imperial administrator, Gregory's political activity began soon after her marriage. During a visit to Egypt in 1881, she met Colonel Ahmed Araby, leader of a mutiny against unfair administrative practices, and she quickly became involved in the campaign for his exoneration (O'Connor 1984, 23–24).

As the mistress of Coole Park, Lady Gregory was a judicious landlord. When the local stores inflated their prices, thus exploiting the local people, she opened her own store to force their prices down. Her interest in Irish language and folklore further developed her connection to Irish culture, and she was even involved in the Gaelic League. She gladly opened her home to Irish thinkers and artists, but, for Yeats, her help was more than financial. She contributed to the style of his Irish folktales and poems, and eagerly listened to and supported his goals.

Yeats[3] had been deeply influenced by the former Fenian and fervent cultural nationalist, John O'Leary, and developed much of his sense of Irish writing and nationalism from him.[4] He had already been involved in a range of nationalist activities. He helped found the Irish Literary

2. Some of the best histories of Gregory's work in the theater include her memoirs, *Our Irish Theatre* (Gregory 1913); *Lady Gregory: Selected Writings* (Gregory 1996); and Saddlemyer and Smythe 1987.

3. The strongest biographies of Yeats are Ellman 1979, Jeffares 1989, and Foster 1998. Thorough historical and critical critiques of Yeats's work in the theater can be found in Miller 1977 and Flannery 1976.

4. For information on Yeats's relationship with O'Leary, see Cullingford 1981.

Society in London and the National Irish Literary Society in Dublin, served as president of the Tone Memorial committee in 1898, and often spoke and participated in nationalist demonstrations. Yet he also had strong opinions about the nature of political art, which invariably led him to choose esoteric over popular forms. "All art is national," Yeats declared as early as 1890 (Yeats 1975, 141), but he was often tyrannical concerning what qualified as art. When the National Irish Literary Society worked to establish lending libraries throughout Ireland, Yeats fought for the inclusion of what he deemed scholarly or artistically sound works—by authors such as Samuel Ferguson, Standish O'Grady, and himself—rather than the highly propagandistic writing of the Young Irelanders of the 1840s. Yeats studied and supported a kind of cosmopolitan Irish sensibility in the restoration of ancient Irish literature and the creation of a new tradition in Irish writing, but fiercely attacked any art counter to his aesthetic. This drive inspired Yeats to create some of the most beautiful poetry and drama of the twentieth century, but it also led him to attack nationalist works that he claimed were outside of the sphere of art.

Yeats was fascinated theatrically by the symbolist drama of Europe, and he claimed that a performance of Villiers de l'Isle Adam's *Axel* in Paris shaped much of his own thinking about theater. His first-produced Irish drama, *The Land of Heart's Desire,* which was staged in London at the Avenue Theatre as a curtain raiser for G. B. Shaw's *Arms and the Man* in 1894, reflects some of that influence. Yeats did not have a strong directorial hand in the project, but it was his first theatrical collaboration with such figures as Florence Farr, Dorothy Paget, and Annie Horniman. The production did not capture its audiences' imagination, but inspired Yeats to pursue writing plays. In 1897, he had a new play, *The Countess Cathleen,* and he was eager to see it performed for a Dublin audience. Thus, Lady Gregory and he determined to try to create an Irish theater in Dublin on the model of the London theater societies.

One of Yeats's greatest gifts was his ability to enlist persons to devote themselves wholeheartedly to his projects, so it is not very surprising that he quickly convinced Edward Martyn,[5] Lady Gregory's neighbor, to help him make an Irish literary theater. An eccentric son of a landed Catholic family, Martyn was a contradictory and troubled man. He was profoundly misogynistic and deeply religious to the point of neurosis: when he discovered that he owned several books banned by the Roman Catholic Church, he had his bishop write Rome for permission to keep them. But he also had money, several unproduced plays that had been rejected by London theaters, and a willingness to see an Irish theater come into being.

The fourth partner in creating the idea of the Irish Literary Theatre was Martyn's cousin and Yeats's friend, George Moore. After living and writing in Paris for several years, Moore established himself in London, where he developed a strong reputation in the literary community with realist novels such as *Esther Waters*. He, too, had produced plays in London and was involved with J. T. Grein's Independent Theatre Club. In fact, of the four, Moore was the only one with significant professional theater experience.

Once they decided to establish the theater, they wrote a letter to solicit funds. Lady Gregory helped compose the letter, typed it out, and mailed it to the list of potential benefactors. It began:

> We propose to have performed in Dublin, in the spring of every year certain Celtic and Irish plays, which whatever be their degree of excellence will be *written* with a high ambition, and so to build up a Celtic and Irish *school of dramatic literature*. We hope to find in Ireland an *un-*

---

5. Martyn's plays are more or less forgotten today, but they—and the playwright who wrote them—were prominent on the Irish theater scene in the first decade of the twentieth century. After his split with the Irish Literary Theatre, Martyn went on to support other nationalist groups such as the National Players and the Theatre of Ireland. He was the first president of Sinn Fein. Martyn's other nationalist activities included donating money for Palestrina choirs and developing a stained-glass window industry in Ireland. Courtney 1952 and Gwynn 1930 recount Martyn's work in a highly eulogistic tone. An even-handed critical analysis of Martyn and his influence on the nationalist movement remains to be written.

corrupted and imaginative audience trained to listen by its passion for oratory, and believe that our desire to bring upon the stage the deeper thoughts and emotions of Ireland will ensure for us a tolerant welcome, and that *freedom to experiment* which is not found in theatre of England, and without which no movement in art or literature can succeed. We will show that Ireland is not the home of buffoonery and of easy sentiment, as it has been represented, but the home of an *ancient idealism.* We are confident of the support of all Irish people, who are weary of misrepresentation, in carrying out a work that is outside all the political questions that divide us. (Gregory 1913, 8–9, italics mine)

This statement makes four important points about the aesthetics and ideology of the Irish Literary Theatre that remained more or less constant throughout the group's three-season history. First, it saw its work as both artistic and anthropological in that the group planned to create a body of dramatic texts based on stories from Irish life that could be appreciated in forms other than performance. In this way, the Irish Literary Theatre followed a procedure similar to that of nationalist intellectuals who collected and translated ancient Irish sagas and Irish folktales.

Second, the Irish Literary Theatre saw artistic experimentation as a nationalist activity. Supporters of the Irish literary revival often attacked what they saw as the decay of English language and culture. The declaration for "freedom to experiment" on an Irish stage, therefore, was both a political and artistic stab at English culture. It pointed out that the English censor did not hold sway on Irish stages, so, technically, the Irish theater had more freedom to experiment. Artistically, the group claimed that, unlike English audiences dulled by the melodrama and the music hall, the Irish, as an "uncorrupted and imaginative" audience, would embrace new forms. However, the Irish Literary Theatre both underestimated the Irish nationalist community's extensive experience as audience members of many forms of performance (and their concomitant set of expectations concerning theater) and overestimated their willingness to see plays that challenged the moral and cultural tenets set forth by the wider nationalist movement.

Third, the Irish Literary Theatre promised an alternative to the denigrating representations of the Irish and their culture on imperialist stages—for example, the "stage Irishman." But the statement claimed that they would get away not merely from the "buffoonery" of the stage Irish melodrama, but also from the "easy sentiment" of Irish nationalist propaganda found, for example, in the political poetry of Young Irelanders such as Thomas Moore. The Irish Literary Theatre stated that it would replace such representations with dramas that reflected Ireland as "the home of an ancient idealism," turning to an Irish identity that was precolonial and pre-Christian, and that transcended intranational conflict.

By claiming that the Irish Literary Theatre's inspiration was to be found in an ancient Ireland, the Anglo-Irish Yeats and Gregory and the landed Catholics Martyn and Moore sidestepped partisan issues of race and class in colonial Ireland, allowing them to speak on an equal footing with "Irish Ireland." In previous decades, Anglo-Irish gentry such as Samuel Ferguson and Standish O'Grady used such a move to establish themselves as leaders of the Irish cultural revival, as they translated and retold the history and legends of an Irish pre-Christian past.[6]

Yet despite the claim of traditional Irish roots, the Irish Literary Theatre's aesthetic goals were neither ancient nor ideal. Their work might have been based on tropes and stories from ancient Irish mythic and folk culture, but those stories were adapted to serve what the authors saw as the needs of Ireland's current situation—what Eric Hobsbawm terms creating an "invented tradition" (1991). Often, the theater's nationalist audience read the "ancient idealism" of its invented tradition as heresy, sedition, or insult.

Still, this notion of creating a representation of Ireland's "ancient idealism" links with the fourth notion of the Irish Literary Theatre— that theatrical performance should serve as a unifying event for Irish of diverse political and cultural backgrounds. Further, the directors insisted that their theater would bring together the Irish people by tran-

6. For a detailed discussion of the role of the Anglo-Irish in the literary revival, see Lyons 1979, Cairns and Richards 1988, and Goldring 1993.

scending political quarrels. They would discover, however, as Gaelic Leaguers would a decade later, that in the passionate milieu of Irish nationalist activism, claiming to be apolitical was itself a political statement.

From their first collaborative act, writing a letter soliciting funds for their theater, the directors of the Irish Literary Theatre separated it from contemporaneous nationalist performance modes in particular ways. They placed higher emphasis on the literary than the performative aspects of theater. Whereas Gaelic League playwrights saw the efficacy of their work in the moment of performance, the Irish Literary Theatre wished to carry that energy into the discussion and dissemination of their dramatic texts. After all, the Irish Literary Theatre was an affiliate of the National Irish Literary Society.

Although the directors' mission statement expressed a desire to unite all classes and creeds in their national theater, the letter soliciting funds was sent to Ireland's political and cultural elite—most of them personal friends of the directors. Some patrons did not seem to care about nationalism or theater, but were supporting what they saw as a charitable interest in which one of their class participated. One theater patron wrote Gregory, "I enclose a cheque . . . but confess it is more as a proof of regard for *you* than belief in the drama, for I cannot with the best wish in the world to do so, feel hopeful on the subject" (Gregory 1913, 11–12).

Others, such as Douglas Hyde, saw the Irish Literary Theatre as a potential contributor to the cultural revival in which they were intimately involved. The final list of patrons was indeed a diverse bunch, including fervent nationalists such as John O'Leary and Horace Plunkett, Irish members of Parliament such as T. M. Healey and John Dillon, and even strict conservatives such as John Mahaffy and Lord Dufferin. In fact, the MP supporters of the theater helped pass legislation that enabled the Irish Literary Theatre to perform in Dublin without obtaining a patent (Gregory 1913, 15–20). These guarantors were publicly acknowledged: their names appeared in the first issue of *Beltaine,* the journal of the Irish Literary Theatre. But they had no authority over the management of the theater or the selection of plays, nor were they ever called on for money because Martyn paid the company's losses.

The success of the patron drive and Martyn's personal financial guarantee gave the company an economic freedom unheard of in other nationalist performance circles. Other nationalist groups had to rely on volunteer efforts, ticket sales, or passing the hat at events to float their theatrical enterprises, which meant that their performances were in a close relationship with the many individuals who made them possible. The Irish Literary Theatre directors, on the other hand, answered to no one but themselves. Whereas Gaelic League events and nationalist melodramas were clearly popular performance modes, the Irish Literary Theatre directors insisted that their work would be high art, experimental, intellectual. They filled all the administrative positions in the group: they were their own authors, business managers, development officers, producers, and publicists. Their ideal audience members, according to Yeats, were persons "who read books and have ceased to go to the theatre" (Yeats 1975, 140)—that is, intellectuals who have grown tired of commercial theater forms. In line with that assumption, the Irish Literary Theatre linked itself with the international movement toward experimental theater among the avant-garde of Europe, whereas other nationalist groups claimed the structures of traditional Irish performance practice—the *ceili* and *feis*, the ballad, the oral folktale.

The Irish Literary Theatre performed its first season in May 1899 in the Antient Concert Rooms. The group chose that week because it coincided with the ancient Irish Beltaine (spring festival) and usually coincided with the annual Gaelic League festival. They produced Yeats's *The Countess Cathleen* and Martyn's *The Heather Field*. Moore chose the actors and directed Martyn's play in London, exporting the production for the Dublin audience. Yeats called on his friend and collaborator on experiments with the psaltery, Florence Farr, to direct his play. Both plays had been published previously, but they were being produced for the first time.

The Countess Cathleen and *The Heather Field* are an intriguing combination, for although both reflect Irish issues, they are designed on different schools of modernism. Yeats's play emerges from the symbolist tradition, but Martyn's reads like the naturalism of Hauptmann or Ibsen. One is set in a medieval Ireland, the other in the 1890s. Both plays, however, evoke the Irish Literary Theatre notion of an elite nationalism, in which the leisured artist/intellectual has a duty to keep the spirit of the nation alive in the midst of the petty materialist concerns of the common person. Unlike the romanticized tradition of the Irish artist—the bard wandering the roads and relying on the respect and admiration of the common people for his survival—the modernist heroes of the Irish Literary Theatre 1899 plays were aloof and alienated from society at large, just as Martyn's financial guarantee of the season kept the Irish Literary Theatre aloof and alienated from the needs and desires of the common Irish nationalist. The nationalism of the Irish Literary Theatre was just as fervent, in its way, but it did not embody the political immediacy and performative intimacy found in other nationalist performance groups.

The Countess Cathleen is a morality play about a beautiful woman landlord who offers supernatural devils her own soul to prevent the starving peasants on her famine-stricken land from selling their souls to the devils in exchange for bread. Yet on the Countess Cathleen's death, an angel intervenes and sends her soul to heaven. The otherworldliness of *The Countess Cathleen*—set in a fairy-tale Ireland, with indistinct, vaguely medieval time and place—reflects aspects of the symbolist plays of such authors as Maeterlinck, Rachilde, or Villiers de l'Isle Adam. This verse drama includes such aesthetic touches as a troupe of minstrels playing instruments and following the countess on her treks to the starving peasants' homes. The stage directions and set design, heavily influenced by Edward Gordon Craig, reflected Yeats's sophisticated understanding of symbol and sign on the modern stage.[7] Martyn's play, however, with its realistic setting and language, psychologically complex characters, and well-made play structure, clearly imitates the naturalist school of Ibsen and Zola. In *The Heather Field,* Carden Tyrrell, a landlord torn between pursuing his spiritual genius and the material needs of his land and family, becomes obsessed with developing a

7. See Miller 1977, 44–47.

heather field on his land into a workable plot. The demands of his wife and the pressures of keeping up the estate finally take their toll on the idealist, and when the heather returns to the field (meaning that the field has gone wild again), he becomes insane, retreating into an imaginary world of his youthful ideals.

Thematically, both plays emphasize the conflict between the imaginative life and material concerns, shown most keenly in the conflicts of the main characters in each play. Both the countess and Carden are profoundly sensitive beings who seem to be surrounded with a few sympathetic confidantes and a mob of materialist proletarians. Both heroes also happen to be aristocrats, which leads to the question: Are they the keepers of the national soul with their sensitive understanding of art and imagination, or has their leisure put them out of touch with the more immediate needs and responsibilities of their position?

The Heather Field, for example, deals with important issues concerning the use and distribution of farmland in 1890. Carden receives a loan from the Board of Works, an organization designed to encourage land improvement, but he uses it for a highly risky venture, taming a heather field into arable land. His tenants, meanwhile, boycott paying rents to Carden that they cannot afford. His obsession with the heather field, however, makes him oblivious to their protests, and he ignores their demands.

Carden's single-minded drive to tame the heather field comes from his disappointment in life. His materialistic wife does not share his ideals, and though he dreamed of being an artist or scholar, he feels yoked to the life of a landlord.[8] Carden's brother, Miles, a Trinity scholar, shakes his head in sympathy with his brother's plight, and his young son, Kit, wonders at his father's brooding nature. But Carden's

8. Martyn hated women and was sickened by the thought of marriage. Although his mother encouraged him to marry so that the family name would continue, he refused. The anxiety the issue of marriage generated in Martyn's life must have contributed to the equation in all his plays of marriage—or sexual desire generally—with materialistic drudgery and the abandonment of spiritual and intellectual ideals.

obsession leads to bankruptcy and madness, leaving his wife and child to fend for themselves.

In the introduction to his cousin's play, George Moore responded to this dilemma in *The Heather Field:* "We forget the ruin he is bringing on his family, and we love [Carden] for his dreams, for his dreams are the eternal aspiration of man for the ideal" (Martyn 1899, xxv). It is also easier to overlook Carden's emotional and economic abandonment of his family because the play makes clear that they will be supported by a wealthy aristocratic family after he goes mad. How much sympathy would a poor farmer, without wealthy friends to take care of his family, receive in such a scenario? And for that matter, how many Irish farmers had wealthy aristocratic relatives?

Despite the class issues raised in the play, the critical response to *The Heather Field* reflects the Dublin theater community's excited interest in seeing an Irish modernism develop on the stage. The play brought in a smaller audience than Yeats's *The Countess Cathleen,* but a healthy one who cheered the play. The *Irish Times* complained that the play was badly structured and did not significantly reflect Irish life. Other papers were much more positive, looking to *The Heather Field* as an Irish form of Ibsenesque naturalism. The *Freeman's Journal* noted, "Here . . . is a play that reveals a tragedy of social and domestic life although there is not the remotest suggestion in it from beginning to end of the disordered eroticism which is responsible for so many stage successes in London and Paris during recent years" (qtd. in Hogan and Kilroy 1975, 46). The *Evening Herald* "called the play 'A fine wholesome drama' " (qtd. in Hogan and Kilroy 1975, 46).

During this period, Irish theater critics railed against dramas that represented immoral behavior, especially those featuring women who rebel against their domestic role. For example, when Pinero's *The Second Mrs. Tanqueray*—a drama about a "woman with a past," whose attempt at respectability is ruined when her former lover appears as her stepdaughter's fiancé—played in Dublin, it was heatedly attacked by nationalist papers. The complaint against this English tour of what they deemed an improper play was more than just anxiety over immorality, however. In a September 1900 article, "The English Mind in Ireland," *The Second Mrs. Tanqueray* was attacked for corrupting not only the morality of the Irish nation, but Irish intellect as well *(Leader,* 8 September 1900, 22). Nationalist critics continually decried in frustration that Irish theaters gave audiences opportunities to see only commercial English plays, but nothing intellectually stimulating or relevant to Irish life and experience. The English society play was a particularly large bone in the throats of nationalist critics such as D. P. Moran, who were infuriated that the Irish were expected to pay money to sympathize with decadent English characters from the class that helped create— and profited from—Ireland's troubles. No wonder that the Dublin critics were delighted to find in *The Heather Field* a play that possessed all the trappings of state-of-the-art naturalism and also reflected the moral and ethical sensibilities of the Irish audience.

Yeats's play was a far cry from the contemporary modern dramas from England and Europe, and from their alleged moral improprieties, but it still created cause for concern in the nationalist community when accusations emerged that the play was heretical. F. Hugh O'Donnell, a disgraced former Parnellite and vehement enemy of Yeats, wrote two letters to the *Freeman's Journal* (the nationalist paper most closely affiliated with the Catholic Church), claiming that *The Countess Cathleen* was sacrilegious. The *Freeman's Journal* published the first letter, but when they refused to run the second, O'Donnell had the two letters printed in a pamphlet entitled *Souls for Gold,* which he distributed throughout Dublin.

O'Donnell attacked *The Countess Cathleen* for presenting "the fine old Celtic peasant of Ireland's Golden Age, sunk in animal savagery, destitute of animal courage, mixing up in loathsome promiscuity the holiest name of the Christian Sanctuary with the gibbering ghoul-and-fetish worship of a Congo negro, selling his soul for a bellyful, yelling alternate invocations to the Prince of Darkness and the Virgin Mary" (O'Donnell 1899, 32). The specific aspects of the play O'Donnell alludes to in his attack include a scene (given in a previously published version of the play but expurgated for production) of a peasant kicking the statue of the Virgin Mary, peasants selling their souls to the devil for

bread, and a woman who is unfaithful to her husband. In his inflammatory diatribe, O'Donnell blatantly takes these moments out of the context of the play.

The pamphlet raised considerable concern among elements of the
Catholic community. Cardinal Logue, although he had not read the
play, wrote a letter condemning it based on O'Donnell's remarks.[9]
Yeats responded by sending the play to two other clergy, who approved
of the play and declared that it was not offensive. Soon the papers began
to take sides on the debate, and by the opening of the play on May 8,
J. H. Cousins remembered, "the house was filled with partizans [*sic*] of
both the critics and the author" (Cousins and Cousins 1950, 57).
Groups of people, such as the young men of the Royal University who
petitioned against the play (Robinson 1951, 8), would hiss or howl at
parts of the play deemed offensive.

Accounts of the actual severity of these vocal protests vary from
source to source, but the protests seemed to have consisted of approximately twelve to twenty persons who hissed at specific lines and at the
falling of the curtain, but did not disrupt the entire play. Also, the detractors were countered with a clique who cheered the play in performance, including the writers J. H. Cousins, Seamas O'Sullivan, and
James Joyce.

Adrian Frazier has noted that although the rhetoric of O'Donnell's
pamphlet was excessive, some of his complaints were valid. The play
does show the Irish peasantry to be sinful, immoral, and willing to sell
their souls. The memory of Protestant "soupers" during the famine
asking peasants to switch faiths for food still made Irish Catholics wince
in the 1890s. The Countess Cathleen, with her orchards and flocks of
sheep, reflects the ways the Irish class system helped create starvation
during the famine, although Yeats has Cathleen give away everything
she has before this point becomes too clear. And most troubling in

9. The cardinal wrote in the *Daily Nation,* "Judging by these extracts [in O'Donnell's pamphlet and the *Daily Nation*] I have no hesitation in saying that an Irish
Catholic audience which could patiently sit out such a play must have sadly degenerated,
both in religion and patriotism" (qtd. in Robinson 1951, 6).

Frazier's eyes is the assumption that Cathleen's rich, aristocratic soul is worth hundreds of times more money to the devils than the souls of any of the peasants (1990, 9–17).

On a more abstract level, any negative representation of the Irish on the nationalist stage potentially challenged the point of the cultural revival. The nationalist community's language, art, and games proved their cultural difference; their religiousness pointed to their purity against the English suspicion of Irish Catholicism; their nationalist organizations pointed to their ability and desire for self-government. To show Irish characters that even hinted at the English stereotypes of the Irish personality seemed a betrayal, even (or perhaps especially) in the arena of nationalist discourse.

Despite the nationalist controversy *The Countess Cathleen* aroused, the majority of the audience appreciated the play and welcomed the Irish Literary Theatre's stated goal of creating a body of national drama. The directors' involvement with already established nationalist groups certainly helped their project along as much as the quality of their productions. Although the National Irish Literary Society had the strongest bond with the group, the Irish Literary Theatre also exploited plenty of collaborations within the nationalist community, forging relationships with persons from a variety of organizations.

In the first issue of *Beltaine*, Yeats announced that the group hoped to perform plays by diverse nationalist writers and desired to produce a play in Irish. The following year they were as good as their word when they produced Gaelic Leaguer Alice Milligan's poetic drama *The Last Feast of the Fianna*. Milligan was an important leader of the Celtic Revival in 1900. For the previous four years, she had coedited with Ethna Carberry (Anna Johnston) the *Shan Van Vocht*, a quarterly nationalist literary journal in Belfast. Her poetry, essays, and other writings had appeared in the *Shan Van Vocht* and in other nationalist organs, and she was deeply involved in the performance of tableaux and short dramas at Gaelic League festivals throughout the country.

One of Milligan's most important dramatic collaborations before her involvement with the Irish Literary Theatre was in the presentation of *The Passing of Conall* at the Letterkenny Aonach Tir Conaill in November 1898 (Hogan and Kilroy 1975, 137), a play that included a scene performed in Irish—namely, the preaching of St. Patrick at Tara *(Shan Van Vocht,* 12 December 1898, 231). She also wrote and produced *tableaux vivants* for Inghinidhe na hEireann in 1900. Her work with tableaux and short plays at nationalist events throughout Ireland made her a highly visible and respected figure, noted for her skill in producing political performance events for the nationalist cause.

Milligan's collaboration with the Irish Literary Theatre, therefore, signals a significant crossing of paths between Irish Literary Theatre high art and Gaelic League popular forms—one that she had encouraged publicly as early as January 1899. In a letter to the *Daily Express,* Milligan responded to Yeats's letter to that paper about the Irish Literary Theatre by detailing her own work in drama and that of the Gaelic League throughout Ireland. The letter concluded, "the fact that the Gaelic League has theatrical ambitions will only increase public interest in the National [*sic*] Literary Theatre's dramas. We will have much to learn from each other, and perhaps our Gaelic production will lead Mr. Yeats to decide on dramatising or adapting his own wanderings of Oisin for the Literary Theatre to produce in the first year of the next century" (21 January 1899, 3).

Instead, the Irish Literary Theatre produced Milligan's one-act dramatization *The Last Feast of the Fianna.* The play depicts the episode in the Oisin legend in which Oisin, a singer among the Fianna, decides to leave the corrupt house of his father, Finn MacCommhail, and his wife, Grania, to follow Niamh of the Sidhe into the fairy world.[10] Milli-

---

10. Because three of the plays discussed in this chapter derive directly from the legend of Diarmuid and Grania, a story from the Red Branch saga of Irish myth, it will be useful to summarize it here. Grania was the promised bride of Finn MacComhail, king of the Fianna. At her wedding banquet, the young Grania fell in love with Finn's handsome knight, Diarmuid. She gave a potion to the other soldiers that put them to sleep, then put a *gaesa,* or oath of honor, on Diarmuid that he would run away with her. Years later, Finn and Diarmuid reconcile, but when Diarmuid is wounded and Finn goes to fetch healing water to save his friend's life, anger fills his heart, and he lets the water slip through his hands twice before finally bringing it to Diarmuid. By that time, it is too late, and Diarmuid dies. *The Last Feast of the Fianna* occurs after Diarmuid's death, when

gan structured the piece in very similar ways to her Gaelic League plays: the characters speak in long speeches rather than interact through quick dialogue, and there is very little action beyond these discourses. Also, Oisin performs three lyrics to music written by Milligan's sister, Charlotte Milligan Fox. The lack of action and the extensive use of music in the play create moments of picturesque stillness on stage, which reflect on one hand the *tableaux vivants* of the Gaelic League or, later, of the Inghinidhe na hEireann, but also the "theatre of unity" Yeats would espouse for plays such as *The Shadowy Waters* and *The Only Jealousy of Emer.*

The Irish Literary Theatre produced another drama in conjunction with *The Last Feast of the Fianna* that also dealt with tropes from Irish myth, Edward Martyn's play *Maeve.* Called a "psychological drama," *Maeve* tells the story of a young Irish woman engaged by her father to marry a bloodless young Englishman, Hugh Fitzwalter. Maeve, however, is enthralled with mythology, and between her studies and conversations with her peasant maid, Peg Inerny, Maeve becomes swept up into the world of her mythological namesake. On the eve of her wedding, she dreams of Queen Maeve, who beckons her to the immortal world of the imagination. On the morning of her wedding, Maeve is found dead. Her father and groom think she died of cold, sitting by an open window, but Peg Inerny knows that she has joined the world of the fairies. She tells Hugh, "If you had only seen her, as I saw her upon the mountain—she was so beautiful—so happy. You would have died at the sight of such beauty, my Englishman" (Martyn 1899, 128).

Both plays reflect the Irish Literary Theatre's commitment to esoteric, spiritual themes and alternative structures in its dramas. Throughout the 1900 issue of *Beltaine,* Yeats, Martyn, and Gregory celebrate the anticommercial nature of their project. Yeats saw a theme of the season being "the war of immortal upon mortal life" *(Beltaine,* February 1900, 4) in that in both plays a thinker or artist chooses to abandon the

---

Grania is established as Finn's wife. Oisin, Finn's son, who had helped Diarmuid and Grania during the years of exile, must then live under the same roof with Grania, who is, in Milligan's play, an Irish Helen of Troy.

real world for one of fantasy and imagination. The directors of the Irish Literary Theatre wished their audiences to make a parallel leap in their opinions about theater.

By retelling an Irish myth using modern theatrical methods, both *Maeve* and *The Last Feast of the Fianna* encouraged Irish nationalists to commit themselves to Celtic idealism. Martyn's choice—psychological drama—received good reviews from the press in the spirit of supporting nationalist efforts, but actually it was poor theater. The audience laughed at the heroine, Maeve. Joseph Holloway commented in his diary in 1900, "I know a good acting play when I see one, and this fairy tale symbolising the unspannable gulf between Irish and English ideals undoubtedly is not one" (Holloway 1967, 10).

Milligan's formal, highly stylized drama was a better choice for dramatizing the binaries between materialism and spirituality, mortal and immortal life, Saxon rationalism and Irish imagination.[11] Critics praised the rich costumes and minimalist setting. The three lyrics in the twenty-minute piece were also noted because they were based on medieval Irish musical structures. The *Daily Express* wrote, "Mr. Martyn follows the school of Ibsen, Miss Milligan reproduces that equivalent to the drama in ancient Gaelic literature—namely the Isheen-Patric Dialogues, which were recited in character by two speakers. If the aim of the Irish Literary Theatre is to create a national drama it is obvious that the development of Miss Milligan's method is the proper road to reach ultimate success" (qtd. in Robinson 1951, 15).

The preference for Milligan's symbolic formalism—which adapts ancient Irish stories, musical forms, and performance structures for a modern stage rather than Ibsenesque drama is intriguing. On one hand, *The Last Feast of the Fianna* seems to be making the same kinds of symbolist experiments Yeats was exploring in his own work, but in it audiences saw both a familiar Gaelic storytelling structure and a reflection

---

11. As discussed in chapter 2, these English/Irish binaries were double-edged swords, often used to explain the lack of economical and industrial advancement in Ireland or to claim that the Irish were incapable of self-government. Here, Milligan uses it to describe the Celtic culture as refined and intelligent.

of the tableaux and pageants being performed at nationalist events throughout Ireland during this period. It established an aesthetic tension between grassroots Irish and avant-garde European modernist aesthetics, pointing toward a dramaturgy simultaneously endogenously Irish and modernist, a theater that validated the viability of Irish culture in the contemporary world.

This tension between European symbolist dramatic modes and the performance tradition of Irish storytelling and Gaelic League events would influence the writing and understanding of Irish dramas in the nonrealistic mode throughout the first decades of the twentieth century. For example, Yeats's *At the Hawk's Well* and *The Shadowy Waters* employ the one-act, dialogic structure and blurring of real and mythical worlds for which Milligan's work was praised in the nationalist press.[12] But despite these playwrights' similarities, critics link Yeats to European modernists, but think of Milligan as a grassroots amateur. The playwright's persona often shapes critical understandings of her or his work, but Milligan was more cosmopolitan and Yeats more Irish than their supporters and detractors have cared to admit.

Two seasons' success raised the prestige of Moore, Martyn, Gregory, and Yeats in the theater and intellectual communities of Dublin and London, but it also served to further the political activism of the Irish Literary Theatre directors themselves. Moore had exiled himself from Dublin after writing a snide satire on his country, *Parnell's Island*. Thanks to the Irish Literary Theatre, he moved back. At a banquet given for the Irish Literary Theatre in 1900, he announced that he

---

12. The third production of the 1900 season, George Moore's rewriting of Martyn's *Tale of the Town*, retitled *The Bending of the Bough*, did not employ the adaptation of myth employed by the other two plays that season. Martyn wrote *A Tale of the Town* as an allegory for Ireland's relationship with England, and several figures directly correspond to famous political figures such as Charles Parnell. When Yeats and Moore saw the text, they insisted on extensive revisions. Martyn replied by "giving" them the play to adapt in any way they saw fit. Yeats quickly dropped out, leaving Moore to make the necessary repairs. See William J. Feeney's meticulous notes on the contemporary political allegories in the play in his introduction to the edition of the play in volume 3 of the Irish Drama Series (Martyn 1969).

planned to pay for his nephews' Irish-language education ("The Irish Literary Theatre," *Freeman's Journal*, 23 February 1900, 6). One of those nephews, by the way, ended up a student at Padraic Pearse's school for boys, St. Enda's. The ideals of high art were merging with the tenets of cultural nationalism.

The 1901 season reflects how earnestly the Irish Literary Theatre tried to blend its high-art, literary, cosmopolitan ideals with the grass-roots goals and aesthetics of other groups, as Moore and Yeats collaborated on the dramatization of the story of Diarmuid and Grania. Their writing process became a nightmare of failed collaboration for both writers. At one point Yeats, fascinated by language and translation, suggested that Moore write the first draft in French, "which Lady Gregory was to translate into English, Taidgh O'Donoghue into Irish, Lady Gregory back into English, and Yeats was to put style upon" (Hogan and Kilroy 1975, 92). Luckily, the idea was scrapped, and the two writers worked entirely in English, with Moore having the final say on structure and Yeats on style. Considering the strong artistic and personality differences between the two men, their collaboration would involve translation enough.

Diarmuid and Grania ended up being a surprisingly good play, but it also reflected the main limitations of the Irish Literary Theatre in the context of the nationalist movement. First, despite the Irish Literary Theatre's desire to develop an Irish dramaturgy and even its proposal for a school for Irish actors, Yeats and Moore insisted on hiring an English company to perform their play. In all fairness, the actors, Frank Benson's Shakespearean company, were one of the finest English troupes available, but they were simply too English. The name *Caoilte* in the play, for example, was reported to have been pronounced by the cast in several ways, including "Wheelchair," "Cold Tea," and "Quilty" (J. C. Trewin, qtd. in Hogan and Kilroy 1975, 96).

English actors were not the only complaint. Moore asked the young composer Edward Elgar to compose some hunting airs and a funeral dirge for the piece. The Irish nationalist community wanted to know why he could not use an Irish musician. C. Milligan Fox, who had composed music for her sister's Irish Literary Theatre play, *The Last Feast of*

the Fianna, wrote to the *United Irishman* that although it was too late
to write Irish music for the October production of *Diarmuid and Grania,* "[t]he ideal music . . . should be written by a person steeped in the
atmosphere of the chants of the early Roman Church . . . in the ancient
modes of early times" (28 September 1901, 1). She then went on to
explain proper medieval Irish musical forms. Nor was the project
helped by Standish O'Grady's criticism of their choice of topic—Grania's seduction of Diarmuid and their elopement from the house of Diarmuid's leader and Grania's betrothed, King Fionn. O'Grady warned
in the *United Irishman,* "Leave the heroic cycles alone and don't bring
them down to the crowd" ("The Dramatic Treatment of Heroic Literature," 3 May 1902, 3).

   Diarmuid and Grania betrayed two of the Gaelic League tenets of
Irish nationalism: buy Irish and always valorize ancient Irish art. Performance was a political act in the eyes of Gaelic Leaguers, and bad acting
by an Irish person was always preferred to good acting by an English
person in a nationalist play. When the English actors mispronounced
Irish words in performances, it foregrounded Moore's and Yeats's own
inadequacy as Irish speakers because they were the ones who managed
rehearsals of the play. And although Elgar's music for the play was beautiful, as Milligan Fox pointed out, there were Irish composers ready to
do the job—the same observation that the Gaelic League made when-
ever any industry looked abroad for workers or goods. Standish O'-
Grady's caveat over the subject matter of the drama emerged at least in
part from anxiety over the previous year's controversy surrounding the
translation and dissemination of Irish texts. At that time, John Mahaffy
and other scholars had spoken out against Irish being taught at the in-
termediate school level because, they claimed, ancient Irish texts were
obscene and of little literary interest. Douglas Hyde had led the pack of
protestors who received letters from European scholars such as Kuno
Meyer, praising the language and pointing out the Trinity dons' inade-
quate understanding and even bad translations of Irish texts. Even
though the Gaelic League ultimately proved the relevance of Gaelic literature and humiliated the Trinity scholars, the wound was still sore in
1901. When Yeats and Moore chose to adapt this tale of star-crossed

adultery, they found themselves and their play the targets of shrewd nationalist scrutiny.

To make matters worse, Moore and Yeats were at wit's end with each other and the play during rehearsal, and their attention had already turned to other ideas. Moore was excited by the future potential of Irish-language plays. Yeats had seen W. G. Fay's work with nationalist amateur actors at an Inghinidhe na hEireann performance and had offered them one of his plays, *Kathleen ni Houlihan*. Edward Martyn had already left the company, and Lady Gregory remained supportive but had plenty of writing projects of her own. Still, the directors did manage to complete the project.

In performance, *Diarmuid and Grania* received mild praise for its writing and no praise for its acting. Moore and Yeats made Diarmuid and Grania human characters, with the concomitant emotional depth but without the heroic stature of the characters in the Irish sagas. A particularly acerbic critic from the *Evening Herald* commented: "The stage version lands one in a world of metaphysical meanderings, whose Grania argues as if she took out her M.A. degree in Boston, and then Diarmuid replies with rocks of thought as if he were a deep student of Herbert Spencer." The critic felt that this humanizing of the heroes "lowered" the drama to the level of the English commercial stage: "Grania is an embryo of Mrs. Tanqueray, B.C.," he wrote, "and every moment one expects her to confide to the audience some passages in her past that would raise her in the interest of all ladies present to the level of the second Mrs. Tanqueray herself" (MJM, "Too Much Grania," 22 October 1901, 4, qtd. in Hogan and Kilroy 1975, 105). In 1899, the Irish Literary Theatre was praised for writing naturalism without Pinero's immoral touch. In 1901, they were accused of putting that immorality back in again. The *Leader* was more blunt: "What have we to do with this English play, or it with us?" (2 November 1901, 158).

The unkindest cut for Benson's company was Yeats's curtain speech. Frank Benson recalled how "[t]he enthusiastic poet, W. B. Yeats, in front of the curtain at the end of the first night's performance, seized the opportunity to indulge in invective against English actors, English companies and all their works. His eloquent periods were abruptly cut short by Mrs. Benson grasping his coat-tails and dragging him back onto the stage" (qtd. in Hogan and Kilroy 1975, 117). After a clear remonstrance from the part-Irish Mrs. Benson, Yeats returned to the front of curtain, apologized and thanked the actors.

The drama that really caught the attention of the Irish Literary Theatre's nationalist audience that season, however, was Douglas Hyde's one-act play in Irish, *The Twisting of the Rope*. Since its founding, the Irish Literary Theatre speculated on producing an Irish-language play. Yeats wrote in the February 1900 edition of *Beltaine:* "We are anxious to get plays in Irish, and can we do so will very possibly push our work into the western counties, where it would be an important help to that movement for the revival of the Irish language on which the life of the nation may depend" (February 1900, 4). But the Irish Literary Theatre directors were far from being innovators in the development of Irish-language drama. Rather, they were grabbing on the coattails of other nationalist dramatic efforts. Irish drama was prevalent enough by 1901 for plays in Irish to have been published, including in 1900 two of Father O'Leary's plays, *Tadhg Saor* and *Bas Dhallain*. In its announcement of the publication of these plays, the *Leader* wrote that "we rejoice that after all these thousands of years there has at last arisen in Ireland an Irish dramatist" ("The Irish Drama," 6 October 1900, 86). And O'Leary was not alone, as the dramas in Irish of other Gaelic Leaguers such as P. T. MacGinley and Father Dineen had already been performed publicly.

The Irish Literary Theatre found its Irish playwright in no less a personage than the president of the Gaelic League, Douglas Hyde. Lady Gregory was the main influence in persuading Hyde to consider shifting his involvement in the Irish Literary Theatre from supporter to contributor. The two had been friends for years, and they had collaborated on recovering and translating the stories of the early-nineteenth-century Irish storyteller Raftery. During a visit by Hyde and his wife to Lady Gregory's home at Coole in August 1900, Gregory convinced him to try his hand at writing a play. He and Yeats discussed topics, and once the story "The Twisting of the Rope" was selected and sketched out by the two poets, Hyde thrust himself wholeheartedly into the project. Three days later he had finished his first play.

Hyde found Irish speakers from the Keating Branch of the Gaelic League to play the parts, and he took the leading role of Hanrahan, the poet. At first, Moore directed the production, but his style of directing clashed drastically with the style of these nationalist amateur performers. A few weeks into rehearsals, he was replaced by a local, semiprofessional actor and producer, William G. Fay. Like Moore, Fay did not speak Irish, so he rehearsed the actors using Lady Gregory's translation of the play, and the actors switched to Irish for performance.

Although W. G. Fay's official profession was electrician, he had established a significant reputation around Dublin for his extensive experience in the theater. In the early 1890s, he worked as an advance man for Lacy's Theatrical Company. In 1901, he and his brother, *United Irishman* theater critic Frank J. Fay, managed two theatrical companies—the Comedy Combination and the Ormonde Dramatic Society. Although they were not above performing works such as the nineteenth-century farce *His Last Legs* and other light entertainments, they also admired modern innovations in the theater. Frank Fay wrote extensively about the actor Coquelin in his column and praised the natural acting style of the continent over the artificiality of the English stage. Yet both brothers were also ultimately practical in their understanding of how to make the theater speak to its audience. For example, in 1901, Frank Fay wrote "a few hints I would give Irishmen who wish to write Irish plays to be played by Irish actors." Because acting at this point must be by amateurs, "simplicity and not subtlety must be aimed at." Death scenes and stage combat are too difficult for amateurs to make look authentic, Fay claimed; thus, they should be described, not acted. Minimal scenery and not too many characters should be used so as not to clutter the stage, and nothing relevant to the plot should happen "for at least five minutes after the curtain rises and until the audience has been given time to settle down" ("Samhain," *United Irishman*, 26 October 1901, 2). The Fays' practical understanding of high and low theater forms, professional and amateur actors, and experienced and naïve audiences would serve Irish theater well in the coming decade.

The Twisting of the Rope is a comic tale of Ireland's simultaneous respect and fear of the poet. Hanrahan the poet enters a party and begins to woo Oona, a young girl engaged to a local man, Sheamus. Maurya, the woman of the house, realizes that Hanrahan is leading her daughter astray, luring her to leave Sheamus and follow him into a life wandering on the roads. But because Hanrahan is a poet and she fears his curse, she cannot throw him out of the house. Finally, Sheamus and Maurya come upon the idea of asking Hanrahan to help them twist a rope. He scoffs at these local people's inability to perform the task themselves, but in twisting the rope he moves backward as the twisted cord lengthens until he crosses over the threshold. Maurya slams the door shut after him, to the laughter and delight of all.

Janet Dunleavy and Gareth Dunleavy (1991) have praised *The Twisting of the Rope* for its beautiful and witty writing and for Hyde's deft employment of both Irish and Greek mythic imagery in the play. By having Hanrahan refer to both Helen of Troy and Grania in his attempt to woo away a woman promised to another, Hyde implies that Celtic myths are as lofty and worthy of allusion as Greek ones—a political assertion made by the Gaelic League every day. He also points to the extensive learning of Irish scholars who were facile speakers of Latin and Greek—a very different image than that of the shiftless, ignorant stage Irishman often seen on the English stage.

But although in *Hail and Farewell* Moore insisted that he felt that *The Twisting of the Rope* was the play in the 1901 season that mattered most, it seemed to have received short shrift from the Irish Literary Theatre. The professional cast of *Diarmuid and Grania* was fitted with elaborate costumes carefully researched by Frank Benson's secretary, and the company and its actors received prominent billing. The amateur actors in *The Twisting of the Rope,* however, were not listed in the program and supplied their own costumes. Hyde enjoyed the extravagance of having a Dublin tailor make his costume. He also paid four pounds for the scenery (Dunleavy and Dunleavy 1991, 219). And because the amateur actors of *The Twisting of the Rope* worked during the day, they did not perform the piece during the matinee (Hogan and Kilroy 1975, 102).

The audience loved *The Twisting of the Rope,* however, and the nationalist papers went wild over a play in Irish being performed in

Dublin's largest professional theater. Stephen Gwynn attended the performance and described it as a wonderful marriage of the Gaelic League's political goals and the Irish Literary Theatre's artistic goals. He remarked not only on the performance on the stage, but on the audience's performance of its response:

> The words were caught up almost before they were out of the speaker's mouth; and I heard from behind me shouts in Irish of encouragement to the performers in the dance. . . . there was magnetism in the air. In the entr'actes, a man up in the gallery with a fine voice, sang song after song in Irish, the gallery joining in the chorus, and an attentive house applauding at the end. One began to realise what the Gaelic League was doing—and one felt a good deal out in the cold because one had to rely on the translation. ("The Irish Literary Theatre and Its Affinities," *Fortnightly Review* [1901]: 1055–58, qtd. in Hogan and Kilroy 1975, 114).

"What the Gaelic League was doing," Gwynn realized, was making its productions interactive events, where the audience could perform its understanding of the play in Irish, cheer the actors in Irish, even take over the focus of performance at particular moments. Gwynn was "out in the cold" not only because he could not understand the play without Lady Gregory's translation in hand, but also because he could not participate in the cheers of the Irish-speaking, Gaelic League-influenced audience members. Hyde's play later became a favorite for performance by professional and amateur troupes, and he continued to write dramas that were popular at nationalist events for decades to come.

A month after these final performances of the Irish Literary Theatre, "Irial," the pen name of future Abbey playwright and actor Fred Ryan, wrote a column in the *United Irishman* asking, "Has the Irish Literary Theatre Failed?" He claimed that the project was too grandly conceived, spending a great deal of money on a few plays a year and, with the exception of Alice Milligan, producing only playwrights with international reputations or influence. "It is not with any disrespect to the work which has been done to the Irish Literary Theatre that I say it seems like a flash in the pan, a nine-days' wonder, which is praised and abused—especially abused—on all sides, and then forgotten" ("Irial" 1901, 3). Instead, he asserted, "the National Theatre should be limited by no literary preferences and should let the Irish drama form itself under the influence of national inclination" (3).

Ryan's critique points to the dilemma confronted by national theaters throughout the twentieth century. By producing large-scale performances of authors such as Yeats and Moore, which attracted the attention of critics such as Max Beerbohm as well as the nationalist community, the Irish Literary Theatre brought national attention to the entire Irish revival and helped legitimate Irish theater as both nationalist activity and art. That degree of attention, Ryan argued, overshadowed less-developed, amateur performance groups. Ryan's model made the national theater a diverse forum for artistic development and cultural debate. Because he was an aspiring playwright and one of Fay's actors, he in fact was participating in the kind of nationalist theatrical activity Fay espoused. It is not surprising, then, that Ryan concluded his article by joining F. J. Fay and others in calling for Irish actors and a small, subsidized house to cultivate new actors and playwrights year round.[13]

Just as the Irish Literary Theatre changed the landscape of Irish nationalist performance practice, nationalist performance practice changed the ideals and goals of those involved in the Irish Literary Theatre. In the 1899 *Samhain,* the Irish Literary Theatre looked to the example of Ibsen and Norway for their path. That issue included a reprint from the *Daily Express* of "The Scandinavian Dramatists" by C. H. Herford. In the 1901 *Samhain,* Yeats recognized that although European structural models were still helpful for Irish playwrights, dramatists outside the sphere of the Irish Literary Theatre—such as O'Leary, Dineen, and MacGinley—were producing uniquely Irish drama. Instead of forcing the Irish dramatic spirit into European high-modern

---

13. In his 1901 columns in the *United Irishman,* F. J. Fay lobbied for amateur actors to produce national drama, perhaps promoting his brother's work with groups such as Inghinidhe na hEireann.

forms, Yeats realized that the modes of the modern Irish theater could learn from the performance tropes of the nationalist movement:

> The truth is that the Irish people are at the precise stage of their history when imagination, shaped by many stirring events, desires dramatic expression. One has only to listen to a recitation of Raftery's *Argument with Death* at some country Feis to understand this. When death makes a good point, or Raftery a good point, the audience applaud delightedly, and applaud, not as a London audience would, some verbal dexterity, some piece of smartness, but the movements of a simple and fundamental comedy. One sees it too in the reciters themselves, whose acting is at times all folk story at Galway feis with a restraint and a delightful energy that could hardly have been bettered by the most careful training.[14] *(Samhain* October 1901, 4)

The end of the Irish Literary Theatre by no means signaled the retirement of Yeats, Moore, or Lady Gregory from the Irish theater, but those three years with the company did provide them with a healthier respect for Irish performance practices already in place. All three were active in new projects by 1902. Gregory's involvement with Hyde encouraged her to write and produce her own folk plays. Moore's next project was producing Hyde's play *The Tinker's Wedding* at a garden party in an attempt to make Gaelic-language performance a high-scale social event. Martyn turned his attention to supporting Irish music and

14. Yeats's claim reflects a comment on nationalist performance practice made by F. J. Fay in the *United Irishman* five months earlier: "The language movement and the revival of our music have brought into being, in Dublin at any rate, a marvelously sympathetic, intelligent, and refined audience. The huge audiences which I have seen at the Davis and Emmet Commemorations organised by the Celtic Literary Society, the Gaelic League Oireachtas, the Leinster Feis Concert, and the Irish Tableaux of the Inghinidhe na hEireann are difficult to describe without seeming to exaggerate; they are the antithesis of the audiences who patronise the Dublin [commercial] theatres; and are, of course, merely the natural result of people being content to be themselves and who do not, like our West Britons, copy the worst traits of the worst types of our neighbours" *(United Irishman,* 4 May 1901, 6).

would later help organize nationalist theater groups such as the National Players Society and the Theatre of Ireland. And Yeats joined forces with a pack of committed nationalist amateurs.

In a way, we can compare Yeats's first three years in the Irish dramatic movement with Hanrahan's experience at the wedding party in *The Twisting of the Rope*. Like Hanrahan, Yeats was so caught up showing the crowd how to "twist the rope"—how to perform the task of building a body of high dramatic art—that he did not realize his ideas had backed him over the threshold. But seven months later he would knock on the door of the Irish dramatic movement again—only this time, not as a blustering poet, but as a Poor Old Woman.

2

Popular Drama's Response to Stage Irish Stereotypes

The Queen's Royal Theatre

A typical Queen's audience, noisy and full of suggestions to the players, filled the cosy little theatre to see Dion Boucicault's . . . *Arrah-na-Pogue*. . . . The Queen's is the home of Irish drama.

—Joseph Holloway, diary

WHEN THINKING ABOUT POLITICAL THEATER, we commonly consider only those companies that define themselves according to a particular political goal. Both the Gaelic League amateur performances and the Irish Literary Theatre attempts at creating an Irish modernism fit into such a definition of political theater. Their central purpose was to establish a notion of Ireland's unique cultural identity and to embody that notion on the stage. The politics of for-profit theaters, even when they produce plays on strident political issues, are more obscure. But in a community where political energy runs high, such as Dublin in the midst of the Celtic Revival, politics influences the performance and reception of theater groups peripherally related—or even unrelated—to the political cause in question. Such was the case for Irish melodrama at the commercial Queen's Royal Theatre. The plays on Irish themes at Dublin's "house of Irish drama" were both admired and reviled by the nationalist community, but they were inevitably part of the discourse of political performance in turn-of-the-century Dublin.

Recent scholarship calls on us to question the political, cultural, and aesthetic roles of melodrama and of popular theater generally in the nineteenth century. Bruce McConachie (1992) and Jeffrey Mason (1993) have examined the relationship between American melodrama and issues of gender, race, and class. Tracy C. Davis's (1991) work on the nineteenth-century actress in Great Britain points to the ways women's experiences as workers in the theater reflected their changing economic and social roles. Such scholarship asserts how, in both the United States and England, the popular stage served to reflect and define developments in the national ideology of a country in the midst of rapid socioeconomic change.

Much of this reevaluation of the social function of melodrama emerges from developments in sociology and cultural studies that urge scholars to read the qualities of a work of art not merely against what Terry Eagleton terms "the ideology of the aesthetic" (1990), a set of structural and thematic rules removed from the experience of the common reader/spectator, but in the context of the use of the work in a given community and social situation. The text of George Lillo's *London Merchant,* for example, presents a formalized, moralistic tale of a young apprentice who betrays his master and ends up on the gallows. Yet in the context of its use in eighteenth-century London, when theaters were filled every Boxing Day with apprentice boys sent to the theater by their employers to see this capitalist morality play, the production signals the development of the British middle class and the regulation of the work ethic in the midst of the Industrial Revolution.

McConachie calls this interaction between a play and the culture from which it emerges a "theatrical formation, the mutual elaboration over time of historical specific audience groups and theater practitioners participating in certain shared patterns of dramatic and theatrical action" (1992, 24). Likewise, Heinz Kosok notes that in the commercially driven popular theater of nineteenth-century Great Britain, "successful . . . plays can serve as first-class sociological documents" (1991, 53), for their success hinged almost exclusively on their ability to affirm the value systems of their audiences, which were in turn conditioned by the ideological position of those spectators in the larger national society.

In Irish theater studies, however, the reevaluation of the cultural and political significance of melodrama concerning Ireland is complicated not only by the shifting of boundaries of high and low art in critical discourse, but also by the role of Irish melodrama in perpetuating or debunking the popular English stereotypes surrounding Ireland and the Irish. In terms of McConachie's theory of "theatrical formation," therefore, each Irish melodrama contained several potential meanings depending on the audience member's geographical and ideological position within the British Empire. For imperialist audiences, Irish stereotypes on the stage affirmed English superiority to the Irish while also expressing a degree of anxiety over the relationship between the two cultures. For Irish nationalist audiences, the plays pointed out discrimination against the Irish within the United Kingdom, so they either boycotted plays with stage Irish characters or developed resistant readings of such dramas. Ireland's opposing interpretations of Irish melodramas garnered new staging practices and acting styles counter to the English reading of Ireland on the stage.

The most obvious derogatory stage Irish stereotype was the clownish Irish peasant character called the "stage Irishman." The character can be traced in English theater history at least as far back as 1599, with Captain Macmorris in Shakespeare's *Henry V.* And this blundering, violent, and verbose "braggart-warrior" (Krause 1982, 174) continued to appear in comedies with names such as "Captain O'Blunder" through the nineteenth century.[1] O'Casey's Captain Boyle from *Juno and the Paycock* alludes to this tradition.

By the 1800s, the stage Irishman had normalized into an unattractive, dirty, shiftless figure, wearing ill-fitting country clothes and smoking an Irish pipe. If he did not own an illegal still, he knew where to get illegal potcheen and drank it often. Although generally friendly and laughable, he was also potentially belligerent. He was crafty with Irish

1. In the twentieth century, Irish playwrights from O'Casey to Behan to Friel to McGuinness reflect, critique, and subvert the stage Irishman in their dramas. At the same time, women playwrights such as Deevey, Devlin, and Carr also challenge stereotypes of Irish women.

eloquence but also could be easily duped. Often a servant, this stage Irish character used his "native wit" to assist in the love plots and schemes of his or her English master. Farces and comedies such as *The Irishman in London, or The Happy African* figured the stage Irishman as a mischievous servant. Other dramas—such as *The Irish Attorney, The Irish Ambassador,* and *The Irish Tutor*—were based on the "joke" of putting a stage Irishman in a position of authority, thus foregrounding classist assumptions regarding the Irish. During the early nineteenth century, Irish actor and playwright Tyrone Power was enormously popular in England, Ireland, and North America for his more dashing characterization of the Irishman;[2] and Heinz Kosok points out that other plays such as John Baldwin Buckstone's *Green Bushes,* Samuel Lover's *Rory O'More,* and some of Boucicault's dramas present Irishmen in a better light. Yet these characters were constricted—at least on most English stages—by their English audience's expectations regarding the stage Irishman.

In the United States, characterizations of the Irish immigrant, such as Mose the B'howery Boy or the portrayals of the comedy team of Harrigan and Hart, became stage fixtures. Although there are similarities in stage Irish characterizations on both sides of the Atlantic, and plays with both American and English versions of Irish caricatures appeared in both countries, the stage Irish immigrant served a different dramatic and ideological purpose for its American audiences than England's colonial stage Irishman. The American stage Irish immigrant reflected—albeit mockingly—the growing power of Irish American communities within American cities and therefore was generally an ambitious, shrewd, and often prosperous figure. England's stage Irishman reflected the United Kingdom's imperialist attitude toward—and anxiety about—Ireland.

The theater of the Irish nationalist movement, on the other hand, presented idealized versions of Irish types, asserting the strengths of Irish identity, Irish difference from the English, and therefore Ireland's

2. As a reporter for the *United Irishman,* F. J. Fay referred to Power's performance in *The Irish Tutor* at midcentury to discuss contemporary actors in Irish melodramas.

cultural as well as political right to national autonomy. Yet representations of the Irish on the English stage—drunken "Paddys" and coquettish "Colleens"—merely confirmed the British belief of Celtic inferiority and the Irish nation's need for Britannia's guiding hand. Nationalists recognized and combated the stage Irishman stereotype in and out of the theater, and papers such as the *Leader* and the *Nationist* pointed out the offensiveness of such representations when they popped up even at pro-nationalist events. Nationalist performance groups such as the amateur actors of the Gaelic League or the Irish Literary Theatre built their work on the premise of ridding the stage of Irish stereotypes in favor of more authentic or flattering representations.

The stage Irishman, nonetheless, provided a rhetorical structure for staging an identifiably "Irish" identity, a structure that remained in use—adapted, transformed, or merely employed for pro-Irish purposes—well into the 1920s. But for Dublin nationalist audiences, Irish melodrama served a significantly different ideological and cultural function that emerged from a conscious subversion of English interpretations of these same dramas. The successful subversion of imperial meanings in these plays occurred for Dublin audiences in at least three ways. First, actors who played the roles of traditional stage Irish characters on Irish nationalist stages were expected to perform those roles sympathetically to Irish nationalist sensibilities. Such a performance served to transform the ideological structure of the role. Second, playwrights wrote new Irish dramas that cast Irish persons as heroes instead of fools. Stage Irish stereotypes appear in these plays, but their vices are turned to virtues. Third, audiences responded to the plot line in ways that further subverted the typical English reading of these figures. This collaboration by playwrights, actors, and audiences to alter the meanings produced by Irish melodrama—this Irish theatrical formation—became the key to the success of the most blatantly nationalist of the three popular houses in turn-of-the-century Dublin, the Queen's Royal Theatre.[3]

3. Recent scholarship on Irish melodrama makes it possible to assess closely the nationalist character of the Queen's Royal, developing a critical analysis of Irish melodra-

The Queen's Royal Theatre had been part of the Dublin landscape since the 1840s. In 1883, the English J. W. Whitbread, who had been working in Ireland for some time, took over its management. Shortly thereafter it was billed "the House of Irish Drama," as it played patriotic melodramas with titles such as *The Famine, The Irish Insurgents,* and *For the Land She Loved* to packed houses. These "rough and ready bits of Irish sentiment" written by Hubert O'Grady portrayed the ravages of the famine or the bravery of the heroes of 1798. Whitbread's own plays, such as *Wolfe Tone* and *Robert Emmet,* played on the sentiment surrounding the centennial of the United Irishman Rebellion to stir patriotic feeling (and full houses) among Dublin theatergoers. In 1909, P. J. Bourke took over management of the Queen's and continued its nationalist Irish melodramatic tradition.

Irish nationalist melodrama at the Queen's ran concurrently with other national performance practices: Yeats and Gregory's notion of Irish national theater as a literary enterprise designed for an imaginative elite, the merging of heroic and religious passions in Pearse's dramas for the students at St. Enda's, the Celtic Revival aesthetics embodied in the festivals and contests of societies such as the Gaelic League and Inghinidhe na hEireann. But unlike these other groups, the Queen's Royal was a nonsubsidized, commercial theater, driven by profit, the desires of the audience, and the conventions of the melodramatic stage. Although it was commercial, its clear, sentimental, truly melodramatic depictions of Ireland's culture and history and its accessibility for working-class audiences made it a site of nation building for many Dubliners—a national theatrical house. Examining the Queen's Royal as a model of nationalist Irish dramatic discourse—another "national the-

---

mas as potentially subversive, anticolonial texts that reappropriate the stage Irish figure in particularly meaningful ways. Stephen Watt's excellent historical and critical work (1983, 1985, 1991) on the Queen's Royal and its drama recovers both the historical significance of the theater in the Dublin theatrical milieu at the turn of the century and the particular influence of the Queen's Royal on writers such as James Joyce and Sean O'-Casey. Herr 1991 includes both information about the Queen's Royal and several play-texts by J. W. Whitbread and P. J. Bourke.

ater"—challenges traditional assumptions surrounding the Irish melo-dramatic stage. Further, it deepens our understanding of the interplay of nationalist theatrical modes in turn-of-the-century Dublin as we read those types of drama in conjunction with, instead of in opposition to, the nationalist discourse of the Irish melodramatic stage.

The Queen's Royal developed a "theatrical formation" that was (1) *popular*—affordable and accessible to all classes, but requiring a nation-alist sentiment among its spectators; (2) *participatory*—the audience responded to the action on stage, thus becoming part of the perform-ance event; and (3) *spectacular*—it produced much higher technical values than any other nationalist theater and usually included famous Irish landscapes and landmarks, allowing the spectator to admire and be proud of the beauty of the country and of the history of its accomplish-ments. Because the Queen's Royal was a commercial house, its budget and resources put it in a different league than all other nationalist per-formance groups, even the subsidized Abbey. The audiences combined these three factors with their own understandings of Irish identity to make the Queen's Royal plays ideologically and emotionally charged events representing a specific idea of Irish nationalism—i.e., political theater.

Queen's Royal Irish melodramas were passionate, simple, straight-forward, but ultimately unrealistic interpretations of the nationalist struggle. Heroes were nationalists, villains were traitors, heroines loved heroes while being stalked by villains. And through it all, a character actor with an Irish brogue would laugh and fight and endure for Ire-land. The tension between the English tradition of stage Irish stereo-types and the Queen's Royal nationalist version, however, created conflicting critical responses to the melodramas in the nationalist press. Critics who hated all popular theater likewise insisted that all Irish melodramas were overrun with stage Irishmen. Yet other critics—in-cluding Frank J. Fay—considered Irish melodrama to be related to the nationalist goals of the Celtic Revival.

To assess the nationalist agenda of the Queen's Royal Theatre, it is useful to conceptualize this argument with an overview of stage Irish personae and their roles in Victorian British political and cultural discourses. The English interpretation of stage Irish stereotypes in the Victorian era reflects the multiple and often contradictory definitions of Irishness employed in English cultural and political thought. The rise in Fenian violence in the 1860s, such as the bombing of Clerkenwell Prison in 1867,[4] made English popular feeling increasingly hostile toward Ireland and the Irish. But the sentimental figures in the pastoral world of Irish melodrama continued to charm English audiences. Although Parliament scoffed at the Irish land-reform movement and condemned the activities of the Irish Republican Brotherhood, Londoners packed theaters such as the Adelphi to see plays that included Irish tenant evictions and Fenian sympathizers in their plots. This contradictory behavior reflects England's complex attitude toward Ireland since its inclusion in the United Kingdom in 1801.

The Irish were officially British, many proudly so, but a great majority of them were not Protestant, not Anglo-Saxon, not really "English." Although the Irish held a modicum of power within the United Kingdom through their seats in the British Parliament, Victorian England anxiously tried to position Ireland in a context with its other colonies. One cannot claim that Irish otherness in Victorian English eyes was equal to that of other colonized peoples: their proximity to England, the presence of Irish persons throughout England, and their physical and cultural similarities to the English made them far less exotic and primitive seeming than more remote colonial subjects. Further, many Irish were loyal to the Crown or were involved in the colonization of Australia, Africa, and India. Different Irish persons, different "Irelands," made Ireland simultaneously imperial and colonial, and conflicting stereotypes in the English imagination emerged out of the ambiguity of Ireland's status within the empire. But every English

4. After the March 1867 revolt, Richard O'Sullivan Burke, the Fenian armaments organizer, had been arrested and was being held at Clerkenwell Prison in London. In a failed rescue attempt, two Fenians blew up the wall of the prison yard. Burke was supposed to have been in the yard, but prison officials had changed the schedule, and the yard was empty. Robert Kee reports that twelve Londoners were killed by the blast, and thirty others were severely wounded. See Kee 1972, 50.

stereotype of the Irish pointed to Irish otherness—Catholicism, language, even supposed physical anomalies—to justify economic and political discrimination against Ireland and to prove Ireland's need of the civilizing force of the English Crown. Hibernia was not Britannia's sister in the United Kingdom, but her helpless ward. Yet this mocking description of Ireland's helplessness actually reflects England's deeper anxiety—or even fear—of the Irish other.

In *The Intimate Enemy* (1983), Asish Nandy points out how colonial discourse requires infantilizing the colonized culture to justify imperial presence as a civilizing, "paternal" force for the childlike, "underdeveloped" people (15–17). The assumed childlike innocence of the subjugated people makes them also "feminized"—i.e., weak, passive, and unthreatening. This idea functioned in Ireland, as farmers and other men victimized by Ireland's poverty were made into childlike "Paddys," characterized by Christopher Fitz-Simon as the "ingratiating rogue" and the "braggart" (1983, 94). The stage Irishman, one of the most visible examples of the Paddy in Victorian England, is such a childlike figure, for his dreamlike, "feminized" view of the world makes him powerless against the paternalistic qualities of his British betters.

The female version of the Paddy, a little discussed but nevertheless powerful figure in Irish colonial discourse, is what I will call the "Colleen," a virginal beauty in need of protection. Some English representations of Irish womanhood, such as images in the popular press of Ireland as Hibernia, represent her as a helpless figure being rescued from the bondage of Irish nationalist rebels by St. George or John Bull. Such a representation, though often claimed to be positive, actually suggests a sense of helplessness in the Irish character. It also reflected the assumption of unmasculine behavior among the Irish people generally, for the waifish Hibernia was clearly weaker than the Minervaesque Britannia, a powerful woman who, although beautiful, was a sturdy figure dressed in armor who could obviously take care of herself.

The theater version of the Colleen was ultimately helpless, like almost all women on the popular Victorian stage, yet she was a more energetic characterization than the press version of Hibernia. The stage Colleen—a character such as Kathleen Mauverneen, Eily O'Connor, or

Ann Chute—was closer to the soubrette than the ingenue, with a co-quettish sexuality seething beneath her fiery temper and quick wit. Her pretty brogue and peasant costume (often including a low bodice and a shorter skirt) usually made her appear to be a country girl, helping to explain critics' references to a Colleen character as a "child of nature." Yet such a description tames the stage Colleen's energy, wit, and sexuality by making her unaware of her own intellectual or sexual power.

Both the Paddy and the Colleen ultimately express an impotence in Irish character that must be overcome by English influence. Even English supporters of Irish culture often implied a "feminine" helplessness among the Irish people. In his essay *On the Study of Celtic Literature* (1867), Matthew Arnold argues for an Oxford chair in Celtic language and literature by pleading that the spirituality and "magic" of Celtic thought will temper the logical, Anglo-Saxon temperament. David Cairns and Shaun Richards (1988) have pointed out that Arnold's designation of the Celt as what Renan termed "an essentially feminine race" (1897, 8) allowed England to position the Irish in a subordinate role, similar to that proscribed for women within nineteenth-century bourgeois sexual norms.[5] Such a representation of the Celt makes the "virtues" of their culture ultimately subordinate to and dependent on the masculine sensibilities of their English neighbors. By "marrying" masculine Saxon logic and feminine Celtic spirituality, Arnold implies that both nations will become stronger, saying, "let us unite ourselves with our better mind and with the world through science; and let it be one of our angelic revenges on the Philistines, who among their other sins are the guilty authors of Fenianism [militant nationalist activity

5. The "feminization" of a colonized culture has been explored from varied perspectives in many colonized countries. Other critics examine not only the feminization but also the eroticization of a subjugated culture. Malek Alloula (1986) reads French postcards of Algerian women as statements of French colonial ideology concerning Algeria. David Spurr develops an excellent analysis of the eroticization of a colonial culture in his book *The Rhetoric of Empire: Colonial Discourse in Journalism, Travel Writing, and Imperial Administration* (1993). For a more detailed discussion of representations of Ireland as woman from both imperialist and nationalist perspectives, see chapter 3.

through the Irish Republican Brotherhood], to found at Oxford a chair of Celtic, and to send, through the gentle ministration of science, a message of peace to Ireland" (1867, 181).[6] The "guilty authors of Fenianism" Arnold mentions, however, are more difficult to fit into this malleable, feminine stereotype. In the 1860s, as Fenian violence became increasingly visible in England and Ireland, a more sinister representation of the Irish joined the laughable Paddy and the spiritual Celt.

Abdul R. JanMohamed (1983) has analyzed how, through what Frantz Fanon terms a "Manichean" rhetoric,[7] the imperialist process of dehumanizing and vilifying a colonial people colors the work of imperial and colonial writers in Africa. The Manicheism of the imperial power justifies its colonizing presence, but at the same time reveals its anxiety over its dominating position. JanMohamed cites Joel Kovel, who wrote: "Whatever a white man experiences as bad in himself . . . whatever is forbidden and horrifying in human nature, may be designated as black and projected onto a man whose dark skin and oppressed past fit him to receive the symbol" (qtd. in JanMohamed 1983, 3). The more Irish nationalists foregrounded English imperialism in their rhetoric and their actions, the more this binary understanding of Irish contra English was implanted in the British imagination.

Earlier in the century, the English press drew caricatures of Irishmen that made them look like pigs, playing on Ireland's agrarian culture (Curtis 1971, 30–31). When parliamentary and violent anticolonial protests emerged out of Ireland as increasing numbers demanded political rights, more menacing images of the Irish emerged in English cul-

---

6. For a cogent description of a modern example of the marriage metaphor for imperialist international relations, see Doris Sommer 1990, 71–98.

7. JanMohamed (1983) quotes a section from Fanon's *The Wretched of the Earth*, in which Fanon defines this notion of a Manichean sensibility in colonial experience: "The colonial world is a Manichean world. It is not enough for the settler to delimit physically, that is to say with the help of the army and the police force, the place of the native. As if to show the totalitarian character of colonial exploitation the settler paints the native as a sort of quintessence of evil. . . . The native is declared insensible to ethics; he represents not only the absence of values, but also the negation of values. He is, let us dare admit, the enemy of values, and in this sense he is absolute evil" (Fanon 1963, 3–4).

ture and began to appear alongside the childlike images of the Paddy and the Colleen. Thus, as Curtis has pointed out, nationalist Irishmen became "Savage Celts" in the English imagination, pictured as gorillas and Frankenstein's monsters in the English popular press. Thinking of Irishmen as dangerous gorillas and monsters certainly smacks of a Darwinian attack on Irish culture as ultimately subhuman when compared to the pinnacle of civilization found in the profile—mental and physical—of an Englishman. But the fact that both characterizations are much closer to human form than a pig makes them in a sense even more unsettling, perhaps reflecting a fear of an Irishman "passing" just enough in English culture to uproot it.

The Savage Celt's female counterpart was an equally monstrous, highly procreative wife. The crowd of ill-dressed children often pictured around her evokes a sense of animal-like fecundity and an aggressive, "masculine"—rather than passive, "feminine"—sexual drive. In fact, her ability to bear children is the only typical female behavior the female Savage Celt retains. No cult of true womanhood exists here, for these gorilla-like characterizations include none of the feminine virtues embodied in Colleen. Whereas the Colleen is pretty and clever, the female Savage Celt is dirty, potentially violent, and possibly drunk. Although the emasculated Paddy/defenseless Colleen and the hypermasculine Savage Celt/unfeminine female Savage Celt are on opposite sides of the spectrum, both require British control. To use Nandy's terms, the "childlike" Paddy is countered by the "childish" and out of control Savage Celt (1983). Yet although docile Paddy can be civilized by English cultural values, the beastlike Savage Celt must be forcibly restrained or killed.

These dichotomous images played themselves out in the representation of the Irish on the nineteenth-century popular stage, and they are found in the multiple interpretations of Ireland that emerged out of Irish melodrama, especially the Irish plays of Dion Boucicault, who first gained fame in England with his 1841 play *London Assurance*—a typical British sentimental comedy. His play *The Poor of New York* gained him a great reputation in North America and was adapted in cities throughout the United States and England. In 1860, he wrote *The*

Colleen Bawn, based on the novel *The Collegians,* in a matter of weeks for Lacy's Theatrical Company in New York. After its successful run in the United States, Boucicault moved it to the Adelphi in London.

Boucicault had a profound influence on the idea of the stage Irishman for several reasons. His plays were internationally popular, played at all levels of the professional and amateur circuits, and therefore were integral to defining the Irish in the empire's theatrical imagination. Also, Boucicault's Irish dramas—*The Colleen Bawn, The Shaughraun,* and *Arrah-na-Pogue,*[8]—were admired in both England and Ireland, but for different reasons, as the traits of the characters and thematics of the plot were interpreted differently in each country. Thus, interpretations of the play from each side of the Irish sea provides an interesting insight into the ways in which the stage Irishman figured in both the English and the Irish political and theatrical imaginations.

In *The Colleen Bawn,* Hardress Cregan, a young Irish gentleman, secretly marries a peasant girl, Eily O'Connor, known about the community as the Colleen Bawn (the blonde or fair girl). His servant, Danny Mann, facilitates their secret rendezvous. Mann was crippled when he and Cregan were playing together as children, yet he dearly loves Cregan and all that Cregan has done for him, such as keeping him in his employ despite the disability. Cregan's mother, ignorant of her son's marriage, plans for him to marry his cousin Anne Chute, the Colleen Ruadh (the red-haired girl), a rich gentlewoman whose income will make it possible for the family to maintain the land. Anne, however, has her eye on Cregan's dear friend, Kyrle Daly. Out of devotion to his master, Danny Mann attempts to drown Eily, but she is rescued by Myles na Coppaleen, the traditional stage Irishman of the piece (played originally by Dion Boucicault). Myles loves Eily but, realizing he cannot have her, devotes himself to her and her husband's service. In the end, Cregan admits to his marriage, his mother embraces her peasant

8. In his essay "The Image of Ireland in Nineteenth-Century Drama" (1991), Heinz Kosok reminds contemporary readers that these were not Boucicault's only Irish dramas. Other Boucicault plays, including *The Irish Heiress, Andy Blake, The O'Dowd,* and *Robert Emmet* were also popular in their time.

daughter-in-law, Mann is killed, Anne and Kyrle become engaged, and somehow the land is saved.

In the world of aestheticized poverty presented in *The Colleen Bawn*, Boucicault dramatized the heated issue of Irish tenant evictions. But the victims of potential eviction are wealthy estate holders, not the poor tenants who typically lost their land—and all means of livelihood—in the economic ravages of the famines. Further, the absence of English characters in the play allowed London audiences to read it as a purely Irish rather than English-Irish conflict. As James Nelson points out, making the Irish Mr. Corrigan, the (absentee) English landlord's agent or middleman, the villain threatening the Cregan home was necessary to get the play past England's official censor (1978, 80). Making Corrigan, instead of an Englishman, the villain helps explain the apparent paradox of Londoners vilifying the Irish land-reform movement in the press while blocking the Strand in "Colleen cabs" to see a play relating to tenant evictions ("Our Dramatic Correspondent," *Punch*, 4 May 1861, 186).

The English audience of 1860 had already established a rhetoric for reading stage Irish characters, and the reviews of the production confirm the ways *The Colleen Bawn* fulfilled particular expectations about the Irish characters on the stage. The *Times* praised the performance, claiming that the plot was "wrought with a skill which none but an experienced dramatist could attain," and praises Boucicault's performance as Myles na Coppaleen, "the plebian Irishman of scampish propensities" in the play ("Adelphi Theatre," 11 September 1860, 5). Yet the *Times* qualifies its praise with the comment that "he is less 'rollicking' than most of the artists who have shown in the Milesian character" (5). Broadly as Boucicault's character was performed, the critic felt it was not comic enough. Further, the critic suggested that "[i]n future representations it might be as well to limit the necessity of speaking with a brogue to those personages who stand as types of Irish character." The critique was made because certain actors had trouble with the Irish accent. Yet the suggestion points out that although the play is set in Ireland, the critic thinks that only Irish "types"—i.e., comic characters—should speak in dialect. The romantic characters, closer to admiration than mockery, should speak in English stage voices.

In fact, dialect marks culture and class identities throughout the play. Hardress hates his wife Eily's vulgar dialect and its unacceptability in high-class circles. But the text indicates that dialect is suppressed (or perhaps repressed) in at least some of the upper-class characters. Anne Chute appears in the first scenes to be a proper Anglo-Irish woman. She speaks of horses with the knowledge and interest (stereo)typical of the Anglo-Irish elite. Yet when she becomes angry, her dialect slips out. When she is alerted to this dialect slip, she comments, "When I am angry the brogue comes out, and my Irish heart will burst through manners, and graces, and twenty stay-laces" (Boucicault n.d., 19). As Watt points out, even a refined, Anglo-Irish woman such as Anne Chute (the Colleen Ruadh) has trouble suppressing her "native" energy. When Chute proclaims (in brogue) that her "common" dialect is aroused by passion and bursts through not only behavioral restraints but also, she warns, the physical restraint of her corset, she in fact points out that her behavior is "unladylike" in that it is Irish, uneducated or lower class, and sexual.

By flattening the distinctions between Eily and Anne, or the Colleen Bawn and the Colleen Ruadh, or "the fair" and "the red-head," Boucicault makes Anne's declaration in brogue an assertion of alliance between the Anglo-Irish lady and her Catholic, peasant fellow ingenue. But that alliance claims that Anne—and young Irish women generally—are actually impulsive, innocent, and childlike Colleens regardless of their education or station. For Boucicault, no English clothing or Anglo-Saxon education can restrain a Colleen's Irish heart; and the plays were acted in this manner to the delight of their English audiences. Whereas in Ireland this moment in the action registered love of country, in England, where Irishness was reviled, it confirmed Irish inferiority.

For example, while *The Colleen Bawn* played at the Adelphi, Josephine Gougenheim, an American actress, performed in another Boucicault play, *The Irish Heiress,* at the Theatre Royal, Lyceum. Her

reviews point out how London audiences typically read Colleen characters. The *Literary Gazette* wrote, "Miss Gougenheim . . . played a
gushing Irish beauty, in the regular impulsive 'child of nature' style"
(qtd. in "Theatre Royal, Lyceum," *Times,* 17 October 1860, 6). The
Times critic called her "a tall, showy figure, with much vivacity, and a
command of the Irish brogue which is effective without being coarse"
("Lyceum Theatre, *Times,* 9 October 1860, 7). This sense of the Irish
Colleen's "country girl" vivacity makes her a figure simultaneously
childlike and sexual, whose animal-like energies (although hers are sexual, whereas the Paddy's are violent) remain visible in her gestures, in
her dress, and in her brogue. Thus, the Colleen's dialect and acting
style on the English melodramatic stage reflected the rationale for
British control of Ireland, for it indicated a wildness and sexual energy
in Irish women that ultimately required the restraint of English will.

"Good" stage Irishmen such as Myles na Coppaleen are not objects of desire for the English audience, but their admiration of the female characters' beauty serves as an index to the women's desirability.
For example, Myles na Coppaleen loves Eily and rescues her, but
never presumes to steal her from her gentleman lover, regardless of
how cruelly Hardress treats her. "Evil" stage Irishmen, such as Danny
Mann, are not childlike but childish and usually threaten the women
characters. Danny's misguided devotion to his master (with the blind
faithfulness and impetuousness of a Savage Celt) causes him to attempt to murder the innocent Eily, and it is mere luck that Myles
stumbles upon the scene (on the way to minding an illegal still) in
time to save her.

The Irish romantic leading men have their dashing moments, but
their lovers ultimately upstage them. Hardress's behavior toward his
peasant wife—keeping her in hiding, only visiting her in secret, and
planning to marry another woman despite his secret marriage— reflects
a selfish, cowardly, "childish" nature. Kyrle Daly is more upright than
his friend Hardress, but he is ultimately a weak character; his love,
Anne, holds the upper hand throughout their courtship. In fact, Anne,
not Kyrle, proposes marriage, showing logic and assertiveness when
Kyrle can express only emotion.

ANNE: Kyrle, come here! You said you loved me, and I think you do.
KYRLE: Oh!
ANNE: Behave yourself now. If you'll ask me, I'll have you.
KYRLE: (Embracing Anne) Anne! (Boucicault n.d., 41)

Hardress and Kyrle are not typical stage Irishmen, yet they do not reflect the assertive, masculine behavior of a proper *English* hero, either.

When Eily and Hardress's marriage is revealed in the final scene of *The Colleen Bawn,* Mrs. Cregan welcomes Eily into the family and all the plot complications are set right. In the midst of these sortings out, Eily utters the word *speak* in dialect as *spake* and instantly corrects herself. Anne replies that "spake is the right sound" (42), and Kyrle concurs. Stephen Watt reads this as an affirmation of the Irishness of the household—a rejection of England and its values (1983, 34). The acceptance of the Irish girl and her Irish dialect into the estate house does in fact bode within the play a utopian unity among the classes in Ireland. In this way, *The Colleen Bawn* subtly raises nationalist issues of language and class within Ireland.

Boucicault's 1875 melodrama *The Shaughraun,* however, is a much bolder assertion of Ireland's right to cultural and political autonomy. The politics surrounding the play emerged even outside of the theater: "Boucicault, as author of *The Shaughraun,* wrote to Disraeli and 'demanded the release of all Irish political prisoners then languishing in British prisons' " (Townsend Walsh, qtd. in Nelson 1978, 104). Also, Boucicault gave benefit performances during the English tour of *The Shaughraun* to raise money for the families of imprisoned Fenians (Fitz-Simon 1983, 103). Although many critics consider Boucicault's action a marketing ploy, it might have been disastrous to his career as a popular, commercial dramatist. His position on the popular stage, however, caused the English ultimately to read these political actions as apolitically as they did his plays.

The Shaughraun clearly implicates England's role in Ireland's troubles, but hedges against making Irish politics too overt for unsympathetic audiences. Robert Ffolliott, the hero, is transported to Australia, falsely accused of Fenian activity. He is sent away by English authority after being framed by an Irish villain, Corry Kinchella, who is jealous of Ffolliott's land and wants to marry his sister Claire. In the first scenes of the play, Claire and Ffolliott's fiancée, Arte O'Neal, are desperately struggling to keep the Ffolliott family land and Claire's honor away from Kinchela, who claims that he will evict the women unless Claire agrees to marry him.

Claire and Arte's hero emerges in the only English character in the play, Captain Molineux. The captain finds himself in the position of protecting Claire, Arte, and the Ffolliott family land in Robert's absence, effectively protecting Ireland for the good Irish people and against the evil ones. Boucicault writes his plot carefully so that Molineux never directly harms the Irish characters or breaks British law. As the love interest of Ffolliott's sister, Claire, Molineux is often torn between his duty as an officer and his desire for Claire and increasing sympathy for her plight. However, by protecting the Ffolliott estate and its inhabitants, Molineux effectively claims the land as his own and in the end "wins" the Irish woman Claire and consequently her land—a microcosm of the ideology of Ireland's relationship with England in the United Kingdom. Ultimately, the love triangle of the play is between the Colleen (Claire), the impotent Paddy (Kinchella), and the valiant rescuer Englishman (Molineaux).

Despite the play's concern with Fenian issues, the staging of *The Shaughraun* insulated English audiences from a political reaction. In the first scene, Molineux flirts with Claire, unaware of her social position. And, like the "child of nature" that she is, Claire does not alert him to her social standing as she flirts with him, shows him how to work a butter churn, and even allows him to steal a kiss before revealing her true station. (Perhaps this scene is also a salute to another Irishman's play, Goldsmith's *She Stoops to Conquer.*) Claire speaks in a brogue, and the dialogue indicates that she has tucked up her skirts, showing her (presumably) bare legs. Yet Claire the Colleen's coy flirtations are politically charged as she debates Molineux's hegemonic assumptions concerning language and dialect. When Molineux calls the community "Swillabeg," Claire corrects him that it is pronounced "Shoolabeg":

> MOL: Beg pardon; your Irish names are so unpronounce-
> able. You see I am an Englishman.
> CLAIRE: I remarked your misfortune; poor crature, you
> couldn't help it. (Boucicault 1984, 173)

The political sentiments of the moment, however, are clouded by the sexual energy of the scene. The rhetoric of the ingenue, the Colleen, and the bare leg were more easily read by the melodramatic theater audience than discussions of language and imperialism. Further, because Claire is pretending to be a dairymaid, thus playing a role, it remains ambiguous whether or not she believes the politically charged comments she makes.

Conn the Shaughraun is in many ways a typical stage Irishman, but he performs his illegal acts, such as poaching game, to help Claire and Arte. Later in the play, Conn helps Ffolliott (who has returned to Ireland and is being chased by Kinchella) escape. He draws the attention of the police away from Ffolliott and is shot and presumed dead. However, in the next scene, Conn reveals that he was not actually shot, but is pretending to be dead so he can help reveal Kinchella's villainy. The heroes admire Conn's bravery, but then he must again "play dead" during his wake to maintain the ruse. During his wake, as two paid keeners mourn over him, Conn steals swigs of potcheen from the jug of one of the keeners, thus fulfilling some of the expectations of the mischievous, childlike Paddy.

In the final scene, Molineux and Claire, along with Conn and Moya (the comic peasants), are about to be married. Although it is traditional to end a comedy with a marriage, these couplings are unusual for Irish melodrama. Molineux's proposal to turn Conn's false wake into a wedding challenges whether the British representative civilizes the Irish or if he is adopting Irish ways. But Claire and Molineux's marriage seems to imply Arnold's plea for a "marriage" of Irish and English temperaments for the good of both peoples.

Despite the political issues raised in the text and marketing of *The Shaughraun,* moments that fulfilled the audience's expectation of the Colleen and Paddy prevailed in the memory of the established English press. The *Times* reviewer described the function of politics in *The Shaughraun* in this way:

Long ago [Boucicault] showed us that he is not one of those who fear
to speak of '98, and now he patronizes Fenianism. . . . Hamlet's uncle-
father would have asked if there was no offense in all this? Not a jot. If
Captain Red, White-boys, Peep o'Day boys, Molly Maguires, United
Irishmen, or Fenians, can succeed in inspiriting one of Mr. Boucicault's
peasants, there is something about them which is not wholly unrepul-
sive in the eyes of the strictest Conservative. ("Drury-Lane Theatre," 6
September 1875, 12)

The *Times* critic named both loyalist and nationalist groups in his rat-
tling off of the names of Irish political radicals—yet another sign of the
simplification of the Irish conflict within English culture. For English
audiences, the shape of the messenger (melodrama) altered the play's
message by coding nationalist sentiments about land reform, language,
and class into a more palatable tale of colorful Irish types. The theoretical position of *The Shaughraun* as popular entertainment and its geographical position as a drama in the heart of the London theater district
occluded the criticism of English-Irish relations inherent in the play.

Stage Irish characters performed an important ideological function
in nineteenth-century England. They affirmed English cultural superiority over the Celt, while claiming that the English presence in Ireland
was necessary for that country's good. In England, even Boucicault's
sympathetic Irish melodramas could not escape the hegemonic interpretation of Irish personality embedded in the English imagination
through representations of the Irish on stage and in the popular press.
And this hegemonic understanding of stage Irish stereotypes on the
nineteenth-century English stage reflected the need for alternative representations or subversive renderings of the stage Irishman on the nationalist stages in Dublin. During the nineteenth century, Dublin
theaters provided much of the same dramatic repertoire as that found in
England; the Irish city was often a stop on British company tours. Thus,
Irish dramas—and stage Irish stereotypes—found themselves on the
boards of Dublin's theaters. Audiences and actors in Ireland developed
techniques to produce different, more positive representations of their
culture when they performed or witnessed these types of works.

In 1860, while the first production of *The Colleen Bawn* was producing traditional stage Irish readings for much of its London audience, the Irish actor John Drew received kudos for his representation (and reappropriation) on the Dublin stage of the stage Irishman O'Callaghan in the revival of the 1822 English farce *His Last Legs*. The *Freeman's Journal* wrote:

> O'Callaghan is certainly one of the least offensive English creations of Irishmen on the stage. He is an average representation—full of good humour, ready wit, inexhaustible resources, and happy temperament which characterise the Irish; and in his portrait of these qualities, Mr. Drew was faithful without exaggeration, witty without coarseness, and irresistibly humorous without burlesquing the alleged peculiarities of our country. ("Theatre Royal, Lyceum," 17 October 1860, 2)

Dublin audiences were clearly sensitive to the stage Irish figure and vigorously—almost polemically—praised actors who could break through that stereotype. Actors in Dublin turned the childlike Paddy of English farces into picaresque heroes, survivors in the face of oppression and adversity. Boucicault's heroes were ideal candidates for this type of representation, both because of Boucicault's identity as an Irishman and—later in his career—as a defender of Fenianism, and because of the relative complexity of his stage Irish characters. Heinz Kosok notes of Boucicault's stage Irishmen, "Myles-na-Copaleen, Shaun the Post, Conn the Shaughraun, Andy Blake and others in Boucicault's plays are underdogs who react to material disadvantages and social discrimination neither with angry rebellion nor with servile submission but with the laughing generosity of the truly superior, and who make up for their faults by tolerance, helpfulness and unselfishness" (1991, 27). Kosok analyzes Boucicault's characters from the Irish nationalist's perspective, claiming that a degree of dissatisfaction and resistance to their position, even if embodied in a kind of stoic superiority, is inherent.

Homi Bhabha, Michael Taussig, and others warn against the danger of ethnocentricity in analyzing hegemonic representations of the other. They point out a disempowered group's ability to generate its own meanings and develop its own epistemologies.[9] Kosok's examination of Boucicault's Irishmen explores how Irish audiences could interpret these figures to make them significant to their lives. Yet, the Irish response to stage Irish characters is not as optimistically subversive as Kosok implies, for the dominant, imperialist interpretations of stage Irish stereotypes never left the imaginations of their audiences. Stage Irish stereotypes appeared in the English papers and on the English stage, and when they were imported to Ireland, it was often in an unaltered form. Even when an actor such as John Drew produced an alternative representation of the stage Irishman, helping his audience form a new meaning for the role and the text, that performance remained a response to the dominant representation, not an independent Irish art form.

By the turn of the century, when alternative theatrical representations of the Irish began to flourish on amateur stages and at political events, critics increasingly called for more politically sensitive renderings of traditional stage Irishmen on the popular stage. Boucicault's dramas (thanks to the playwright's connections to Ireland, his work in the 1870s and 1880s for Irish nationalism, and the quality of his work) were staples of the repertoire of Dublin houses, but nationalist critics insisted on appropriate interpretations of the Irish character on the Dublin stage.

Derogatory interpretations of the stage Irishman generally received heated reviews. In 1899, the *United Irishman* warned theaters that plays that used Irish stereotypes—such as the drama *Muldoon's Picnic,* then playing at the Queen's Royal—"would not be tolerated in Ireland" ("The Dublin Stage," 4 March 1899, 3). When the *United Irishman* reported on a performance of *The Whiteboys* by an amateur society in 1902, it commented: "This society produced the play as it was written—an indefensible thing, since it was written for an English and not for an Irish audience, and it degrades the Irish character in many ways." Yet the review goes on to comment that the company could have es-

9. See Taussig 1993 and Bhabha 1986.

caped this censure—and the violent response of its audience (the company called in police protection)—by adapting the play to make it sympathetic to the cause. "[They] might have saved their self-respect and their reputation," Frank Fay remarked, "if they had gone through the book of the play with a judicious pen. It does not require any great literary skill to excise what is at once objectionable and incapable of alteration, and to alter what is objectionable and capable of alteration" ("All Ireland," 3 May 1902, 1).

Even plays more or less accepted as nationalist called for editorial scrutiny. Frank Fay warned actor Tyrone Power, with an Irish theater company called the Kennedy-Miller Combination, about playing the stage Irish types in Boucicault's melodramas according to traditional English strictures: "Read your text carefully, Mr. Power, and I know you will come to the conclusion that Miles, Shaun, and Conn are three different types of Irishmen. It ought to be your business to distinguish them; but you can achieve considerable reputation by not doing so" (*United Irishman*, 1 June 1900, 3).

A year later, Fay had the opportunity to show Mr. Power what he meant. In July 1901, the *United Irishman* ran a review of an amateur production of *The Colleen Bawn* by the Ormonde Dramatic Society, a company led by the Fay brothers. The critic pointed out the care with which an actor, "Mr. Murray," performed the death scene of the Irish character, Danny Mann, writing that "the tradition on the stage is to clown this scene, and the audience seemed to expect that tradition being adhered to and were inclined to laugh at every remark of Sheelah. But the stage manager, Mr. F. J. Fay, must have had it otherwise rehearsed, for the tension of the scene brought out the tragedy to its true degree. It reminded me of how the part of Shylock in *The Merchant of Venice* was played as a clown until Macklin's time" (6 July 1901, 3).[10]

10. The eighteenth-century Irish actor Charles Macklin (1697?–1797) revolutionized English acting with his more realistic acting style. His most famous contribution to the English theater was his 1741 performance of Shylock at Drury Lane, in which he replaced the clownish characterization of the Venetian Jew with a more complex, sympathetic portrayal.

The *United Irishman* comments on the Fays' *Colleen Bawn* reflect the brothers' subtle understandings, even in 1901, of ways to humanize and complicate traditional representations of stage Irishmen. By comparing Danny Mann to Shakespeare's Shylock—or, more accurately, Murray's interpretation of Mann to Macklin's interpretation of Shylock—the review points to an Irish understanding of the "othering" of particular Irish groups through melodrama. Fay's production exposed one of the ways a nationalist sensibility could define a performance that subverted a strictly derogatory understanding of the character. Willie Fay's work with a popular Irish touring company and Frank's years studying elocution and working as a theater critic for the *United Irishman* helped them understand the rhetoric of popular Irish stage business, and they sought ways to produce more complex interpretations of characters in many popular Irish plays.

They would carry this knowledge into their work with the Irish Literary Theatre, Inghinidhe na hEireann, and the Irish National Theatre Society. For example, in the director's script to Yeats's play *The Pot of Broth,* Fay wrote notes for blocking that called for "business" at particular moments in the action, adding much-needed energy to the text. Occasionally, Yeats and W. G. Fay's styles worked at cross-purposes—for example, when the first audience of *Kathleen ni Houlihan* giggled at Fay's antics as Peter Gillane. Both Fay brothers were interested and involved in the study and practice of naturalism, realism, and experimental theatrical practices. Fay wrote several essays in the *United Irishman* regarding the need for a more natural style of acting. But that did not stop them from engaging in the work of Dion Boucicault and other Irish popular playwrights. Their experience with Irish melodrama was fundamental to their training in the theater, thus helping them develop what would become known as the Abbey style of acting.

In the midst of these discussions, Dublin's Queen's Royal Theater developed an industry of producing Boucicaultian melodramas on Irish themes and, more than other Dublin popular theaters, cultivated a nationalist audience for the popular theater. J. W. Whitbread, the Queen's manager from 1883 to 1907, promoted historical Irish melodramas that would appeal to his audience's political and aesthetic tastes—both of which ran national. But the identity of the Queen's Royal as a kind of national theater was formed beyond its choice of dramas. Whitbread's inclusion of benefit performances for nationalist causes and the behavior of his audiences were integral elements of the Queen's identity as a national theater.

From the 1870s through the early 1900s, Dublin supported three professional theaters—the Royal, the Gaiety, and the Queen's Royal. Although all three theaters included a wide range of entertainments—including variety shows, melodramas, musical events, and "pantos" (pantomimes)—each had its own niche in the community as well. The Royal was most closely connected to the Anglo-Irish community, and British officials occasionally held benefit performances there. The Gaiety usually performed typical commercial fare, but also brought in internationally acclaimed guest artists, such as Sara Bernhardt and Henry Irving. The Irish Literary Theatre performed its 1900 and 1901 productions there.

The Queen's Royal was the most proletarian of the licensed theaters, and its drama came to reflect the aesthetic desires and political beliefs of its mainly lowbrow, working-class and middle-class audience. All three theaters performed occasional Irish melodramas or plays with Irish themes, but the Queen's found its niche in the commercial theater scene by identifying itself with Irish nationalist dramas that would appeal to a popular audience.[11]

In the 1880s, Hugh O'Grady, the author of what Dublin's *Evening Herald* called "rough and ready bits of Irish sentiment" (qtd. in Watt 1985, 3), was the dominant nationalist playwright on the Queen's Royal stage. He introduced the role of Conn to Dublin in the 1876 production of *The Shaughraun* at the Gaiety Theatre (Watt 1985, 3). From the late 1870s until his death in 1899, O'Grady was a dominant figure of the Queen's Royal stage as an actor and playwright, and his

---

11. The Queen's Royal repertoire was not exclusively Irish, however. It also included sensational dramas with other themes, such as Charles Reade's *Drink* and George Gray's *The Football King,* which included a dramatization of "the final for the English cup at Kensington Oval" (Hogan and Kilroy 1976, 14–15).

plays continued to be performed at the Queen's Royal for decades after his death.

"Rough and ready bits of Irish sentiment" truly reflects the style of O'Grady's plays, which pack as many moments of sensation and intrigue as possible into a plot set against a moment of Irish political crisis. The title of each O'Grady play—such as *Emigration, The Famine, Eviction,* and *The Fenian*—reflects the political leanings of the play, which were subversive enough to attract the attention of the government. In his defense of his play *The Fenian* to the Lord Chamberlain's Review in 1888, O'Grady claimed that "this Drama is simply a Romantic Irish Love Story and has nothing to do with *Patriotic, Political,* or *Social* evils. It takes its title from the fact that the scene is laid in Ireland—and is supposed to take place during the Fenian movement which gives the opportunity for the *villain* to accuse the hero (Lieutenant Tracy) for complicity with the Fenians" (qtd. in Watt 1985, 10, O'Grady's capitalization and emphasis). This same argument was used to defend or interpret Boucicault's *The Shaughraun* as well as later Irish melodramas.

The politics of O'Grady's dramas lies in their presentation of the suffering and survival of oppressed Irish people in the face of actual moments of imperial injustice in Irish history. The meaning of the play in performance lay in where the audience and producers focused their attention: Does the historical placement of the drama serve as a backdrop for the characters' actions, or are their actions in fact shaped by—or allegorical for—the historical situation in which they are placed?

O'Grady's curtain raiser *Emigration,* for example, tells of a family who cannot afford to pay their rent after the failed potato crops of the late 1870s and spend almost every penny they have to leave for America. O'Grady uses this tragic story line, however, to describe a series of comic events. As Paddy Burk, his wife Mary, their daughter Kitty, and future son-in-law Hughey gather up their money and make the trek to the harbor, the land agent, Jerry Naylor (who wants to marry Kitty) and his clerk, Skinner, try to have Hughey arrested, sabotage the family's arrival at the ship, and even steal their money. They fail every time, often with comic effect. When Naylor and Skinner attack the family in the woods, Hughey knocks them into a hole, and as they try to crawl out, Kitty *"pelts fellows in hole with turf"* (O'Grady 1985, 22). These comic effects not only allowed the play to slip past the censor, but also pointed to the Irish people's ability to survive with spirit the social disaster of famine and emigration. And even if the play does not overtly address the imperialist policies that created the need for emigration, O'Grady implicitly presents (and his audience may critique) those policies simply by presenting famine and emigration on the stage.

By the 1890s, as nationalist sentiment ran high among Dublin's working class, Whitbread himself wrote Irish plays. Formally, Whitbread's plays are imitations of Boucicaultian plots. But since they reflected actual people and historical events, audiences could read them in a more clearly political context.

On 26 December 1898, Whitbread commemorated the centennial of the United Irishmen uprising by presenting his drama *Wolfe Tone*. Works relating to the 1798 United Irishman Rebellion were popular in nationalist circles not only because of the centennial of that struggle, but because of the connection that could be made between the 1798 rebellion and nationalist Ireland's involvement against the English in the Boer War, 1898–1901. The play describes Tone's work in Ireland with the United Irishmen as he plans the nation's liberation, eludes traitors, and woos his bride, Susan. Then the action moves to France, where Tone and his wife convince Napoleon and Josephine to aid the Irish cause. The play ends with Tone sailing on the French ships for Ireland, conveniently omitting the failure of the insurrection and Tone's ultimate death by suicide in prison.

Whitbread couches the plot in a double love story between Tone and his wife and between their friends/servants, Shane and Peggy. Shane and Peggy fulfill many of the Boucicaultian versions of Paddy and Colleen characters. Tone and Susan, however, are unapologetically straightforward romantic leads. Rather than labeling it a history play, Whitbread called it an "Irish Romantic Drama" (Herr 1991, 171). In fact, Whitbread's manipulation of both love stories further removes the characters—and the play—from the stereotypes of stage Irish melodramas.

First, the imperialist version of the stage Irishman is typically a bachelor. When he does marry, his abilities as a husband and father remain questionable. Tone and Shane not only woo their women, but also win them. And when their marriages produce children, the audience is assured that they are responsible, loving fathers, even when their duty to Ireland calls them away from their families to France. Second, Shane is extremely generous to Tone and to the Irish cause. He works as a servant at Trinity College, where he is paid well but regularly beaten and kicked about by the Anglo-Irish, loyalist students. Yet he uses this money to help Tone and his struggling family so that Tone can continue to lead the United Irishmen. Shane's situation both reflects his nationalist loyalties and serves as a metaphor for Ireland's still-racist class system with regard to economic and educational opportunities.

But despite the potential attack in the play on the iniquities of the colonialist Irish class system, there is an inherent class bias in Shane's relationship with Tone. Whereas Wolfe Tone and his wife, Susan, do not speak in a brogue, Shane and his wife, Peggy, provide traditional brogue-filled banter in their courtship and their professions of devotion to the Tones. Shane and Peggy provide comic moments for the audiences, but they also employ many standard tropes of the stage Irish character.

Likewise, the heroines of the play are trapped in the gender roles of traditional melodrama. Susan and Peggy do not really move beyond the childlike, gushing-beauty characterizations of the distressed Colleen: ultimately they become Hibernias upon whose bodies the Irish struggle is fought. The Irish traitor, Samuel Turner, is motivated to destroy Tone out of his desire for Susan. Susan was promised to Turner by her father, so when she and Tone elope, Turner and his sidekick, Rafferty, begin a personal vendetta against the Irish hero, betraying Tone and the Irish cause to gain revenge on Susan. Thus, the plot conflates the possession of Susan with the fight for Ireland.

The idea of woman as metaphor for Ireland is especially clear in act 3, scene 3, when Turner and his men capture Susan and Peggy. Peggy is gagged and tied to a chair, while Susan is held by two men. Turner threatens Susan: "Do you know what I am going to do with you (with suppressed passion). In an hour you will be on board [a] ship bound for South America. When you arrive you will be disposed of—Sold—to a man half nigger-half spaniard [*sic*] who lives fifty miles up the country from Buenos Ayres [*sic*]. He is waiting to receive you with open arms. What a prize you will be. . . . You would have done better to marry me, eh?" (Whitbread 1991, 239). Susan responds, "I would sooner prefer the death in life you say you have meted out to me, than endure the ignominy of being for one single instance your wife" (239).

Susan's spirited reply to Turner's threat to make her literally a colonial slave embodies Hibernia's refusal to acquiesce to John Bull's control under any circumstances. When Shane rescues the women later in the scene, he metaphorically liberates Ireland. Yet the staging of Peggy and Susan's violation, with verbal intimations of sexual assault, objectifies the actresses playing these roles, exposing the ultimate lack of agency or autonomy the metaphor of Ireland as woman/Hibernia really allowed women in the nationalist movement.

Like most of Whitbread's dramas, *Wolfe Tone* was a popular success, and it received some critical acclaim as well. In the *Irish Playgoer*, Joseph Holloway wrote, "it is a step in the right direction to try to create a new type of true Irish play without too much of the 'arrah-begorra' element in it, so inseparable from the old form of Irish drama, where everybody, from the highest to the lowest, spoke with the vulgarest brogue (often mingled with a Cockney accent)" (qtd. in Herr 1991, 9). Holloway's reaction to *Wolfe Tone* is moderate, but it does remark on ways in which Whitbread's work subverted the "old form of Irish drama"—that is, the imperialist constructions of the Irish character on the English stage. In Whitbread's texts, Irish persons are kind, intelligent, and ultimately more complex characters than English stage Irish personae.

In the Queen's Royal production, Whitbread's characters were performed by Kennedy-Miller combination actors who differentiated among their characters and—unlike the Londoners playing stage Irishmen—who had authentic Irish accents. The controversy regarding Irish accents—that is, the need to use Irish actors in nationalist drama—was a contemporaneous issue surrounding the work of groups such as the Irish Literary Theatre.

Frank Fay's review of a revival of *Wolfe Tone* in August 1899 comments that what Whitbread's plays lacked in literary merit, they made up in ideological influence:

> Of the many plays written and produced at the Queen's Theatre by Mr.
> J. W. Whitbread, *Wolfe Tone,* his latest, is to my mind, his best. The the-
> atre-going public were evidently of the same opinion, for the play con-
> tinued to attract large audiences for a full month after its production on
> St. Stephen's Day, 1898. . . . We have not yet had a real historical Irish
> drama, and the author of *Wolfe Tone* cannot give us one, but with the
> skill born of a long connection with and knowledge of the boards and
> of the class of audience to which he appeals, Mr. Whitbread has con-
> structed an exceedingly effective play. (Fay 1970, 24).

Fay was never very impressed by the quality of the acting or subtlety of plot at the Queen's Royal,[12] but here he was impressed by the emotions generated from Whitbread's plays in performance. In other words, Fay's review remarks on the theatrical formation of a highly patriotic nationalist performance event at the Queen's Royal. A closer examination of particular factors of performance that shaped the meaning of Queen's Royal productions, such as audience response to its plays and Queen's Royal marketing strategies, points out ways in which dramas such as *Wolfe Tone* could carry significant nationalist weight.

Understanding the significance of the audience's behavior to the political valences at the Queen's Royal Theatre requires moving away from a purely textual understanding of the Irish dramas performed there and instead thinking of the productions in the context of their performance before their rowdy, but nationalist-leaning audiences. The two "performances" at a Queen's Royal event—the nationalist play on the stage and the singing, cheering, and heckling in the audience—oc-

12. For example, Fay was quite frustrated with the conventionalism and unprofes-
sionalism of the production of Whitbread's play *The Irishman* in September 1899. He
wrote, "I positively loathe the virtuous persons of melodrama and would have their
blood were it not that, between us, intervenes that horrible instrument of torture, the
orchestra of the Queen's theatre" *(United Irishman,* 9 September 1899, 5).

curred simultaneously and fed on each other in the production of meaning. Karen Gaylord observes that a "performance takes place on at least two levels of 'reality' simultaneously and within at least two frames. The outer frames always embraces [*sic*] both audience and performers. The inner frame demarcates the playing space" (qtd. in Bennett 1990, 148–49). The event, therefore, creates a "double consciousness" for all its participants—an awareness of both the events on stage and the multiple relationships between actors and audience (or inner and outer frames) during performance.

Many nineteenth-century theaters, especially those geared toward the middle class, developed increasingly restrictive rules of spectatorship for its audiences. Such rules did not take hold at the Queen's Royal, where much of the evening's entertainment was produced by the activities of the audience. Cheering the hero, hissing the villain, and singing along when a character sang a patriotic song were par for the course at the Queen's Royal (Maguire Colum 1961, 90). The *Freeman's Journal* noted at a production of O'Grady's *The Famine* in 1899 that "[t]he pit and galleries were simply packed. . . . [They] were noisy, but that was evidently caused by the incidents of the play, and the characters . . . were constantly applauded or hissed according to their merits or demerits" (10 October 1899, 5; qtd. in Watt 1985, 5).

Such cheering or hissing was motivated by politics as well as by aesthetics. Harold Balfe recalled that when Frank Breen, an actor famous for his portrayal of melodramatic villains, took curtain calls, "he was received with howls of execration and catcalls—and sometimes had to retreat from an avalanche of missiles" (de Burca 1983, 13). This response was not an insult to Breen's acting, ultimately, but a celebration of it as the audience reacted to the villainy of the character he portrayed. In other words, when the audience hissed Breen off the stage, they were really attacking the imperialist villains whom he portrayed (Hardress Cregan in *The Colleen Bawn* and Michael Feeney, the informer in Whitbread's play *Michael Dwyer*). To cheer a patriotic sentiment by an Irish hero or to hiss a British sympathizer/villain on the Queen's Royal stage was, effectively, to register your own nationalist sentiments within this particular public sphere. This performance within the "outer frame" of the production was clearly visible and influential to the production of meaning within the performance.

Most of this kind of activity occurred in the sixpenny seats in the gallery. Dublin slang termed these spectators "the gods" because they were so close to heaven high up in the balcony of the theater. Additionally, galleryites were godlike in that they wielded a great deal of control over the conditions of performance. F. J. Fay commented in 1899 that "the galleryites at [the Queen's Royal] were wont on Boxing Day to turn Mr. Whitbread's theater into pandemonium, the play being quite inaudible to the majority of the audience" ("Irish Drama at the Queen's Theatre," *United Irishman,* 30 December 1899, 7). Fay's call for a semblance of order in the theater—at least enough for the audience to follow the play—is in keeping with the habits appropriate for a realist play, but disruptive behavior among the Queen's Royal audience actually showed that the performance of Irish nationalism within the walls of the Queen's Royal extended beyond the proscenium of the stage. By critiquing, directing, and encouraging the actors from the seats, audience members effectively made themselves part of the performance event, collapsing the outer and inner theatrical frames. To see a melodrama about Wolfe Tone in "the house of Irish drama" was to identify oneself publicly as a supporter of Irish nationalism.

In *Performance Theory,* Richard Schechner distinguishes between "accidental" and "integral" audiences at a performance event. His distinction is simple: whereas an accidental audience is a group of people who choose to go to the theater, an integral audience "is one where people come because they have to or because the event is of special significance to them" (1988, 194).

Although some audience members, such as "relatives of the bride and groom at a wedding" (Schechner 1988, 194), have a clear relationship to the "performers," an integral audience member also may be simply a person "in the know" and prepared to respond to the production in a knowledgeable way. "In short, an accidental audience comes 'to see the show' while the integral audience is 'necessary to accomplish the work of the show' " (195). Those audience members knowledgeable of the tropes of melodrama and the rhetoric of Irish nationalist history did in fact become an integral audience for Queen's Royal productions, performing in the outer frame of the event their allegiance to the patriotic Irish sentiments enacted within the inner frame. And the presence of this integral audience shifted the Queen's Royal performance from an aesthetic production to a ritual event—moving the productions from the realm of popular to political performance.

The Queen's Royal cultivated this notion of itself as a political as well as popular theater. In September 1899, the theater performed a benefit matinee performance of Whitbread's *Wolfe Tone* to raise money for the Tone Memorial Fund. The *United Irishman,* announcing the event, encouraged "all [its] Dublin readers who possibly [could]" to attend (16 September 1899, 3). On 22 December 1902, the Queen's Royal performed *The Insurgent Chief* or *Michael Dwyer* as a benefit to raise funds "for the erection of the National Memorial to Michael Dwyer and Sam MacAllister at Baltinglass" *(United Irishman,* 20 December 1902, 4). These benefits provided Queen's Royal audience members the opportunity to publicly support nationalist causes through patronage at the theater, while allowing the theater to align itself with other groups involved in raising money for these monuments. Audience members who attended these events were integral rather than accidental audiences, for they could identify themselves through their patronage as supporters of the memory of the rebellion of 1798, supporters of current Irish nationalism, knowing interpreters of the rhetoric of Queen's Royal performances, and perhaps even readers of the nationalist newspaper, the *United Irishman.*

In 1902, J. W. Whitbread developed a scheme that would identify his theater with not only Irish nationalism but the Irish dramatic movement as well. After a performance of his play *The Insurgent Chief,* he took the stage to announce a play contest in which he offered one hundred pounds for a new Irish play about the 1798 uprising. "[W]ho knows?" he remarked, "[whether or not] among the writers and authors we may not discover another Goldsmith, a Brinsley Sheridan, or a Dion Boucicault" *(Freeman's Journal,* 7 April 1902, 6).

This contest, significantly, occurs at the moment when the Irish National Theatre Society is getting off the ground: the same weekend that

Whitbread announced his contest, *Kathleen ni Houlihan* debuted at the Antient Concert Rooms. Controversies surrounding what makes an Irish play—and an Irish playwright—filled the nationalist newspapers and literary journals. But for the Queen's Royal, a good nationalist playwright was not an experimental author such as Milligan, Yeats, or Hyde, but a popular dramatist such as O'Grady, Whitbread, or Boucicault.

Whitbread retired in 1907, and the Queen's Royal floundered until actor/playwright/manager P. J. Bourke took it over in 1909. Of the three playwrights/managers of the Queen's Royal during this period, Bourke was, I believe, the most flexible, the most political, and the most talented. His success as a political playwright is owing, at least in part, to the increased number of political performances in Dublin generally during the period, along with the nationalist energy of the times. But even his productions of traditional Irish melodramas were obviously subversive.

For example, Bourke's son, Seamas de Burca, published an adaptation of his father's version of the Irish classic *Kathleen Mavourneen*.[13] In the source story, a young landlord woos a lovely peasant girl, Kathleen Mavourneen, and he impetuously proposes marriage to her. As Kathleen considers the proposal, she falls asleep and dreams of the outcome of the marriage. In her dream, her rich husband grows tired of her, ostracizes her, and even plots to have her killed. Likewise, her marriage to the rich landlord breaks the heart of her peasant lover. Kathleen awakes a wiser woman and politely refuses the landlord's offer, happy with her station in life.

The landlord is a villain in Kathleen's dream, but he does not actually do anything to harm Kathleen. Rather than pointing out the inequities in the class structure, *Kathleen Mavourneen* points out the folly

---

13. When de Burca says he "adapted" the play, he claims that he "modernised" it. "The asides are written there as my father had them" (Bourke 1959, 3). This text really seems to be a reconstruction of *Kathleen Mavourneen* as it was *performed*. I cannot claim it is an historically accurate text, but I believe it to be a fairly accurate recollection of the *performance* of plays at the Queen's Royal during Bourke's tenure as manager.

of a young peasant girl trying to move beyond her "station." Thus, the play simply reasserts the class status quo.

P. J. Bourke's *Kathleen Mavourneen,* however, celebrates the energy and cleverness of the Irish peasant or working class against the soporific idleness of the (Anglo-Irish) ruling class. In the first scene, Kathleen is hauling wood into the house as her father, David, prepares for a visit from the landlord, Bernard, and his sister, Dorothy. When the landlord arrives, Kathleen takes Dorothy in for a cup of tea while Bernard is offered a glass of potcheen. Later, Bernard demands a gallon of it from David. Although the request is good-humored, it does reflect the iniquity of the landlord/tenant relationship, as the landlord demands valuable gifts from his comparatively poor tenant. Meanwhile, Dorothy answers Kathleen's questions about the life of a lady. Dorothy—a clear figure of fun—describes her day as a tedious process of being dressed and undressed by her maid for various social events. In contrast to the robust Kathleen, Dorothy constantly yawns and complains of the fatigue generated from her upper-class lifestyle.

Whereas Bernard is a rather indolent and impetuous character, Kathleen's peasant lover, Terence, is an ideal subversive stage Irishman. He owns a still, but he gives a portion of his product to Kathleen's father (who in turn hands it over to Bernard). He is intelligent, knows his own mind, and is devoted to Kathleen. Terence proposes, and Kathleen clearly prefers him to Bernard, but, tempted by the notion of being a lady, she asks Terence to wait for her answer. In scenes 2–4, Kathleen has her dream, and in scene 5 she awakes clearheaded and satisfied with the prospect of marrying Terence.

But rather than humbly begging the landlord's pardon for Kathleen's decision to marry Terence, Terence takes advantage of the situation to mock Bernard. He talks Bernard into giving him and Kathleen a farm and furniture to start their married life and even two barrels of porter for their wedding. The play ends with songs from each of the main characters, an Irish dance, and the curtain closing as Kathleen and then all the company sing "The Dear Little Shamrock" (Bourke 1959, 35). Bourke's *Kathleen Mavourneen,* like the original play, celebrates an idealized notion of Irish country life, but the cleverness and energy of

Kathleen, Terence, and David undermine the shiftless stereotypes found in English representations of Irish character. Likewise, the soporific Dorothy and selfish Bernard portray the landlord class as a lazy, elitist drain on Irish culture and the economy. Dorothy comments in the play, "Too many people nowadays want to better themselves. If we were all ladies and gentlemen who'd do the work?" (Bourke 1959, 9). Such a line is designed to trigger a response among the gallery gods.

Along with such comic subversions of traditional Irish drama, Bourke also wrote historical dramas such as *When Wexford Rose* and *For the Land She Loved*. These dramas, like O'Grady and Whitbread's historical plays, used settings and characters from Irish rebel history, and engaged in issues of gender and class in their representation of historic nationalist events. *For the Land She Loved,* for example, recounts the story of Betsey Gray, "the heroine of Ballinahich," who led a troupe of rebels during the United Irishman insurrection at Ballinahich. Betsy is in love with Robert Munro, general of the United Irishmen, but Colonel Johnston wants Betsey (and her money) for his own. Likewise, Lady Lucy Nugent, the daughter of a British general, is desperately in love with Munro. Throughout the play, Betsy must escape attempts of abduction or rape by Johnston and murder by Lady Nugent, both of whom are obsessed more with desire than with politics. Yet Betsy and Robert manage to lead the insurrection despite the obstacles Johnston and Lady Nugent put in their path.

Betsy's body, in a similar situation to that found in almost every other play mentioned in this chapter, becomes a metaphor for Ireland, as Johnston and Munro fight to possess her or defend her. But Betsy Gray has more autonomy than most melodramatic heroines do. She often defends herself and, at one point, even manages to rescue Munro. Likewise, the triangle created by Betsy, Munro, and Johnston is paralleled by the love triangle created by Munro, Betsy, and Lady Nugent. Munro's body is also an object of desire and a metaphor for the conflict between the two women.

For the Land She Loved can ultimately be read as a call for unity among Irish nationalists of different class and religious affiliations, as the characters in the play rally around Betsy Gray and go into battle.

And the play contains lines that are not necessarily specific to 1798. For example, at one point Betsy exclaims, "Curse on the laws that set class against class and creed against creed, that can only rule us by sword in our disunity. But God shall give us strength that some day we shall yet be a nation free" (Bourke 1991, 328).

Such phrases did not go unnoticed. In 1915, P. J. Bourke's No. 1 Company rented space at the Abbey Theatre to perform *For the Land She Loved*. World War I and increasing intimations of violence among nationalists and unionists throughout Ireland had made officials nervous, and, Cheryl Herr notes, they had since 1914 determined Bourke's theater to be potentially dangerous. With the production of *For the Land She Loved*, "de Burca states that the Castle 'remonstrated with the Abbey manager St. John Ervine, for permitting 'this piece of sedition to be performed.' Ervine responded by barring Bourke from the Abbey from 1915 forward" (Herr 1991, 15). When removed from the commercial melodramatic house, the subversive potential of Bourke's plays came to the fore. *For the Land She Loved* points out that the tradition of the Queen's Royal Theatre had helped create a rhetoric for the writing, acting, and comprehending of Irish history, Irish politics, and Irish culture within the discourse of popular melodrama that was relevant enough to be recognized by the imperial authority.

Understanding the relationship between the rhetoric of the nineteenth-century popular theatrical tradition, the Queen's Royal Theatre, and the increasingly politicized Dublin public is essential to understanding the effectiveness of Irish melodrama as a nationalist performance mode and, more generally, the role of the Queen's Royal in the Dublin community as a kind of national house. The Queen's Royal provided a laboratory for Irish nationalism and Irish theater. Theater critics (both for and against popular theater) tested their ideas regarding the representation of the Irish on stage as they critiqued Queen's Royal melodramas. Audience members, many of whom could not have afforded a ticket to the Abbey, could perform their nationalist sentiments by attending a performance and responding to the production. And dramas were written for the melodramatic stage that—with varying degrees of success—subverted the imperialist stereotypes of stage

Irish characters. The Queen's Royal Theatre often performed before thousands of persons in a single evening, and it continued throughout the early years of the Irish dramatic movement. Its massive presence on the Dublin theatrical scene, its effect on all Dublin theaters' understanding of nationalist drama and of the representation of the Irish on stage, and the positive and negative responses it generated in all factors of the cultural revival made it an important ideological as well as physical site for the building of Irish drama—and of the Irish nation—at the turn of the century.

3

Women's Work and the Irish Nationalist Actress

Inghinidhe na hEireann

Inghinidhe na h'Eireann has promoted the first Irish entertainments we have had, and it has laid, with its plays in English and in Irish, and its Irish celidh, the foundation of an Irish national theatre. While others have been talking the women have been working.

—*United Irishman,* 7 September 1901

JUST AS THE QUEEN'S ROYAL THEATRE occupied a dual position on Dublin's theatrical landscape as simultaneously commercial and political, other organizations negotiated similarly tricky identity positions in the nationalist movement. Feminism, nationalism, and workers' rights activity often pulled women in contradictory directions. Some women felt compelled to table gender issues in favor of other political goals. Others saw nationalism, feminism, and workers' rights as interrelated and fought for them in that manner. But tracing a woman's involvement in one field often means losing sight of her simultaneous activity in others. And, worse, women's activity in political groups not directed exclusively toward women's issues often drops out of the historical record altogether.

The history of the Irish dramatic movement is such a gendered history, for it focuses on the work of men such as William Butler Yeats, George Moore, and the Fays, while, until recently, devaluing or ignoring the group contributions of organizations such as Inghinidhe na hEireann (Daughters of Erin) or of individual women such as Alice Milligan, Maire Nic Shiubhlaigh, Annie Horniman, Lady Gregory, Maud Gonne, and many others. Women are usually represented historically as they were perceived by the men in the movement. Works that record the women's work in this way occlude the true diversity and complexity of the early Irish dramatic movement, while denying the significant aesthetic, organizational, and political contributions women made both in the context of Irish theater and in the nationalist project of which that theater was a part.

On 2 April 1902, several nationalist organizations, led by the women's group Inghinidhe na hEireann, performed two Irish plays before an enthusiastic nationalist audience. W. G. Fay combined actors from Inghinidhe, the Celtic Literary Society, and his own Comedy Combination into a group of actors called the Irish National Dramatic Company. W. B. Yeats and George Russell (Æ) wrote the plays. The Workman's Club band played Irish music at the intervals. The collaborative venture transgressed several boundaries within the nationalist movement, as Catholics and Anglo-Irish from all classes participated, and the women involved played important roles in the production and performance. Because the playwrights and most of the actors went on to form the Irish National Theatre Society one year later—the organization that became the Abbey Theatre—the evening is often marked as an originating moment for the Irish National Theatre.

Historically, the playwrights, Yeats and Russell, and the director, W. G. Fay, receive credit for the production, but Inghinidhe na hEireann members' vital roles as producers, financiers, ticket sellers, trainers, and actors have been reattributed, devalued, or forgotten. Recovering the women's roles in this production—and Inghinidhe's performance activities beyond stage performance—reveal the richness and power of women's activism in the nationalist movement during the Celtic Revival.

Inghinidhe na hEireann crossed gender stereotypes and class lines to create a united body of nationalist women, one of the few avenues for Irish women to become active leaders in the public sphere. The members considered their collaborative work with men's organizations a partnership, not a subordinate relationship, as it is often recounted. Putting Inghinidhe's dramatic work in the context of its other activities in the public sphere points out how the women's involvement was instrumental to the success of the Irish dramatic movement and the ways in which Inghinidhe's social influence was ultimately both nationalist and feminist in scope.

Understanding the relevance of Inghinidhe and the kinds of gender and political issues it negotiated in its work requires a brief overview of women's positions in late-nineteenth-century Irish society and how women were perceived culturally. A morally conservative country, Ireland contained carefully delineated male and female spheres. Women's identity hinged on their familial relationships to men as wives, daughters, or sisters. A woman's work, likewise, was valued only as auxiliary to men's activity, and her primary duty, regardless of whatever outside labor she performed, lay in her position within the family—maintaining the household, bearing children, respecting the familial status quo. A woman gained respect by performing well her function within the family, but women's work was not considered equal to men's labor. Cynthia Enloe has noted how typically female tasks, such as sewing and caring for children, are deemed natural or "unskilled" labor (1990, 162), which makes a woman's talent at typically female jobs go unrecognized. Women especially skillful at their work are deemed "accomplished": their talent exemplifies their success in the feminine role, without acknowledging the work involved in achieving and maintaining that skill. This devaluing of women's labor applied to the occasional opportunities they were given in the public sphere.

Particular representations of women within Irish nationalist discourse further impeded women's personal involvement in the public sphere. The "aisling" ("Dark Rosaleen") poetry of the Young Ireland movement in the mid-nineteenth century played on the image of Ireland as a young maiden in need of rescue from subjugation or rape by her (English) conqueror. As discussed in chapter 2, the popular press often drew pictures of "Hibernia," a young, virginal beauty in need of protection from (or the protection of, depending on the politics of the cartoonist) John Bull or Britannia. Along with the notion of Hibernia,

Ireland as Maiden, nationalists used the metaphor of "Mother Ireland" through the myth of the Shan Van Vocht or "Poor Old Woman." Typically, the old woman calls Ireland's men to rescue her land from the invader by dying in battle for her. This sacrifice of Ireland's sons renews the youth and beauty of the Poor Old Woman and revives the land. Women inspire men to action in both idealized images, but they are personally helpless—unable to defend themselves, much less contribute actively to the rescue of the nation. Irish women's assumed helplessness put Irish men in a hypermasculine position, from feminized colonial to powerful champion. Irish women became merely passive symbols of the nation—their bodies literally the terrain on which the colonial battle is fought.[1]

Just as women's activity was limited in their representations in nationalist rhetoric, so were they limited in everyday life. At best, a woman could enter the public realm in a role that was—or at least appeared to be—complementary to men. Such was the case for Anna and Fanny Parnell, sisters of the leader of the Irish Parliamentary Party, Charles Stuart Parnell. In the late 1880s, leaders of the Land League, the radical land-reform movement, were imprisoned. A group of women, many of whom were related to men in the movement, responded to the leadership crisis by forming the Ladies' Land League.[2]

1. See Herr 1990 and Innes 1993.

2. The Land League was founded by Michael Davitt, Charles Stuart Parnell, and John Devoy in 1879 to protest unfair landlord practices, including exorbitant rents and evictions during times of poor crops. Their tactics included funding evicted families, boycotts, "no rent" campaigns, and actual confrontations at the site of an unfair eviction. Although the Land League never supported violence outright, the threat of violence and actual acts of intimidation were affiliated with Land League activity. Obviously, Land League actions were often potentially dangerous for the participants. Although the women of the Ladies' Land League performed mostly administrative duties during the period discussed here, their involvement in such an organization was indeed radical for this time, and their aggressiveness toward land reform commendable. Anna Parnell would later describe her disappointment in the ultimate ignoble treatment of the Ladies' Land League in her book *The Tale of a Great Sham*, which was finally published decades after her death. See Ward 1983, 31–39.

Ladies' Land Leagues had already been established in the United States and Canada with enormous success. With Fanny Parnell and her mother heading up the campaign in the United States and Anna Parnell (along with such women as Jenny Wise-Power and Helena Moloney) working in Ireland, the Ladies' Land League became an important force within the movement.

The male Land League applauded the women's work when it seemed that they were bearing the torch for the absentee men. But ultimately the women became more radical than their brothers, stepping up the number of public demonstrations in the West of Ireland and generally increasing the visibility of the issue (and themselves) within the land-reform movement. Once the men were released, however, they coerced the Ladies' Land League into disbanding. After this personal and political betrayal, Anna Parnell never spoke to her brother Charles again.[3]

With the dissolution of the Ladies' Land League, the only group in which women could take an equal role with men in 1890s Ireland was the Gaelic League. Although participating in Gaelic League activities

3. The story of the tensions between the Land League and the Ladies' Land League in the months following the men's release from prison is full of anecdotes of passive and active protest. The men of the Land League wanted the Ladies' Land League to perform clerical duties, but leave the major decisions (and public credit) for them. In a response to this kind of treatment, as Margaret Ward notes, Charles Parnell and John Dillon once entered the Ladies' Land League offices, and the women dropped their work and greeted them with a rendition of Gilbert and Sullivan's "Twenty Love-Sick Maidens, We." Meanwhile, the Land League ultimately squelched the Ladies' Land League by ignoring it. The women paid for their activities through a fund set up in Paris. The Land League simply cut off this funding until the women found themselves with a five-thousand-pound overdraft. At that point, the Land League agreed to honor the debt only if the women agreed to relinquish their organization, yet stay on to review requests for funding submitted to the Land League. In a revision of the document stating these provisions, the wording was changed so that the women would review only requests for funding submitted to the *Ladies'* Land League, effectively freeing the women from working for the men who had betrayed them. Historians have speculated whether the men overlooked the change in the agreement or if they consciously ignored it to save face. See Ward 1983, 31–39.

did allow Irish women—like Irish men—to construct and perform national identities on the streets at rallies and outings, and on the stage through the *feis* and the *ceílí,* the universal success of the organization among Ireland's diverse population hinged on its nonsectarianism and nonpartisanship.[4] Overt political activity required joining another group, such as the Irish Republican Brotherhood or the Irish Parliamentary Party. But because these other political organizations either had only auxiliary branches for women or did not allow women at all, it was difficult for Irish women to make their voices heard within the nationalist movement in anything other than a social or cultural context. And even when a woman performed "men's work" on her own—manual labor, military activity, political involvement—her gender position tended to devalue this labor. In the political forum, a woman's work, regardless of its "feminine" or "masculine" nature, tended to be represented in the feminine terms of natural labor or feminine accomplishment: she received few opportunities for public activity and leadership.

Political women struggled against the grain for visibility in several ways. After 1898, the Local Government Act permitted women to vote for and be elected to political seats beneath the county level of government (Owens 1984, 30). Although many women entered the political establishment with this law, they were typically elected into "feminine" positions as advocates for the poor, the sick, and children, but not given a strong legislative voice.

Irish women could not transgress their society's rigid gender roles by "passing" as men in doing men's work in the public sphere. Rather, to perform typically male political tasks in the nationalist movement,

---

4. To insist that Gaelic League members did not lean toward a more radical nationalism by 1900 would be specious. Its 1900 campaign to force the British Postal Service to accept officially any letters addressed in Irish, for example, ultimately challenged the authority of the English language (and English rule) within Ireland. Furthermore, the organization of chapters according to more than merely geographic affiliations points to an awareness of social and political differences within the movement, at least in urban areas. Yet, officially, the Gaelic League did welcome everyone interested in Ireland's cultural revival and certainly remained the most heterogeneous of nationalist groups during this period.

such as making political speeches or assuming leadership roles, they had to transcend both the masculine and feminine spheres by becoming "extraordinary" women. Represented as atypical of their sex, these women did not pose a threat to male authority in the public realm, nor did they set precedents for typical women's involvement. In fact, they often appeared to support both the everyday and idealized roles for women in the nationalist movement.

Women who were deemed truly extraordinary, such as Maud Gonne and the Sheehy sisters, created visible positions for themselves in the nationalist public eye, but only by characterizing themselves in or allowing themselves to be characterized by feminine ideals of beauty, performative skill, and accomplishment. Such women were admired for their extraordinary talents, but they were not exactly "real" women to their nationalist audiences. Rather, they took on idealized personae developed consciously and unconsciously from the rhetoric of Irish femininity found in figures such as Hibernia, Dark Rosaleen, and the Shan Van Vocht.

Ireland's most famous extraordinary woman in this revolutionary period was Maud Gonne. Throughout the 1890s, Gonne, an ardent political nationalist, used her beauty and economic privilege to increase her visibility in the public sphere. Her charm gained her admittance as a visitor in nationalist men's organizations, and her friendship with nationalist leaders gained her opportunities to speak publicly on Irish issues. Strikingly beautiful, six feet tall, with a strong voice and a keen sense of performance, Gonne knew how to make her presence felt at the most disorganized meetings. She fought for Irish independence in Ireland, England, and France, where she edited *L'Irlande Libre* and wrote for other French papers about the Irish cause. Her activism increased her fame and power in the movement, as she risked arrest to speak before audiences, some of whom were as enthralled by her personality as they were by her political ideals.[5]

---

5. Such seems to have been the case for William Butler Yeats, whose love for Gonne inspired some of his most memorable love poetry (i.e., "When you are Old, Grey and Full of Sleep" and "No Second Troy"). Yeats's sometimes idealizing, sometimes patron-

Gonne was as committed and talented in her way as any male nationalist figure. Yet in the eyes of many men in the nationalist movement, her encroachment into the male sphere—speaking publicly about abstinence, English influence in Ireland, or military insurrection—was balanced somewhat by her characterization as an ideal of feminine beauty. Arthur Griffith, who published her politically potent articles in the *United Irishman,* "affectionately dubbed her, 'Queen' " (Ward 1983, 47). Indeed, Gonne seemed to cultivate this regal persona for herself as she walked the streets of Dublin in long flowing robes, with her dog, Dagda, by her side. Considering Irish nationalists' affection for images of Ireland as *Kathleen ni Houlihan,* Hibernia, and Queen Maeve, such a public representation of herself was a shrewd one. Gonne's identity as "Ireland's Joan of Arc" was a construction in the deepest sense. Her father, an English army officer, was posted in Ireland when she was a child. In her autobiography, *A Servant of the Queen,* Gonne claims that she witnessed and protested a tenant eviction in her youth and that her father converted to the Irish nationalist cause on his death bed, but these stories are probably apocryphal. Yet Gonne's commitment to nationalism throughout her life cannot be challenged. She was bolder than many of her male counterparts, encouraging violent protest and actually planning violent activities herself. Her separation from her husband, John MacBride, made her lose favor in nationalist circles, but she persevered. After MacBride's death in the Easter Rebellion of 1916, Maud Gonne MacBride put on widow's weeds that she would wear for the rest of her life, creating a new nationalist image for herself. Well into the 1930s, Gonne remained a visible and influential presence in Irish political life, from holding political office to giving speeches in the street.

Gonne's bold political activism in the 1890s and early 1900s seems

---

izing approaches to Gonne's life and career in his writing have come to shape the way Gonne is often remembered. However, as Elizabeth Cullingford (1981), Norman Jeffares (1989), and others have pointed out, Gonne was actually quite influential in the radicalization of Yeats's politics in the 1890s. Her actual interests and activities rarely coincide with the images Yeats created about her.

weirdly anomalous to the hyperfeminine representations of her in the nationalist press. In an 1896 edition of the nationalist literary journal *Shan Van Vocht,* Barry Delaney described Gonne in this way:

Uncrowned save by a nation's love, our island's maiden queen,
By spell of her young voice alone, unfurls the standard green.
Oh, fairest flower of womanhood, her weakness is her strength:

Yet well too is she known at home, in cottages that fear
The vengeance of the evictor cursed, that ever hovers near.
Well is our Maid of Erin known to solace there and cheer. (1896, 33)

This poem refers to Gonne's protests of tenant evictions in the West of Ireland and her incendiary writings in *L'Irlande Libre*. Acts that would have been read as aggressive political confrontations if men performed them were read as docile, nurturing actions when the beautiful Gonne performed them.

Other women, lacking Gonne's physical and economic advantages, performed as extraordinary women by displaying their feminine "accomplishments." When Margaret M. Sheehy performed in Sligo to raise money for the Dominican Fathers in 1902, she showed her skill at the art of recitation. "This talented lady," the *Freeman's Journal* recorded, "who is the daughter of Mr. David Sheehy, ex-member of Parliament . . . delighted the large and fashionable audience" ("Miss Margaret M. Sheehy in the Provinces," 7 April 1902, 2). Yet her political commitment is evident in her elocutionary selection, "Robert Emmet's Speech from the Dock." Although her performance is in a culturally devalued "feminine" form, the political resonance derived from reciting the speech of the hero of the military rebellion of 1803 could not have been ignored by the audience. Her representation in the newspaper puts her work in the feminine sphere, but her speech embodies the commitment of the nationalist movement to Irish independence.[6]

6. Margaret's sister, Hannah, employed this tactic to some extent in the years after her husband's murder in a British prison during the Easter Rebellion of 1916. Hannah

The personal commitment of women such as Gonne and Sheehy drew them into the public sphere as speakers and activists, but the interpretation of their acts by their audiences, male colleagues, and the press forced them to negotiate the ideological tension of female bodies doing men's work. Other women were able to avoid the gender complexities inherent in performing physically in the public sphere because their work was through writing. Ethna Carberry (Anna Johnston) and Alice Milligan, for example, edited the *Shan Van Vocht* from 1896 to 1899. Contributing writers, besides the editors, included Katharine Tynan, W. B. Yeats, and socialist leader James Connolly (Innes 1993, 135–36). Apparently, writing, even about and in the public sphere, was deemed "private" enough a task for women to perform it without appearing to cross into the public, male realm. But, at the same time, as more women insisted on a role in the public sphere of the nationalist movement, they loosened the boundaries between women's and men's nationalist work, degendering many tasks and increasing opportunities for women's influence. In 1900, a group of Irish nationalist women made such a forum for public involvement for themselves.

On Easter Sunday 1900, fifteen women met in the Celtic Literary Society Rooms to plan a gift for Arthur Griffith, editor of the radical paper the *United Irishman* and future founder of Sinn Fein. Griffith had broken his *jam bok* (a South African walking stick) over the back of a writer for the society journal *Figaro*. The reporter had accused Maud Gonne of being a British spy, and Griffith had been defending her political honor (Ward 1983, 47). Besides being a close personal friend and political ally, Gonne wrote for Griffith's paper and gave him money so that he could devote himself to his political work. Griffith's gratitude

---

Sheehy-Skeffington certainly had been an independent thinker and vocal activist for nationalism, socialism, and women's suffrage in the years before her husband's death. His death, however, added the ideological weight of being the widow of a revolutionary martyr to her already powerful image. Sheehy-Skeffington, Padraic Pearse's mother and his sister Margaret, Kathleen Clarke, and Gonne MacBride, among others, were not above manipulating their relationships to the martyrs of 1916 to lend authority to their voices and their causes.

and admiration for Gonne accounts at least in part for his chivalry regarding her good name as well as for the detailed and laudatory articles that Gonne's and, later, Inghinidhe na hEireann activities received in his newspaper.[7]

The women's conversation ultimately turned to Queen Victoria's recent visit to Ireland to increase Irish enlistment into the British army to fight in the Boer War. During her visit, Victoria sponsored a Children's Treat in Phoenix Park, and five thousand children attended (Ward 1983, 48–49). The nationalist women decided to retaliate against this overt English propaganda by sponsoring an Irish Patriotic Children's Treat that summer, on the Sunday following the commemoration of Wolfe Tone.

Men and women throughout the nationalist movement enthusiastically supported the idea. By summer, more than fifty women were involved in organizing the event, and in the four days before the treat more than one hundred men and women packed twenty thousand lunches for the children (Gonne MacBride 1974, 294–95). Dozens of individuals made financial contributions, including Anna Parnell (who was practically destitute at this time). The Irish National Club and Hibernian Club collected money for the event ("The Patriotic Children's Treat," *United Irishman,* 30 June 1900, 6), and the Phoenix Brewery Company gave a kilderkin of ale for the chaperones ("Patriotic Children's Treat," *United Irishman,* 7 July 1900, 7).

The treat itself became a kind of nationalist rally for the children who attended, the stewards who supervised, and the adults who looked on. An hour before the children arrived, "23 vehicles [bearing food and drink for the treat], adorned with Irish, American, French and Boer flags, started for Clonturk an hour ahead of the children, and presented an imposing spectacle" (ibid.). The children gathered around Beresford Place to march in a kind of parade to the site of the treat at Clon-

---

7. Other nationalist papers (including *An Claidheamh Soluis,* the *Irish People,* the *Freeman's Journal*) also discussed Inghinidhe activities, but not in the same detail. Mainstream papers, such as the *Irish Times,* usually ignored the group, as they ignored most nationalist organizations.

turk Park. This procession of more than twenty thousand children took ninety minutes and was two miles long. Along the route, the children waved flags and sang patriotic songs (ibid.). The *United Irishman* noted that when the children passed the Orange Hall in Rutland Square, "from which a Union Jack was flying, the youngsters threw redoubled vigour and energy into their admirable rendering of 'God Save Ireland,' which was followed by lusty cheering" (ibid.).

But children were not the only parade participants. The article goes on to describe how members of nationalist organizations marshaled the children on the march to Clonturk Park, and "about half-a-dozen bands" also attended. Also, "the footpaths were thronged with people all along the line of route, and spectators occupied windows commanding a view of the procession" (ibid.). Arthur Griffith commented in the *United Irishman* that "Dublin never witnessed anything so marvelous as the procession through its streets . . . of the 30,000 schoolchildren who refused to be bribed into parading before the Queen of England" (Cardozo 1978, 189).

The Patriotic Children's Treat became an incredible spectacle of the strength and fervor of Irish nationalism in Dublin—the largest political rally in the city up to that time. Within the park, the children participated in games, the Gaelic Athletic Association played a demonstration game of hurling, and four speakers gave speeches from platforms in different areas of the park. In her autobiography, Maud Gonne (then Maud Gonne MacBride) commented that, years later, "middle-aged men and women would come up to me in the streets and say: 'I was one of the patriotic children at your party when Queen Victoria was over' " (Gonne MacBride 1974, 295). On one hand, the Irish Patriotic Children's Treat seems like unempowering "women's work" because it was geared toward children. Daphne Spain (1992) points out how giving women contact with and authority over only typically disempowered groups, such as the ill and children, gains women no real power in the public sphere (172–83). Additionally, such positions allow women to do only what is regarded as private, feminine work—healing and nurturing—even if these acts are performed in public. Further, although the Patriotic Children's Treat enabled women to extend their nationalist activity into more visible arenas, it did not necessarily espouse a new role for women in Ireland. In her speech to the children, Maud Gonne, the only woman of the four speakers that day, urged the little boys in the audience never to wear a British uniform. Only after speaking to the boys in the audience did Gonne add that the girls should encourage their fathers, brothers, and male friends not to join the British forces. True, Gonne herself had spent much time in the past few years discouraging men from joining the British army to participate in the Boer War, and such activity was politically useful. But no political work outside encouraging and supporting men's activity was presented as an option for the girls. However, the girls may have found role models in the women running the event, even if many of these women were still too timid to speak before the crowd.

The Patriotic Children's Treat was ultimately an empowering moment for nationalist women. The women who organized the treat had full control over the event and the nationalist message it carried. They educated thousands of children about the nationalist cause, while giving them an opportunity to perform their political allegiance. Male volunteers (who took on "domestic" tasks such as making sandwiches and marshaling children at the treat) were subordinate to the women leaders, giving women an opportunity to lead men as well as women. Organizing the treat allowed women to find a public voice by uniting with other concerned women, thus empowering both the nationalist women's community as a whole and the individual women in it.

Inspired by their success and with some money left over from the Children's Treat, the women created a permanent organization—Inghinidhe na hEireann, which attracted "many brilliant young women—but more than brilliant—illuminated by an idea and devoted in support of it" (Colum 1988, 61). Most of the women were middle-class Catholics (although there were some working-class, Protestant Anglo-Irish, and wealthy women, as well) who had already gained a degree of personal autonomy through receiving a good education and working or participating in activities outside the home. In this uncertain period, when the nationalist movement was torn between supporting radical or parliamentary measures to achieve independence, Inghinidhe was committed to achieving Irish nationhood by any means, including military force. Some of the women—such as Maire Nic Shiubhlaigh (Mary Walker), Hannah Sheehy, and Maire Killeen—were members of nationalist families who sought a vehicle for personal involvement in the movement. Others—such as Jenny Wyse-Power, Sinead O'Flanagan, Ethna Carberry, Alice Milligan, and, of course, Maud Gonne—had established nationalist reputations as authors and editors, but wished to increase the visibility of the women's community in the cause of Irish nationalism.

Inghinidhe na hEireann significantly contributed to integrating the nationalist movement by blurring the boundaries between private and public, personal and political, and individual and communal in women's political activity. The objects of the society included:

> 1. To encourage the study of Gaelic Irish Literature, Music, and Art, especially amongst the young, by the organising and teaching of classes for the above subjects [and]:
> 3. To discourage the reading and circulation of low English literature, the singing of English songs, the attending of vulgar English entertainments at theatres and music-halls, and to combat in every way English influence, which is doing so much injury to the artistic taste and refinement of the Irish people. *(Programme for Deirdre and Kathleen ni Houlihan* [1902], 4)

The rules of the organization corroborated with the groups ideals, stating that: "Each member must adapt a Gaelic name by which she shall be known in the Association" and "Each member shall pledge herself to aid in extending and popularising Gaelic as a spoken tongue and to advance the Irish language movement by every means in her power" (ibid.). Thus, the political act of affirming and proliferating Irish culture in order to weaken colonial English influence was confirmed by the personal imperatives placed in the rules.

Inghinidhe's second object, "To support and popularise Irish manufactures," called for the public act of strengthening Ireland's economy and decreasing its material dependence on England. This reflected the organization rule that "[e]ach member shall pledge herself to support Irish manufacture by using as far as possible Irish-made goods in her household and dress" (ibid.). In other words, an Inghinidhe member's public economic choices about maintaining her private sphere (dress, food, household goods) were recognized as politically charged activities that carried economic weight. Inghinidhe na hEireann was not alone in this ideal: stores often pointed out that they sold Irish goods in their advertisements in Irish nationalist papers.

Finally, Inghinidhe members' commitment to this women's community is confirmed in the first rule of the organization: "The *Inghinidhe na h-Eireann,* remembering that they are all workers in the same holy cause, pledge themselves to mutual help and support, and to stand loyally by one another" (ibid.). Each member's talents supported the organization, and the organization supported each member, providing a place where women's nationalist work would be not only allowed, but also valued.

Although the wealthy, Anglo-Irish Maud Gonne was their leader, the large number of middle-class and working-class young women in Inghinidhe na hEireann were not by any means docile followers of their colorful leader. Ella Young's recollection of the members points out that the group was far from an idle diversion for them: "The Society is composed of girls who work hard all day in shops and offices owned for the most part by pro-British masters who may at any moment discharge them for 'treasonable activities.' To be dismissed in such wise means the semi-starvation of long-continued unemployment. These girls dare it, and subscribe, from not too abundant wages, generous amounts for the hire of halls to be used as class-rooms and for theatre rehearsals" (Young 1995, 19).

Inghinidhe na hEireann immediately began classes in Irish language, history, and music for children older than the age of nine (Ward 1983, 52), and they planned a Christmas children's treat for January 1902 *(Freeman's Journal,* 31 December 1901, 2). Yet their work included adult classes and entertainments as well. Inghinidhe sponsored a monthly *ceili* and invited members of other nationalist organizations, such as the Celtic Literary Society (Ward 1983, 52). An Inghinidhe member would read a paper on a Celtic heroine or famous woman in Irish history at each of these events, providing female role models for the other members and a public platform for the speaker (Inghinidhe na h'Eireann 1901, 6). Many more women felt at ease on the speaker's platform than had at the children treat months before.

Other Inghinidhe projects, however, were less-traditional women's work. One of the most daring Inghinidhe practices was their campaign on O'Connell Street against Irish enlistment in the British army. English soldiers frequented a section of this main thoroughfare and the saloons on it, leading to frequent confrontations between nationalists and loyalists. Inghinidhe members distributed leaflets to Irish women on O'Connell Street, urging them not to consort with British soldiers (Gonne MacBride 1974, 292). Carrying a tract by the Rev. Father Cavanagh claiming that fighting in unjust wars (i.e., on the English side of the Boer War) was equal to committing murder, other women would follow soldiers into saloons—places the women would not go normally—to distribute these leaflets. These actions often led to shouting matches and fistfights between soldiers and male Irish nationalists coming to the women's "aid" (ibid.).

O'Connell Street, being Dublin's main thoroughfare, was a dangerous place for the bodies—and reputations—of "respectable" Irish women to be performing political acts and walking into saloons. Nationalists were quick to question the political and moral reputations of any woman accompanying a British soldier there. Inghinidhe members who campaigned on this street, therefore, were taking both a political and a personal risk. In *Women in Public: Between Banners and Ballots*, Mary Ryan notes how the geography of cities was gendered in the nineteenth century, segregating men's and women's participation in the public realm. Ryan further points out that "[t]he politics of the public streets divided women by race and class, and between the dangerous and the endangered" (1990, 94). Entering streets considered dangerous to women threatened a woman's respectability, making her, in turn, seem dangerous to men. Although their involvement in this Inghinidhe action allowed the women to keep their reputations in the community, the male nationalists' "rescue" of the women harkens back to the rhetoric of Hibernia and the Shan Van Vocht; it comes dangerously close to usurping the women's control over their political act. Yet Inghinidhe's actions were also attempts to reclaim O'Connell Street as a female as well as a male space, calling for equally respectable, nationalist behavior from the male and female inhabitants of the street. Again, Inghinidhe subverted gender codes by rewriting them in the name of nationalism.

Ultimately, Inghinidhe's performances of Irish nationalist woman-hood would include not only the speaker's platform and the street corner but the traditional stage as well. By 1901, the women had begun to perform *tableaux vivants* on Irish themes, enlisting the help of Alice Milligan, by then an active member of Inghinidhe and a noted play-wright among nationalist circles. Her one-act play *The Last Feast of the Fianna* had been performed by the Irish Literary Theater in 1900, and other works by her had been performed at Gaelic League events. Milli-gan's *tableaux vivants,* such as "The Battle of Clontarf," "The Children of Lir," and "The Fairy Changeling" (Reynolds 1902, 258), contained many of the kinds of tropes one would expect to find in a British panto—fairies, beautiful ladies, fantastic settings—but (as noted in chapter 1) her dramas were actually politically charged.

The Irish nationalist community warmly received these tableaux, which were performed by Inghinidhe members and male collaborators in the project, including Douglas Hyde, the leader of the Gaelic League. When Inghinidhe's April 1901 production was performed be-fore a full house in the Antient Concert Rooms, the *Freeman's Journal* noted that "[t]he whole production reflects the greatest credit on all concerned, not only for the faultless manner in which the several per-formers acquitted themselves, but for the evident attention that was given to historic accuracy by those who had the difficult task of arrang-ing and grouping of the figures conceived in accordance with the tradi-tion or story represented" ("Inghinidhe na h-Eireann: Gaelic Tableaux Vivants," *Freeman's Journal,* 10 April 1901, 5). Six months after ap-pearing in this production, Hyde would star in the Irish Literary The-atre production of his first play, *The Twisting of the Rope.*

The *Freeman's Journal* represented the evening of *ceilithe* and tableaux as a much more docile event than it actually was. More than one hundred people took part in the production, including a choir that provided musical background to the images. W. G. Fay stage managed the event, and along with Inghinidhe actors, noted figures in the movement such as Douglas Hyde and Seamus McManus appeared in the *ceilithe* (Inghinidhe na h'Eireann 1901, 8). The hall was "crammed in every part" the night the *United Irishman* reviewer attended ("The Gaelic Tableaux," 13 April 1901, 5). The success of the event is further confirmed by the profit the group made: net proceeds of the tableaux came to twenty-two pounds (Inghinidhe na h'Eireann 1901, 8). Some of the tableaux presented typical images of women in Irish nationalism. "The Battle of Clontarf," for example, told the story of King Brian's army driving the Danes out of Ireland. The *United Irishman* stated that the tableaux "brought vividly back to us the fateful Good Friday eight hundred years ago when the Irish warriors broke for ever the power of the Vikings, and changed the current of European history" (13 April 1901, 5). Rather than beginning with the story of the battle, however, the first tableau established the well-being of Irish persons—most notably Irish *women*—under Brian's reign. It presented "the bejewelled lady who wandered through our island, protected only by her maiden smile," while a "bewildered knight—more than likely a Saxon knight-errant" looked on, puzzled that the woman needed no protection from harm during King Brian's reign (ibid.).

This image implied that eleventh-century (and, correspondingly, nineteenth-century) Irish followed loftier ethical and moral codes than their English counterparts. It also drew the audience's attention to an image of the Irish woman as beautiful and pure. But unlike the beautiful, pure image of a poor Hibernia in the contemporary popular press, this rich woman in a precolonial Ireland needed no protection or vengeance. Still, the puzzled "knight-errant" was a confusing image in the tableau. In precolonial Ireland, he looks on in wonder at the bejeweled maiden, but in the rhetoric of nationalism he is the one who steals her jewels, her virtue, and her four green fields.

Although the bejeweled maiden was a passive image in the performance, other tableaux portrayed women in more active roles, including "Maeve, greatest of Ireland's ancient heroines [and] Grania Mhaol vis-

iting Elizabeth and pulverising the virgin monarch, who strove to im-
press the splendid Irishwoman" *(United Irishman,* 13 April 1901, 5).
The historical figures Ann Devlin and Sarah Curran from the days of
the United Irishman Rebellion were also presented. One of the most
powerful images of the performance, however, occurred in the tableaux
of Ireland Fettered and Ireland Free. Ireland Fettered is a typical nationalist Hibernia image, "crouching over her unstrung harp at the base
of the Celtic cross" (ibid.). Here, Hibernia was presented as a weak figure crouched limply against the cross, her unstrung harp leaving her
voiceless. In the next tableau, however, the audience saw "Ireland Free,
erect against the cross, her harp newstrung at her feet, her green robe
flowing around her, the cap of Liberty on her head, and in her hand a
shining sword" (ibid.). This strong, "erect" woman, with the red cap of
the French Revolution on her head and a "naked" sword in her hand,
appropriated masculine imagery, representing Hibernia as a strong,
protective, aggressive fighter. "This tableaux evoked a tremendous out-
burst of enthusiasm," the reviewer reported, "and the shouts of 'Aris!
Aris!' [Again! Again!] caused the women to repeat the scene again and
again" (ibid.). Another tableau picturing "the Boer fight for freedom"
was replayed four times (ibid).

Inghinidhe na hEireann was also active in the production of Irish
plays, performing the works of Irish playwrights such as Alice Milligan
and Father Dinneen (Hogan and Kilroy 1976, 85). The actresses were
Inghinidhe members, and male actors were recruited from other nationalist groups such as the Celtic Literary Society and the Gaelic
League. They had hired William G. Fay, who had served as stage manager for the tableaux, as a teacher, and as a director. Along with teaching, acting, and directing plays for Inghinidhe, W. G. Fay even attended
some of the group's meetings. Inghinidhe na hEireann's dramatic
events quickly became popular throughout the nationalist community,
and it even earned the distinction of being the first group in modern
Dublin to perform a play completely in the Irish language—P. T.
MacGinley's *Eilis agus Bhean Deirce* (Ellis and the Beggarwoman)
(Reynolds 1902, 258).

Although the production of these plays points to increasing public, political activity among nationalist women, the plays themselves did not overtly reflect a new role for them, but relied on traditional representations of women currently shown on the stage. In *Eilis agus Bhean Deirce,* for example, a son plays a trick on his miserly mother by giving away her things to a beggarwoman. Milligan's *The Last Feast of the Fianna* portrays the Irish heroine Grania as a cruel and vain adulteress, and Niamh, the queen of the Sidhe, as a femme fatale.

But there are several possible reasons for such traditional representations of women in these plays. First, many of these dramas are based on heroic and folktale sources that already contained gender biases. Second, even potentially subversive theater tends to be read—and even performed—in the rhetoric of dominant acting and writing tropes (an especially common trap for amateur actors and playwrights). Third, Inghinidhe members had to negotiate the relationship between nationalism and feminism in their political work, and although many members were involved in feminist activity, the fight for women's equality was a subordinate issue within the organization to the fight for national independence. But their work did give women an organized, public voice in the discourse of Irish nationalism and highlighted the importance of traditional (and nontraditional) female tasks to gaining Irish independence.

By 1901, Inghinidhe performances were known throughout Ireland and had established themselves as a part of the Dublin political performance milieu. In October 1900, the moonlighting Willie Fay directed *Robert Emmet* by the American Robert Pilgrim, using the Dramatic Society of St. Teresa's Total Abstinence and Temperance Association for his cast (Hogan and Kilroy 1975, 85). As discussed above, also within this milieu, Gaelic League events often included play performances; the Queen's Royal Theatre presented commercial melodramas based on nationalist themes; and the most remembered company of the period, the Irish Literary Theatre, published its plays and critiques. By 1901, however, the directors of the Irish Literary Theatre determined that their third season would be their last.

Inghinidhe na hEireann's June performances, however, turned W. B. Yeats's eyes back to the Dublin theater. Inghinidhe produced an entertainment to provide a nationalist alternative to the events surrounding the Dublin horse show, which were deeply associated at that time with loyalist elements of the Anglo-Irish aristocracy. Along with a series of tableaux, Inghinidhe presented Alice Milligan's *The Deliverance of Red Hugh* and *The Harp That Once,* along with P. T. MacGinley's *Eilis agus Bhean Deirce* (Ward 1983, 56). In his autobiography, Yeats remembers, "I came away with my head on fire. I wanted to hear my own unfinished *Baile's Strand,* to hear Greek tragedy spoken with a Dublin accent" (1936, 72). Yeats had found the Irish actors he craved, and he was ready to appropriate them.

Meanwhile, Willie Fay read George Russell's dramatization of a scene from the Irish legend of Deirdre in the *All-Ireland Review* (Hogan and Kilroy 1976, 9) and was so enthralled that he urged Russell to finish it. Russell reluctantly agreed, and Fay helped him with the writing. Because the completed play was too short for a full evening's entertainment, Yeats contributed *Kathleen ni Houlihan,* a one-act drama set around the United Irishman Rebellion of 1798, as a second production. Although Yeats has traditionally received full credit for the play, he actually collaborated with Lady Gregory, who was responsible for the bulk of the dialect writing in the play. Yeats dreamed of Kathleen's final, haunting lines; Gregory contributed most of the rest.

In this most blatantly nationalistic of Yeats's plays, the Gillane family prepares for the marriage of their son, Michael, looking forward to happier economic times thanks to the bride's dowry, when an old woman enters the house. The "Poor Old Woman" turns out to be Kathleen ni Houlihan, a mythic folk figure who beckons Ireland's young men to defend the nation. Kathleen woos Michael away from the house, and the young man abandons his bride to die for his country. But his blood sacrifice renews the land, represented in the transformation of Kathleen. After Michael rushes out of the house, his younger brother, Patrick, reenters. His parents ask him if he had seen an old woman on the road. Patrick replies, "I did not, but I saw a young girl, and she had the walk of a queen" (Yeats 1953, 57).

Yeats wrote the part of Kathleen with Maud Gonne in mind and asked her to play it. Gonne had refused to perform in Yeats's *The*

Countess Cathleen with the Irish Literary Theatre a few years earlier, but recognizing the political influence her presence would create on the stage and wishing to support the event, she agreed to perform the role. In her autobiography, *A Servant of the Queen,* Gonne remarks that she performed the role because "it would have great importance for the Nationalist Movement" (Hogan and Kilroy 1976, 19).

Gonne's visibility in Irish nationalism at demonstrations, meetings, and other events and as the founder of Inghinidhe na hEireann made her a controversial and, some argued, unfeminine public figure, whose work was already too "theatrical" to be taken seriously. Dudley Digges, an actor in the 1902 performances, commented on the danger implicit in her taking the stage: "[Gonne] hesitated to give the loyalists a chance to ridicule her and say: 'Ah . . . yes . . . of course . . . the stage, that's where she belongs' " (1988, 33). Gonne was aware of the emotion her identity in the movement would generate when she played Kathleen ni Houlihan, the ghostly figure beckoning Irishmen to die for national independence. Theatrical performance potentially could have broken the balance Gonne constantly negotiated between her presentation of the nationalist cause and her representation as an "extraordinary woman." She hoped her reputation as a nationalist figure would make the play more political, but it could easily have made her political activity seem, in retrospect, pure theater. Perhaps that is why she served the Irish theater later as an administrator rather than as a performer and reserved her public presentations for strictly political events unmediated by the traditional stage.

But Gonne enthusiastically took the risk to show her support for the production and the groups involved in it, and the gamble with her reputation ultimately paid off. The actress Maire Nic Shiubhlaigh, who would later perform the same role at the Abbey Theatre, commented on Gonne's performance: "in her, the youth of the country saw all that was magnificent in Ireland. She was the very personification of the figure she played on stage" (qtd. in Ward 1983, 56–57).

When a political actor (such as an Inghinidhe na hEireann actress) takes the stage, she registers at least two representations for the audience. She is the character she portrays, and she is also recognized as a political actor. If she is a famous political figure or recognized as an activist by someone in the audience, a third representation—that of her identity in the movement—arises out of her performance for those audience members in the know. These three significations from the one body—as character in a political play, as political actor, and as political activist—build on and reflect one another in performance. Gonne's ability to play on her political identity as nationalist activist and founder of Inghinidhe na hEireann in her portrayal of Kathleen ni Houlihan—the female embodiment of Ireland—made her performance one of the most remembered in Irish theater history.

Kathleen ni Houlihan, despite its folklore theme, is set at an actual moment in Irish history—the landing of the French at Kilalla during the United Irishman Revolt of 1798. Russell's *Deirdre,* however, is based on a story from the Red Branch cycle of ancient Irish myth, making the political overtones of the play more oblique. By using a mythological story, Russell sidestepped an overt discussion of contemporary issues of cultural identity or national history. Yet, to tell a story from Ireland's ancient past was to mythopoeticize Ireland's ancient heroes, making them and their stories metaphors for contemporary issues. Russell's manipulation of his source story and its performance by Inghinidhe members and nationalist actors with other affiliations transformed the myth into a metaphor for the need for unity and inclusion among different groups within the nationalist movement.

In the source story, Deirdre, a beautiful woman promised to Concobar, high king of the Red Branch (an alliance of kings in Ireland), runs away with the warrior Naoise, and they exile themselves in Scotland. Concobar, in his jealousy, convinces Fergus, another Red Branch king, to persuade them to return to Ireland, assuring Fergus that he has forgiven the lovers. Deirdre and Naoise return to Ireland, but Fergus stays behind to attend a feast, planning to join them later. Concobar betrays his word and kills Naoise. Later, Deirdre commits suicide.

Usually, Deirdre is portrayed as an Irish Helen of Troy—a passive beauty whose treachery brings down the alliance of the Red Branch. In Russell's story, however, a divine vision, rather than uncontrollable passion, brings Deirdre and Naoise together. Their elopement is not as much selfish as it is inevitable obedience to divine will over earthly law. Russell also adds another strong female character, the Druidess, Lavarcam. Acknowledged as a wise woman by all the characters, Lavarcam foresees the ensuing tragedy and advises Naoise and Concobar to set aside their quarrels and maintain unity among the Red Branch at any cost. Deirdre, likewise, understands the political consequences of Naoise's and her own actions, and urges Naoise to avoid conflict with Concobar, knowing it will lead to their destruction.

Deirdre and Lavarcam, thus, are not femmes fatales or benign beauties passively awaiting rescue, but active and sympathetic figures. Russell's play gives them a high degree of agency, and both characters are respected by the men in the play for their wisdom and bravery. Inghinidhe na hEireann members who played these roles, therefore, portrayed Irish women as brave, intelligent, willing to live or die for their ideals, and worthy of the respect of their male counterparts. This is the same role for Irish women that Inghinidhe na hEireann cultivated on stage in its own dramatic performances and offstage among the nationalist community.

Deirdre in performance looked much like an Inghinidhe tableau. The actors performed the play behind a gauze "lit by green lights, giving an eerie atmosphere" (Hogan and Kilroy 1976, 12). In a January 1899 *Daily Express,* Milligan discussed her plan to use a gauze curtain in a play she was developing for the Gaelic League, *Oireachtas* (21 January 1899, 3, qtd. in Hogan and Kilroy 1975, 53). Two years later, the Irish National Theatre Society used the same staging method for Yeats's play *The Shadowy Waters.* In his enthusiastically flattering review of the performers in *Deirdre* in his essay "The Acting at St. Teresa's Hall," Yeats admired the "gravity and simplicity and quietness" of the acting, describing how "the actors moved about very little, they often did no more than pose in some *statuesque* way and speak; and there were moments when it seemed *as if some painting upon a wall,* some rhythmic processional along the walls of a temple had begun to move before me with a dim, magical life" *(United Irishman,* 12 April 1902, 3, italics mine). Yeats's interrogation into such areas of European theater as symbolist drama and the designs of Edward Gordon Craig nurtured a passion in the burgeoning playwright for stillness and beauty on the stage. But Yeats was already witnessing this kind of performance in Fay's work among Inghinidhe nationalist actors.

Yeats's *Kathleen ni Houlihan* did not receive the same positive response; the first night performance was anything but "gravity and simplicity and quietness" as the audience laughed at W. G. Fay's interpretation of the father of the Gillane household. Fay played the dialect role in the style of the melodramatic stage and received the usual response among Dublin audiences for that stylization. "He was not played as a Mayo peasant, perplexed and frightened by some vague terror impending," Edward Martyn admonished, "but as a Dublin jarvey whose reputation secured for every remark a laugh from his fare" *(United Irishman,* 19 April 1902, 1). Although unfortunate for Yeats's play, the audience's response to Fay's acting in this tragic drama does point out the audience's ability to identify particular acting styles and that they tended to respond to a drama according to the performance mode before them.

Inghinidhe's involvement in the first production of *Kathleen ni Houlihan* and *Deirdre* was highly visible to the audience and to the Dublin community. The organization was listed first on the program cover, and its members also received credit for sewing the costumes. The house—which was "too crowded for comfort" with "an audience vibrating with enthusiasm and quick to seize every point and to grasp every situation" ("Two Irish Plays: by Mr. W. B. Yeats and A.E.: The Performance Last Night," *Freeman's Journal,* 3 April 1902, 5)—can also be accredited to Inghinidhe, which publicized and sold tickets for the event. The actors in W. G. Fay's company were all either members of the Inghinidhe na hEireann (Maire Nic Shiubhlaigh, Maire Quinn, Maud Gonne) or members of the Celtic Literary Society who had performed in prior Inghinidhe performances. "[T]he large banner of the '*Inghinidhe na h-Eireann,*' having a gold sunburst on a blue ground, hung near the stage" (ibid.). But in the gendered language of more mainstream presses (and ultimately historical memory), these signs of Inghinidhe's involvement faded in favor of a celebration of Fay, Yeats, and Russell. The press and later recollections by participants in the event deemed the tasks performed by Inghinidhe —such as sewing costumes, organizing the event, and selling tickets—as unimportant, anonymous, or simply "women's work." Thus, they were relegated to devalued labor and not worth notice. Although Inghinidhe originally gathered the actors together and hired Fay to direct them, Fay's position as director has made him remembered as the only developer of the Irish National Dramatic Company.

The closing review of the *Freeman's Journal,* 7 April 1902, recorded the speeches Russell and Yeats, the playwrights, gave, expressing their excitement over the future of Irish national theater. The only acknowledgment of the production itself that the reviewer recorded was a comment by Yeats, who "congratulated Mr. Fay upon the great success of his effort at the formation of an Irish National Dramatic company which in his opinion had already shown itself well fitted to carry on the work of the Irish Literary Theatre" (7). Yeats's comment obliterates Inghinidhe's involvement by crediting only Fay with gathering the actors, when actually he had originally been hired by Inghinidhe. Further, by implying that the company would carry on the work of the Irish Literary Theatre, Yeats appropriated the successful history of Inghinidhe's dramatic efforts, aligning it to his own failed project.

Thus, the collaborative effort of this performance project by several groups was ultimately recorded as the work of a few individuals. Inghinidhe members who performed in the play were regarded as actresses, not nationalist actors on and off the stage. Ultimately, Gonne's performance would become the most-remembered aspect of the performances, but with the disappearance of Inghinidhe in the history of the production, her involvement is remembered mainly as a favor to Yeats, not a dangerous act in support of her organization and of the nationalist movement generally.

Likewise, Maire Nic Shiubhlaigh, another Inghinidhe member who performed in *Deirdre* in 1902, continued to work with Fay and the Irish National Theatre and acquired a great reputation on the Irish stage. Not only was Nic Shuibliagh active in Inghinidhe, she fought as a senior member of the Cumann na mBan (the Women's Association) in the Easter Rising of 1916. But just as the Inghinidhe has receded from the historical memory of the Irish dramatic movement, Nic Shuibhliagh's political activity has receded in light of her acting career. Other Inghinidhe members achieved prominence in the women's suffrage, nationalist, and workers' movements—inspired to and educated in public activism through this first political group.

By the time the Irish National Theatre Society was established in 1903, Inghinidhe had discontinued its official dramatic activity, although some of its members were involved in both organizations (Ward 1983, 57). In fact, Inghinidhe members would become visible everywhere in the Irish national movement. They were stars of the Abbey Stage, leaders of Sinn Fein and Cumann na mBan, union leaders, suffrage leaders, and, during the Easter Rising, soldiers. They were performing women's work, not as auxiliary women in male-dominated groups, as they were in the 1890s, but as women in increasingly integrated political organizations.

To ignore women's work in Irish political history is to obscure the range of political activism surrounding Ireland's quest for independence. To deny Inghinidhe's place in the history of Irish theater is to veil the true heterogeneity of cultural identity within the Irish nationalist movement and the wide aesthetic and ideological scopes of performance practices at this volatile time in Irish national history. The marginalization of Inghinidhe na hEireann in the dominant narrative of Irish theater history reflects the increasing hierarchization of performance groups with the establishment of the Abbey in 1904. As the Abbey Theatre and its directors—W. B. Yeats, Lady Gregory, and J. M. Synge—centralized more and more economic power and cultural authority throughout the first decade of the theater, its narrative, its ideology, and its aesthetics increasingly overshadowed other significant contributions to the Irish dramatic movement.

4

Nationalist Performance Becomes Profession
The Abbey Theatre

[R]elieved of the necessity to obtain an audience, the artist becomes self-conscious and self-contained; and it is considerably a question of the personality of Mr. Yeats whether the new theatre is to retain a bond between itself and the people.
                    —Maurice Joy, "The Irish National Theatre"

MAURICE JOY MADE THE ASTUTE OBSERVATION given in the epigraph on the eve of the official opening of the Abbey Theatre, the permanent, endowed home of the Irish National Theatre Society. Two and one half years after the collaborative performances of *Deirdre* and *Kathleen ni Houlihan* by the Irish National Dramatic Company—made up of members of Inghinidhe na hEireann, the Celtic Literary Society, the Ormonde Dramatic Society, the Gaelic League, and the Irish Literary Theatre—the descendant of that company had a permanent home on the Dublin landscape. But artistic, political, and organizational conflicts were already causing dissension—and even resignations—among the company. The added weight of their own building—and a very temperamental benefactor—exacerbated the conflicts regarding the aesthetics, ideology, and goals of the theater running rampant through the company.

The Abbey Theatre building, as the Irish national theater, was identified as a physical site in the Dublin town center and an ideological focal point for nationalist Irish drama; it was the only permanent performance space in Dublin in which one was assured that the evening's entertainment would always have something to do with the Celtic revival. And because the space could be rented to other nationalist groups, often it would serve as a communal site for groups with diverse ideas. Although the Abbey Theatre Company became increasingly exclusive, the Abbey Theatre space was open to an array of diverse representations of Ireland, nationalism, and theater.

The Abbey Theatre simultaneously occupied multiple, often contradictory identity positions as theater building, theater company, and theatrical movement, reflecting the conflicting ideas of Irish culture and nationalism in turn-of-the-century Ireland and different opinions in the movement concerning the proper use of theater as a political tool. Traditionally, the turbulent years 1903–10 of the Irish National Theatre Society have been read through a literary lens as purely textual controversies, looking at the internal and external disputes surrounding the Abbey (the 1903 decision not to produce *The Saxon Shillin'*, public incomprehension of *The Shadowy Waters* and other verse plays by Yeats, outcry against Synge's *Shadow of the Glen*, and the riots around *The Playboy of the Western World*). But the arguments between directors and company and between company and community were not based solely on the proper balance between ideology and art in a national theater. Equally if not more important was the role of the theater in the wide spectrum of nationalist activity in contemporary Dublin and the theater's responsibility to the people it claimed to represent as Ireland's national house. Although almost everyone in the Irish cultural revival believed that a national theater was an important goal, the politics of that theater—what kinds of productions it would serve up and to whom—remained a hot controversy. Everyone who entered the Abbey Theatre—be it as actor, playwright, patron, guest company member, spectator—entered into the larger nationalist debate.

The history of the Irish National Theatre Society in these formative years does not read like the linear narrative found in most traditional accounts, but like a farce, with entrances, exits, complicated plots, mistaken motives, and unlikely collaborations. As Yeats commandeered authority over the management, texts, performance style, and ideology

of the Abbey Theatre, he also created a focal point for the argument between different nationalist dramatic practices to the point that the
Abbey stage became the literal and figurative site of contest for Ireland's
nationalist theatrical ideals. By examining some of those entrances and
exits of texts, ideologies, policies, and personnel—by reading some of
the Abbey's "stage directions" in its formative moments—this chapter
reveals the mercurial nature of the company in its first decade and its
multiple roles in the increasingly active Irish nationalist performance
community.

Yeats's initial involvement in the company that would later be
shaped into the Irish National Theatre Society—the Irish National Dramatic Company—was peripheral. After the tremendous success of the
performances of Yeats's *Kathleen ni Houlihan* and Russell's *Deirdre* in
St. Teresa's Hall, the Fays and the actors of the Irish National Dramatic
Company continued to work together and decided to form a permanent society to be called the Irish National Theatre Society. The actors
of the company were all members of nationalist organizations around
Dublin—Inghinidhe na hEireann, the Celtic Literary Society, and the
Gaelic League—and (except for their organizers, the Fays) were amateurs who saw their work in the theater as primarily a nationalist enterprise. Thus, they created their company on a similar model to the
political groups from which they came, in which energy and commitment to the nationalist cause, rather than acting ability, were the marks
of a good member.

All members of the Irish National Dramatic Company were involved in planning the mission of the new theater society. They agreed
on two main principles for the company: that the society be a "purely
co-operative one," with all members involved in the artistic and administrative decisions of the group, and that "all the members were to be
amateurs" (Nic Shiubhlaigh 1955, 22). This amateur status gave the
company political freedom, while undermining the possibility of competition over actor status among the company members. In 1903, the
Irish National Dramatic Company reorganized as the Irish National
Theatre Society.

In their statement of aims, The Irish National Theatre Society claimed that they planned "to continue—if possible on a more permanent basis—the work begun by the Irish Literary Theatre, to create an Irish national theater by producing plays in English and Irish, written by Irish writers or on Irish subjects, or such dramatic works of foreign authors as would tend to educate and interest the public in the higher and more vital forms of dramatic art" ([Irish National Theatre Society] 1903, 1). Clearly the Irish National Theatre Society admired and adapted the intellectual principles of the Irish Literary Theatre, but it rejected its organizational structure. The Irish Literary Theatre had been hierarchically structured and carefully controlled by its directors in its quest to create a body of good Irish dramatic literature and to produce this literature in polished, professional performances, even if that meant importing professional, English actors. The Irish Literary Theatre directors established careful, hierarchical control over its employees and its product. The Irish National Theatre Society, however, initially structured itself according to egalitarian and nationalist principles, and the main goal of its performances was to encourage the spirit and growth of the nationalist movement among Irish nationalists. In that spirit, the society structured itself according to the more egalitarian principles of groups such as the Gaelic League or Inghinidhe na hEireann.

Yeats was the only Irish Literary Theatre director involved in the Irish National Theatre Society in its earliest days and then only marginally. At the meeting at which they appointed officers, Russell declined the presidency in favor of Yeats, who was not even present at the time. Making Yeats the head of the organization gave the new society clout in artistic circles, but the structure of the society did not give him any authority over the group: his involvement was limited to that of an invited figurehead. Russell, along with Douglas Hyde and Maud Gonne, became the vice presidents of the organization, with W. G. Fay as stage manager and Fred Ryan as secretary.[1] Hyde had written a play for the Irish Literary Theatre, *The Twisting of the Rope*, but it had been per-

---

1. The founding members were W. G. Fay, Frank Fay, Dudley Digges, P. J. Kelly, Mary Walker (Maire Nic Shiubhlaigh), Sara Allgood, Maire T. Quinn, Padraic Colum,

formed in Irish by members of the Keating Branch of the Gaelic League, with W. G. Fay directing. The Irish Literary Theatre's real involvement in the production of Hyde's play, outside sponsoring the event and encouraging Hyde in the early writing of his play, was minimal.

The actors and enthusiasts who formed the Irish National Theatre Society admired the dramatic legacy of the Irish Literary Theatre's three-season existence, but they brought their own experience, ideals, and aesthetics to the new group. They wanted to produce good plays, but they were a nationalist political group first. And they wanted to have fun. Nic Shiubhlaigh and Cousins both note in their memoirs that during that first summer the organization met informally over tea at one another's homes for lessons from the Fays. They also held what Cousins called in a 1938 letter " 'Pic-nic' rehearsals . . . Frank Fay believing that speakers who could make themselves heard in the open air could be intelligible in the back of the hall" (ms. 11,000, National Library of Ireland, qtd. in Hogan and Kilroy 1976, 29). Nic Shiubhlaigh recalls that after rehearsal the company would hike through the countryside, and Russell often joined them with his easel and paints. Like most political organizations, the Irish National Theatre Society recognized that one of the main interests of members of a volunteer organization, outside any particular goals, is to establish a community of individuals with similar interests and beliefs. Thus, a strong element of the Irish National Theatre Society's early experience was social as well as political in intent. Such a friendly attitude must have contributed to the volunteerism among the group in the early days, as everyone spent hours after work rehearsing, building, painting sets and properties, or installing seats in their first performance space in Camden Street. Meanwhile, Irish National Theatre Society members continued nontheatrical activities with groups such as Inghinidhe na hEireann and the Gaelic League.

The Irish National Theatre Society's first performances at the

---

Fred Ryan, James H. Cousins, James Starkey, George Roberts, George Russell (Æ), and Frank Walker.

Samhain Festival—an annual cultural festival sponsored by Cumann na nGaedheal (an umbrella organization for Dublin nationalist groups with a more politicized platform than the Gaelic League) reflected the democratic, nationalist spirit of the group. Maud Gonne performed the role of the Poor Old Woman for the last time in the restaging of *Kathleen ni Houlihan,* and the company produced Russell's *Deirdre* again, along with Yeats's new play *The Pot of Broth.* Yeats and his collaborator, Florence Farr, were on the bill twice under the auspices of the Irish National Dramatic Company to lecture and demonstrate their experiments with verse speaking to the psaltery. The repertoire also included a play produced by the company before Russell and Yeats joined in the theater venture: P. T. MacGinley's play in Irish, *Eilis agus Bhean Deirce* (Ellis and the Beggarwoman). J. H. Cousins, a nationalist from Belfast, contributed two new plays—*The Racing Lug* and *The Sleep of the King*—and Fred Ryan offered an Ibsenesque drama with socialist themes, *The Laying of the Foundations.*

Just as Cumann na nGaedheal was an umbrella organization for Irish political activity, the Irish National Theatre Society was a kind of umbrella organization for nationalist performance. It included individuals from practically every regional, ethnic, and economic group in Ireland, all united to serve the cause of cultural nationalism. Its repertoire also encompassed the spectrum of nationalist performance modes. The group produced plays in both Irish and English, poetic dramas on mythic themes, and folkish peasant plays, and it even made room for Yeats's esoteric performance experiments with the English Florence Farr. And by performing at one of the most visible and important cultural events of the nationalist movement, they also were aligning themselves with Cumann na nGaedheal and its populist ideals. The actors' populism even rubbed off on Yeats's rather elitist image in the nationalist community, as shortly after the performance of *Kathleen ni Houlihan* he was recommended for directorship of the *United Irishman* (Foster 1998, 265).

But even at this early moment in the history of the company, signs of division were apparent. J. H. Cousins wrote of Yeats's appropriation of the efforts of the Irish National Theatre Society after the production of Cousins's play *The Sleep of the King*—a production around which Yeats had little or no involvement. Backstage after the production of the play, Cousins remembered, "W. B. Yeats lifted his hand and uttered solemn words in his minor-canon voice: 'Splendid, my boy. Splendid. Beautiful verse beautifully spoken by native actors. Just what we wanted.' The suggestion that [the rest of the company] were contributory to him, and not he to us gave a twinge to some of the company who were within hearing" (Cousins and Cousins 1950, 75–76). Like after the Inghinidhe performances in April, Yeats was already positioning himself at the head of the group, although his work and methods were a fraction of the total activity of the organization at the time.

Over time, Yeats would influence the company away from its philosophy of inclusiveness toward an increasingly narrow, focused style of presentation—one that favored art over ideology, text over performance, and the unity of the mise-en-scène over the individuals who took part in it. This distilling of the purpose of the Irish National Theatre Society caused not only ideals, but also individuals to be squeezed out of the society's sharpening focus.

Nine months after the individual members of the Irish National Theatre Society agreed to collaborate, the first resignations from the company occurred over the refusal to produce Padraic Colum's patriotic play *The Saxon Shillin'*.[2] A twenty-year-old railroad worker, Colum became involved in the theater through Inghinidhe na hEireann and acted in the 1902 productions of *Kathleen ni Houlihan* and *Deirdre*. He had already shown his potential as a national writer, winning awards at Gaelic League festivals and receiving Russell, the Fays, and Yeats's attention and encouragement. *The Saxon Shillin'* and other plays by Colum had been published in national papers such as *The Nation* and the *United Irishman*.

---

2. R. F. Foster notes that Abbey directors ended up in such groups as Cumann na nGaedheal Theatre Company and Edward Martyn's Players Club. See Foster 1998, 294. Others involved, such as Dudley Digges, would seek success in the United States.

The Saxon Shillin', a one-act play, opens on two sisters in the West of Ireland preparing to be evicted from their home by British soldiers. The soldier who appears at their door turns out to be their brother, who joined the army as his only opportunity for social and economic advancement. He offers the women money so that they and their father can stay in their home, but his sisters refuse to accept "the Saxon shillin'," even if it means homelessness for them. His sisters' patriotism makes the soldier comprehend his betrayal of Ireland, and he resolves to protect his sisters and father against the force of the other soldiers and from eviction from their home. He is shot by one of the soldiers, but he dies having redeemed himself from his betrayal of his nation.

The Saxon Shillin' brings up important concerns within the nationalist movement, such as enlistment, the need for land reform and decent housing, and even the need for Irish nationalists to learn the Irish language. But there is no significant action in the play, as it consists almost entirely of the soldier and one of his sisters debating nationalist issues by the door of the house. The drama is too short for the characters or the ideas they debate to be developed in any real depth.

The Irish National Theatre Society rejected the play on artistic grounds—Willie Fay felt that it had staging problems—but Maud Gonne and Arthur Griffith felt that the decision was based on Colum's play being politically inflammatory, and they resigned from the organization. The play had already been published in Arthur Griffith's paper, the *United Irishman,* and had won the Cumann na nGaedheal one-act play award at the Samhain Festival, so it is possible that Griffith took personal offense at the Irish National Theatre Society determination that the play was faulty.

W. G. Fay's response to Gonne and Griffith's accusation was vehement. He wrote in a letter to Yeats, "I take a devil of a lot of scaring, for I don't care a damn for any man, woman or child alive. I've been in the mud and walked on velvet, but I am not scared of any political play that anyone in Ireland had backbone enough to write. . . . As for the piece it's puny enough from a political point of view, and could be done much better at the Queen's Theatre than we could manage it for they have more soldiers [*sic*] coats and rifles."[3] Fay's adamant insistence that good political theater had likewise to be good art, a decision with which even the author of the rejected play concurred, also expressed itself in his theatrical practice. The Fays drilled the actors on clear elocution and a simplified acting style, devoid of the mannered gestures of the English Victorian stage. Colum remembered how "Frank Fay would spend hours getting the line of a poem right. He cultivated the voice and would make the actors say 'oohs' and 'aahs' until their voices changed completely and were capable of speaking verse" (Hickey and Smith 1972, 18). W. G. Fay designed beautiful and simple sets, "calculated to centre the onlookers' attention principally on the dialogue and action" (Nic Shiubhlaigh 1955, 33), using symbolic color schemes.

During the interval of the Irish National Theatre Society March performances of *The Hour Glass* and *Twenty-Five*, Yeats gave his lecture "The Reform of the Theater," which explained the technical choices made by the company but also reflected Yeats's increasing focus on the play rather than on the players. Yeats claimed that "they were endeavouring to restore the theatre as an intellectual institution" by simplifying gesture and setting, and concentrating the audience's focus on the language and ideas of the performance *(Freeman's Journal,* 16 March 1903, 6). Years earlier, F. J. Fay had written in the *United Irishman* in favor of such acting, and the actors likewise were committed to developing this simple, poetic style. But Yeats wished to control the bodies of the actors to the point that they would disappear and become instruments of his text.

3. W. G. Fay, letter to W. B. Yeats, 30 January 1903, W. B. Yeats Papers, SUNY Stony Brook. It did not help matters that Maud Gonne had been vehement in her defense of the play at highly improper moments. In a letter to Yeats, Fay claimed that Gonne berated him in front of the company at an Irish National Theatre Society rehearsal and later in front of strangers at George Russell's house. Two weeks earlier, Fay had complained to Yeats that Maire Quinn had asked Gonne if she could play the title role in *Kathleen ni Houlihan,* thus sidestepping Fay's authority to cast roles. Whereas Yeats negotiated his way to leadership, Gonne simply took charge.

In his Irish Literary Theatre days, Yeats expressed his desire to rehearse the actors in barrels: an interesting exercise, but one that suppresses the corporeality of the theater.[4] And it was the corporeality of nationalist theater in Dublin—its ability to embody the movement, its potential and its ideals—that made it so effective a political and artistic vehicle for the nationalist movement. One of the great strengths of the performances of *Kathleen ni Houlihan* and *Deirdre* in 1902 was the triple meaning of the actor's bodies on stage, for they were recognized as the nationalist characters they portrayed, as nationalist actors on the stage, and as nationalist activists in real life. Yeats's reform of the theater, however, called for the individual identities of the actors to be subsumed by the authority of the text, thus making the performers mere instruments of the "theater of unity," symbiotically attached to other aspects of the mise-en-scène, but unable to survive outside the total context.

Just as bodies on stage were being suppressed in favor of text, the bodies of the actors were being controlled offstage by increasingly restrictive by-laws written into the rules of the society. In April, Frank Walker proposed that any society member request permission to perform in any engagement outside the society (Hogan and Kilroy 1976, 58). The new rule was designed to rein in Dudley Digges and Maire Garvey, who began taking numerous professional engagements outside the organization, but it carried controlling implications for the entire company. In June, Russell proposed that a reading committee of Yeats, himself, Colum, and the Fays approve of plays to be submitted to the rest of the society, and that the plays had to pass with a three-quarters majority vote of those present (Hogan and Kilroy 1976, 64–65). These amendments took care of pragmatic problems in the society, but reflected the increasing trend to solidify set rules to which society members were expected to conform.

---

4. In a 1902 edition of *Samhain,* Yeats declared that "I had once asked a dramatic company to let me rehearse them in barrels that they might forget gesture and have their minds free to think of speech for awhile. The barrels, I thought, might be on castors, so that I could shove them about with a pole when the action required it" (Yeats 1923, 20).

In October 1903, the Irish National Theatre Society produced *The King's Threshold* by Yeats, along with *Kathleen ni Houlihan* and John M. Synge's first-produced play, *In the Shadow of the Glen*. *Kathleen* was a success to most of the audience, although some critics complained that it was not as well performed as before (perhaps in part because, for the first time, Maud Gonne did not play Kathleen). The other productions pointed toward the company's future. In *The King's Threshold*, the poet has been banned from his seat on the king's cabinet, and he goes on a hunger strike before the king's threshold, putting shame upon the kingdom. The play is significant for two reasons at this point in Irish National Theatre Society history. First, it reflects Yeats's assertion that art should have an honored place within a culture. Second, the design and construction of the costumes for the play were the first gifts to the Irish National Theatre Society from its future benefactor, A. E. F. Horniman.[5]

The new society also had its first real taste of controversy over the production of Synge's *The Shadow of the Glen*. In this play, an old man, Dan Burke, feigns his death to test the faithfulness of his young wife, Nora. The curtain rises on the old man stretched out on his bier while his wife keeps vigil. A tramp comes by, and Nora offers him shelter. When she goes out briefly, the old man rises up and tells the tramp of his plan, but warns the tramp not to reveal it.

Nora returns accompanied by Michael Dara, a young herdsman with an eye for Nora, who proposes to marry her. Dan jumps up from his bier, accuses his wife of unfaithfulness, and banishes her from his house. She turns to Dara for help, but now that she has no fortune, he is no longer interested in her, and he timidly suggests that she might go

---

5. Even in 1903, in this limited capacity, Horniman displayed her irascibility and frustration with the attitude of the players. The George Roberts Collection contains several letters from Horniman to W. G. Fay, complaining that actors were not sending her their measurements or properly describing their parts. "I do not know whether I am to laugh or to cry. Only Senhan's [*sic*] costume is finished—no one else will confide in me the size of his neck and waist. . . . Miss Hackett calls herself '2nd girl' and you took no notice of my telegram asking if that meant Court Lady or Princess so I cannot even begin her dress." Annie Horniman, letter to W. G. Fay, 21 August 1903, George Henderson Papers, Harvard Theatre Collection.

to the workhouse. The tramp, however, offers to accompany her on the road, and she leaves with him, choosing the hard but free life of the wanderer over the petty existence chosen by Dan and Michael.

The *Daily Express* and the *Irish Times* praised the acting of the piece, but much of the nationalist press was taken aback that this play was being set before the people as a representation of Irish peasant life. The Celtic Revival idealized the peasant as the keeper of the national spirit. Although *The Shadow of the Glen* is set in Wicklow, an area south of Dublin on the east coast of Ireland, rather than in the Gaeltacht (the Irish-speaking parts on the west coast), the audience did not want to be confronted with a representation of poverty, loveless marriage, "unfaithful" wives, and violence among the peasant class in a play presented by the self-proclaimed national theater. Synge claimed that he had heard the story during one of his visits to Aran, but other critics, such as Arthur Griffith, insisted that he stole the story from "Widow of Epheseus" in *The Decameron;* thus, it was not even an Irish story ("All Ireland," *United Irishman,* 17 October 1903, 1). But the play raised typically Irish problems, such as the rise of familism, poverty, and the land crisis.

The play created tremendous rifts within the theater company, as well. Douglas Hyde withdrew from the theater in protest of the production, as did the actors Dudley Digges and Maire Quinn.[6] "Conn" wrote one of the more cloying essays in the *United Irishman,* "In a Real Wicklow Glen," the story of a young woman who married an older man, turning down a younger lover. But this woman, being conservative Irish nationalism's idea of a real Irish woman, is happy with her choice and the joy of her settled, moral life.[7]

6. In some ways, *The Shadow of the Glen* was an excuse for Digges and Quinn, then husband and wife, to leave the organization. One of the finest male actors in the movement, Digges was aware of his potential in the professional theater. He had already been reprimanded for taking roles outside the company. He did make a very successful acting career for himself in the United States. Among his roles was Mr. Zero in the original production of Elmer Rice's *The Adding Machine.*

7. For the text of "In a Real Wicklow Glen," see Hogan and Kilroy 1976, 148–52. Rarely did arguments against *The Shadow of the Glen* even allude to Dan Burke's emotional and physical cruelty to his wife in the play. In the original story, according to

In the midst of this controversy, Yeats addressed the nationalist community's moralistic response to Synge's play in his essay "The Irish National Theatre and Three Sorts of Ignorance" published in the *United Irishman*. This essay is one of Yeats's most specific public refutations of the aesthetic practices common to most nationalist events. The "ignorances" Yeats believed were holding back Irish art included: (1) an insistence on a country Gaelic dialect, which usually appeared as a tacky form of English; (2) the " 'obscurantism' of the more ignorant sort of priest" that demanded only very simple themes; and (3) the "obscurantism" of the politicians who want art to serve immediately the needs of a particular cause (1975, 307). Such attitudes may have been considered ignorant in the sphere of the Irish National Theatre Society, which had the luxuries of rehearsal time, a procedure for training committed and gifted actors, and some of the most talented and best-educated writers at its disposal. But the political directness, thematic simplicity, and clumsy attempts to capture the spirit of the Irish language in English-language productions—all of which Yeats criticized in other nationalist dramas—can also be attributed to the haste and inexperience with which most other nationalist theatricals were put together.

The Irish National Theatre Society was capable of doing work at a much higher artistic level than the patriotic dramas at rural or Gaelic League events; thus, many nationalists hailed it for the quality of its productions. But many critics of *The Shadow of the Glen* still wanted positive politics with their good art. In the 24 October 1903 *United Irishman,* Arthur Griffith stated plainly much of the real concern among nationalists regarding this Irish National Theatre Society production: "Mr. Yeats does not give any reason why if the Irish National Theatre has now no propaganda save that of good art it should continue to call itself either Irish or National. If the Theatre be solely an Art

---

Synge, the old man beats his wife, and the tramp helps him. See Roche 1994, 147. Catholic Ireland's strict rules surrounding marriage, sex, and family made a woman being wooed by another man, hours after her husband's death, seem sexually deviant, regardless of her late husband's behavior toward her.

Theatre, then its plays can only be fairly criticized from the standpoint of art. But whilst it calls itself Irish National its productions must be considered and criticised as Irish National productions" (2).[8]

An audience sensitive to immoral "foreign influences" in its theaters and negative representations of itself in British stage Irish stereotypes was naturally also concerned about representations on the self-proclaimed national stage. Nationalist performance practice up to this point had served either to educate the audience about and celebrate Ireland's mythic past or to create positive representations of Irish culture and life in the face of clownish English stereotypes. When oppression was presented on the nationalist stage, so was Ireland's ability to conquer it, in spirit if not in body. In a theater of moral, political, and cultural absolutes, a play such as *The Shadow of the Glen* challenged the theater's role in the community it served. By producing the play as a national drama, the Irish National Theatre Society magnified—not for the last time—the larger aesthetic and ideological debates surrounding art in the nationalist movement.

In 1904, further shifts in the company stirred even more questions about the Irish National Theatre Society's authority to call itself a national house. Yeats realized that to fulfill his vision of an Irish theater he needed a patron who would free him from relying on ticket sales. He found his angel in Annie Horniman, a devoted admirer of Yeats with an interest in the theater, whom he convinced to contribute approximately fifteen hundred pounds annually for six years to create a permanent theater house. W. G. Fay suggested that they purchase the theater attached to the Mechanics' Institute on Abbey Street. It had served as a theater in the nineteenth century, but its most recent incarnation had been as a morgue. In the spring of 1904, Horniman wrote a letter to Yeats offering him the theater, under a few conditions. The company agreed, and the building was underway. Joseph Holloway, architect and avid theatergoer, was chosen to design the renovations for the building, and W. G. Fay quit his day job to oversee the work (Hogan and Kilroy 1976,

---

8. Arthur Griffith added this comment to an editorial by W. B. Yeats, "The Irish National Theatre and Three Sorts of Ignorance," *United Irishman,* 24 October 1903, 2–3.

106). Irish artisans Sarah Purser and Lily Yeats designed artwork for the new building, and Jack B. Yeats was commissioned to paint portraits of some members of the company, as well as a portrait of Horniman. The refurbished Abbey was beautifully designed with brass railings, red velvet seats with good views, and a tearoom in the lobby.

The Abbey was an excellent site for a burgeoning theater. It was a five-minute walk from the General Post Office in the city center and a few blocks from the train station. With only 562 seats, it was much more affordable to run and fill than the other professional houses in Dublin, and its rich history as a theater in the nineteenth century increased the romance of the space.

But Horniman, although having "great sympathy with the artistic and dramatic aims of the Irish National Theatre Company, as publicly explained by [Yeats] on various occasions" (Horniman 1904, 53), did not comprehend or care about the theater's accessibility to or relationship with the Dublin nationalist community. Her allegiance was unshakably with Yeats's art, not Ireland's politics, and she demanded artistic input and respect from the company in return for her generosity. In fact, one of the ways Yeats seduced her into supporting his dream of a theater was allowing her to design the costumes for the first production of *The King's Threshold*. Perhaps her desire to be taken seriously as an artist, along with her affection for Yeats and her distaste for Irish politics, made her so critical of even the smallest administrative and artistic details of the theater. She was no silent partner; rather, she contributed to some of the most volatile conflicts in the Abbey's first decade.

Horniman agreed that other groups could lease the space for a fee, although the company would let it for free if the Irish National Theatre Society received the proceeds. She further stated that the prices of the seats could be raised by other groups, but they could not be lowered. Considering that the lowest-priced seat was a shilling (half a day's wages for a working-class regular laborer), instead of the sixpence charged in every other Dublin theater, this stipulation created considerable controversy. Not only did the Irish National Theatre Society have prohibitively high ticket prices for much of the Dublin public, it had separate entrances for the gallery and the pit (Frazier 1990, 171–74).

The theater that was meant to unite the Irish in the cause of Irish art divided those people on strict class lines, "with a door for aristocrats, another door for the middle class, and no seats for the poor" (Frazier 1990, 172).

Horniman's design for the management and building of the Abbey Theatre reflects her designs for the theater's identity on Dublin's cultural landscape. Horniman hated Irish politics: the theater was a gift to Yeats, the artist and man she adored, for the furtherance of his aesthetic vision, which she determined transcended politics. As a woman of business, she designed the theater on a model that allowed only the audience she deemed suitable for Yeats's work—educated professionals, wealthy aristocrats, or artistic elite (given complimentary tickets). Such a model served Mary and Squire Bancroft enormously well at the Prince of Wales and Haymarket Theatres in London, where they dressed up the theater houses and hiked up their prices so that their theaters would cater to a middle-class clientele with high-class aspirations.[9] But constructing a theater to cater to the comfort and fashionable exclusivity of more moneyed classes—who in Dublin were mostly those who profited from England's economic control over Ireland—weakened the theater's ability to attract an audience who wished to be challenged and educated by new theater forms, much less by dramas that promoted social and political change.

Yeats, like Horniman, wanted an exclusive theater, but a theater for Ireland's intellectual, not economic, elite: he wanted to escape the middle class, not cater to it. From his perspective, the Abbey was to be a subsidized theater on the model of the national houses of France and Norway in the nineteenth century. Unlike theaters designed on the subsidized system, however, the Abbey in 1904 was not allowed to reduce its price of admission for anyone. Only in the fall of 1906 did Lady Gregory finally convince Horniman to allow sixpenny seats; and it took another year for the Abbey to sell subscription discounts.

The company did make at least one exception to Horniman's strident rule. A group of nationalist university students called the Twilight

9. See Frazier 1990, 171–74.

Literary Society requested a reduction of prices to eightpence for their twelve members because they went to every production. Yeats agreed. It was a good investment. Mary Maguire Colum, a member of that society, remembered that "[t]he audience was so slender in those days that we visibly augmented it, and Yeats would cast a pleased eye on us as we entered in a body. We could be depended upon to listen ecstatically to a verse play and to applaud with hands and feet" (Maguire Colum 1966, 116). If the Abbey had been allowed to admit more young or not-so-rich enthusiasts into its doors in the first two years, it might have earned fuller houses and more warmth from proletarian nationalist groups.

The new Abbey opened 27 December 1904 with a production of *Kathleen ni Houlihan*, Lady Gregory's *Spreading the News*, and *The Shadow of the Glen*. The plays were generally well received, and Maire Nic Shiubhlaigh and Sarah Allgood received strong reviews for their performances. But Yeats gave one of his stranger speeches to the supporters of the theater at the curtain. He told the audience, "[A. E. F. Horniman] has given us . . . the free use of this theatre, and as our salary list and our expenses are very small, we shall be able to ask ourselves when we put a play on, first, 'Does it please us?' and then, 'Does it please you?' " ("Yeats's Speech on Opening Night of Abbey" 1904, n.p.). Most theater directors do not declare on opening night that they do not care primarily whether or not their work pleases the audience. Yeats was celebrating his freedom from relying on the box office, but his passion for high-art experimentation in the theater was distancing him from almost every faction of the nationalist movement his theater claimed to represent. The English Horniman's patent meant that the Irish National Theatre Society no longer relied on the populist, collaborative spirit of amateur nationalist performances, which made them so powerful for their audiences. The gatekeeper of the Abbey was ultimately Yeats, and, at least in Irish National Theatre Society productions, the Abbey would be his idea of a theater. Yeats never wanted to be Ireland's only dramatic voice, even if he could have been. Often, other nationalist theater groups thrived while the Abbey struggled. And he could be very generous to other playwrights and organizations. But within the Irish National Theatre Society, the establishment of the Abbey and his relationship with Horniman allowed Yeats effectively to erase the amateur, collaborative spirit of the first years of the Irish National Theatre Society.

The hierarchization of the Abbey became a legal fact with the reshuffling of the society into a joint stock company in November 1905. Adrian Frazier (1990) recounts the brilliant political machinations Yeats performed between campaigning key individuals in the late spring and forcing his reforms through the society that fall. Yeats first enlisted Russell to approach the actors with the reorganization. Russell had left the Irish National Theatre Society in 1904, but Yeats hoped he, as one of the first leaders, could influence the actors to Yeats's side. After Yeats suggested the idea to Horniman, she wrote an approving letter to him, which he then showed to the company as a way of making it seem her idea. Frazier notes that "after getting the actors to agree that the theatre should be incorporated to limit its liability and to raise further capital, Yeats had it registered under the Friendly and Industrial Societies Act, according to which no member could own more than two hundred shares, and members had a vote for each share held. Under this arrangement, Horniman could not keep enough and the actors could not buy enough to threaten Yeats, Synge, and Lady Gregory. The writer-directors each held one hundred shares, and the actors were given one vote each" (1990, 120). "Before the crucial meeting of 22 September 1905, when Yeats proposed turning the Irish National Theatre Society into a joint stock company, he wrote to John Quinn that he was 'going to Dublin to preside at a meeting to put an end to democracy in the theatre' " (Allan Wade, qtd. in Frazier 1990, 117). The actors were aware that these revisions threatened their original vision for the society: "it was pointed out that the old Irish National Theatre Society had been founded in 1902 on the understanding that its independence as a national movement was to be secured only through the efforts of its members. . . . If such a subsidy was accepted the individual character of the movement would be completely destroyed" (Nic Shiubhlaigh 1955, 72). Nic Shiubhlaigh discreetly avoids pointing out the way the new structure effectively emptied the individual actor's participation in the company of any relevant, self-determined political meaning. The rules of the National Theatre Society, Ltd., read that "[t]he Directors shall appoint and may remove the stage manager, business manager and all other employees of the Society, fix their salaries and arrange their duties" (National Theatre Society, Ltd., n.d., 13). In other words, "Once actors signed contracts, they stopped being primarily artists and nationalists; they became employees, valuable according to their walk, their voice, and their general capacity for theatrical dissimulation. . . . Turning professional led toward a system of bosses and workers, the breakdown of relations between workers through unequal pay and competition for scarce labor, the alienation of the workers from their work, and reification of their skills" (Frazier 1990, 123).

Nor could the workers express certain opinions. Rule sixty-four, on "Contentious Subjects," stipulated: "No sectarian discussion shall be raised, nor shall any resolution which deals with irrelevant and contentious subjects be proposed at a General Meeting of the Society" (National Theatre Society, Ltd., n.d., 14). This rule effectively squelched political activism among the members within the rubric of the theater. The Abbey actors may have lost their vote on what plays the company would produce, but they still had the right not to act in them. Thus, faced with the prospect of becoming the directors' hired help, rather than collaborators, all but four members of the original Irish National Theatre Society resigned from the company.

Arthur Griffith made the snide remark in the *United Irishman* that "[e]verybody will be sorry for the conversion of our best lyric poet into a limited liability company" ("All Ireland," 10 March 1906, 1). But in a way, Griffith's comment reflected the Abbey's establishment as an institution and Yeats's recognized position as its head. The Abbey Theatre Company had a building; it had a subsidy; it had earned international recognition; it toured England regularly; and it even published a series of its plays and two annual journals. But its emphasis on professionalism, slick marketing techniques, and international reputation did not earn it exclusive rights to Irish nationalist theater in turn-of-the-century Dublin. Groups with less theatrical professionalism but a more intimate relationship with the movement continued to draw huge crowds.

Even within the Abbey repertoire, Yeats, Gregory, and Synge found some competition for their vision for Irish national drama, as tensions over the company's new, hierarchical structure seethed even among the playwrights at the Abbey. The most famous playwrights of the period were the Abbey directors. W. B. Yeats's symbolist-influenced verse dramas were always highlighted in the Abbey repertoire, and they received mixed but generally favorable reviews. Lady Gregory's peasant plays in Kiltartan dialect provided a brightness and wit to what might otherwise have been dolorously somber evenings of theater. In some ways, Synge captured the best of both playwrights: his knowledge of Gaelic language and culture helped him capture a sense of the colors of the Irish language in his elaborate style of dialogue, just as Gregory's searches for Raftery's writings influenced her dialect writing. The beauty of Synge's turns of phrase and—in *Riders to the Sea,* for example—the emphasis in his dramas on spirituality and imagination in the face of bleak environmental, social, and economic circumstances evoked the dramatic concerns of W. B. Yeats. But against these three, other Abbey playwrights wrote dramas in a style more accessible to the Dublin community, which often gained more attention and box office than their more intellectual counterparts. From 1902 to 1908, the most important of these playwrights were Padraic Colum and William Boyle. Colum, who got his start in the nationalist movement with Inghinidhe, caused one of the Irish National Theatre Society's first major controversies in 1903 and wrote dramas that exposed many of the harsh realities of Irish peasant life, but in a way sympathetic to the people, pointing out the social, moral, and material conditions that shaped the conflicts in his characters' lives. His 1905 play *The Land,* for example, is a polemic against Irish emigration, but its characters wrestle with complex social and psychological issues. The characters are made up of two tyrannical fathers and their two sets of children. Murtagh Cosgar has a "vapid" daughter and an intelligent son. Martin Douras has "a gentle, verbose fool" of a son and a daughter who wants a more genteel, educated life. Set after the "land wars" of the 1890s and the passage of the Land Purchase Act (which allowed peasants to purchase land from the large estates with money advanced from the government), the young characters in the play are torn between staying on their farms to work the land and leaving home to pursue other dreams. Ultimately, Murtagh's bright son decides to escape his father and emigrate to America, where Martin's daughter will join him after spending a year at school. The fathers despair that their weaker children will be the inheritors of the land, while Ireland's brighter, more aggressive minds move away to more economically and psychologically amenable conditions.

In the final speech, Martin's less-intelligent son urges his father to give a speech begging the group of departing emigrants to stay. Martin's grief leaves him speechless, but his son struggles to find the words he thinks his father should say: "stay on the land, and you'll be saved body and soul; you'll be saved in the man and in the nation. The nation, men of Ballykillduff, do you ever think of it at all. Do you ever think of the nation that is waiting all this time to be born?" (Colum 1986, 37). Putting the theme of the play—and the nationalist movement—in the mouth of one of the weakest characters makes it resonate as both political and transcendent truth. Yeats uses the same approach in *The Hour-Glass,* when the Fool recognizes the Wise Man's need for redemption, or in *On Baile's Strand,* when the Blind Man and the Fool recognize that the warrior Cuchulain has just killed is in fact Cuchulain's son.

Against Colum's strident psychological realism, William Boyle's plays—even in their bleaker moments—use broad and bold characters. Boyle was a broad and bold character himself. He was older than Yeats and did not appreciate taking suggestions from the poet. The directors found him and his plays vulgar (Frazier 1990, 138–39). In Boyle's first Abbey success, *The Building Fund* (1905), a miserly woman takes in her orphaned granddaughter to the distress of her own son, who believes his niece will receive the family inheritance. In the end, the grandmother gives all her money to the building fund of the church, even though she never attended the church when alive and died without a priest. The old woman's son and her granddaughter, stripped of the inheritance they had both coveted for so long, decide to remain together and earn their own fortune. In many ways, the plot of *The Building Fund* echoes MacGinley's *Eilis agus Bhean Deirce,* but its resolution also can be read as a call for unity among differing factions of the nationalist movement with competing claims for the "national inheritance."

Boyle was extremely popular with Dublin audiences, and his plays were also produced in England and the United States. His work was considered broadly comic when it first appeared—a judgment D. E. S. Maxwell, among other contemporary readers, finds difficult to imagine (1984, 71). But the prompt scripts in the Fay Papers in the National Library of Ireland point out that W. G. Fay blocked a good bit of traditional comic stage business in Irish National Theatre Society productions. *The Building Fund* and *The Mineral Workers* read as serious, ironic commentary on the economic conditions of Irish life. By inserting physical comic action, Boyle's dramas became dark—but funny— satire.[10] Imagine Stanley Kubrick's 1961 film *Dr. Strangelove* without the comic business of Sellers, Scott, and Pickens. In *Who's Who in the Theatre* of 1936, W. G. Fay claimed that his favorite role was the title character in Boyle's play *The Eloquent Dempsy*, a shyster politician who was an excellent vehicle for Fay's comic gifts (Saddlemyer 1982, 74).

The Abbey Theatre gave many playwrights a leg up in the theater, such as George Fitzmaurice, Norreys Connell, and W. F. Casey, who represented a range of dramatic styles. Still, Yeats, Gregory, and Synge were the gatekeepers of the Abbey, and although they opened the door for new writers, those writers were more often than not fitted lower in the hierarchy of the theater repertoire. The directors' work was inevitably given the central position in the theater seasons and in the Abbey theater journals, *Samhain* and *The Arrow*. The dramas of other playwrights were often relegated to the position of "fillers" in the dra-

---

10. Act 2 includes the following stage business: *"O'NEILL comes in. He whispers to MRS. DEMPSY. Meanwhile MARY KATE is assisting DEMPSY to take off his coat. MRS. DEMPSY picks up his dressing-gown and throws it towards them. It is turned inside out. MRS. DEMPSY sits down in the easy chair in a sulky, uninterested attitude, and as MARY KATE goes over to the side with the torn coat, DEMPSY hastily puts on his dressing-gown inside out. The dressing-gown is green lined with orange, the opposite party colours. None of them notice the accident. The noise goes on outside. DEMPSY (going towards the window).* Make way, O'Neill, I've got my fighting harness on" (Boyle n.d., 72–73).

matic repertoire. Ironically, those *dramatic* fillers were often better *theater* fillers than the work of Yeats, Gregory, and Synge. When the company produced Fitzmaurice's *The Country Dressmaker,* a saucy satire on romance and marriage, the play was such a hit that they extended the run an extra weekend. Yeats wrote to Synge in 1907, "How can we make them understand that [Synge's] *The Playboy* which they hate is fine art and that [Fitzmaurice's] *The Dressmaker* which they like is nothing?" (qtd. in Hogan, Burnham, and Poteet 1978, 171).

At the end of 1905, the Abbey Theatre Company's attempt to regulate the behavior of the players caused several key players to defect. Then, in early 1907, the Abbey attempted to regulate the behavior of its audience and very nearly received the same response. The Abbey directors' confrontation with the audience led to the riots surrounding the performance of J. M. Synge's *The Playboy of the Western World.*

Today, J. M. Synge's *Playboy of the Western World* is considered a masterpiece of Irish drama. In this wild, darkly comic play, Christy Mahon, a frightened, frail young man enters a West of Ireland community claiming he has killed his father and fires up the imaginations, passions, and desires of the people of the community with his tale of patricide to the point that he becomes a hero in their eyes. When the "dead" father appears with nothing but a bad bump on the head, the people turn on Christy for being a liar. The lavish attention they bestowed on Christy, however, has made him think of himself as a hero. The bullied boy now bullies his father and leaves the town and his beloved, Pegeen Mike, for new adventures. A few scenes earlier, Pegeen had threatened to scald his shins with a hot coal, but when he leaves, Pegeen can only cry, "I've lost the only Playboy of the Western World" (Synge 1968, 229).

The Playboy parodies the conflict between passionate imagination and strict moral codes within an Irish culture struggling under economic oppression and the rigid strictures of the church. Christy Mahon is "the Playboy of the Western World" to the villagers because he becomes an empty signifier on which the townspeople can project their own repressed desires surrounding sex, violence, and heroism. These desires, however, can be expressed only in economic terms: by offering shelter to a murderer, Michael James feels like an accomplice in the crime. The village girls express their desire for Christy by offering him material gifts. One young woman offers him a laying hen and urges him to feel the fat on the chicken breast, which he does; her erotic desire is thus transferred comically onto her gift. Only Christy's interactions with Pegeen touch on direct expression of desire.

The Abbey committed itself to producing *The Playboy,* but they knew they were sitting on a powder keg. Even Joseph Holloway, a friend and constant patron of the Abbey, was banned from attending rehearsals of the play (Hogan, Burnham, and Poteet 1978, 123). At the first performance, the audience listened with tolerance to the curtain raiser, *Riders to the Sea,* and to the first two acts of *The Playboy.* But in the middle of act 3, a line by Christy offended the colloquial, moral, and sexual sensibilities of many in the audience: "It's Pegeen I'm seeking only, and what'd I care if you brought me a drift of chosen females, standing in their shifts itself, maybe, from this place to the eastern world?" (Synge 1968, 212). The audience broke into hisses. The next night, the audience went from hissing to shouting their protest of the play, but the Abbey announced it would run the drama for the full week. And for the rest of the week, *The Playboy* did appear, albeit in a kind of dumbshow over the noisy performances of protest, outrage, and, conversely, support of the play going on in the audience.

The Abbey chose two ways to deal with the protests. First, Yeats announced that a debate on the play would be held in the Abbey the following week. Second, the theater determined to squelch all audience attempts to silence the play. On 30 January 1907, the *Daily Express* recorded the announcement Yeats made before the curtain at a *Playboy* performance:

"We have put this play before you to be heard and to be judged, as every play should be heard and judged," Yeats remarked. "Every man has a right to hear it and condemn it if he pleases, but no man has a right to interfere with another man hearing a play and judging for himself. . . . and I promise you that if there is any small section in this theatre that wish to deny the right of others to hear what they themselves don't want to hear—(a voice: 'We will put them out')—we will play on, and our patience will last longer than their patience." ("The Abbey Theatre," 5, qtd. in Hogan, Burnham, and Poteet 1978, 127–28)

When members of the audience booed the play that night despite Yeats's admonitions, constables entered the building and arrested individuals causing a disturbance. Police representing an English government arresting Irishmen in the national theater raised the furor of many nationalist protestors, but the directors remained adamant. Lady Gregory said in a 29 January 1907 interview with the *Freeman's Journal,* "We have already declared publicly this winter that, in the opinion of those conducting this theatre, it is the fiddler who chooses the tune. The public are quite at liberty to stay away, but if they come in they must take what is provided for them" ("What Lady Gregory Said," 7, qtd. in Hogan, Burnham, and Poteet 1978, 130). Lady Gregory's comment is ironic because before the production of *The Playboy of the Western World,* many nationalists had habitually expressed their displeasure with the Abbey by staying away or patronizing other nationalist performance groups. The Abbey was used to playing to sparse houses. The week of the *Playboy* riots, the theater grossed one hundred pounds more than its usual take. The Abbey charged half the usual price for a seat at the debate regarding *The Playboy,* and again the house was full. Considering that none of the speakers at the debate were paid, again the Abbey made a healthy profit.

People were not going to the Abbey that week to see *The Playboy of the Western World;* they were going to witness or participate in the debate between the stage and the house. Only a few persons actually created the real disturbance (about forty out of five hundred): most of the audience watched this turn-of-the-century performance intervention with minimal participation. Despite—or perhaps because of—the arrests and the urgings in the newspapers for order, the disturbances lasted the full run of the play. Outraged by the event, William Boyle resigned from the Irish National Theatre Society and did not allow his plays to be performed there again until 1912.

The debate, held a week after the production, attracted many leaders of the nationalist movement, including Francis Sheehy-Skeffington, the critic W. G. Lawrence, and Cruise O'Brien. Synge, upset by the response to his play and not in good health, did not attend, so Yeats was the primary defender of the Abbey and the play. He appeared in evening dress and at one point silenced the audience by declaring himself the author of *Kathleen ni Houlihan*. The progressive nationalist Sheehy-Skeffington summed up well the anti-Abbey sentiment of the crowd when "he declared that the play in his opinion was bad; the organised disturbance was worse (uproar), and the methods employed to quell the disturbance the worst of all. Sheehy-Skeffington went on to say that Yeats's calling in the police was as out of place as if the Western Board of Guardians had condemned the drama without having seen or heard it" ("Abbey Theatre Disturbances," *Daily Express,* 5 February 1907, 8, qtd. in Hogan, Burnham, and Poteet 1978, 149).

On one hand, Sheehy-Skeffington's analogy is specious: the reason Yeats called in the police was so the people could indeed "see and hear" the play. Sheehy-Skeffington's point, however, was that quelling the audience was a form of censorship and that the audience was participating in a widely practiced mode of nationalist—and theatrical—discourse in booing and cheering the play. At the Queen's Royal and other commercial houses, the audience regularly hissed the villain, cheered the hero, yelled advice to the characters, and sang patriotic songs. *Ceili* and *feis* performances by the Gaelic League, Cumann na nGaedheal, and other groups likewise created a more relaxed relationship between audience and actor because these productions were often given in informal spaces and occurred amid other kinds of activities.

The Abbey, on the other hand, insisted on solemn dignity. There was always the show of seeing nationalist playwrights there; Yeats, Gregory, and Synge were invariably in the audience when they were in town. Maguire Colum remembers the way intermissions were spent discussing the play in the tearoom or listening to Arthur Darley and the Abbey orchestra perform, and anyone who attended might rub elbows with the playwrights, the leaders of the nationalist movement, or famous intellectuals from England or Europe (Maguire Colum 1966, 91). But when the gong sounded, patrons were expected in their seats, their attention focused intently and quietly on the stage. Any noises made by the audience were to be positive and polite, and given only at the fall of the curtain.[11]

Una Chaudhuri describes how this mode of spectatorship, which emerged with the rise of realism/naturalism on the early modernist stage, "installed a logic of representation to which the spectator was, essentially, an obstacle, a hindrance, an inconvenience." It involved the spectator "in an impossible displacement, where s/he was asked to play the role of ultimate hermeneutic authority while being reminded simultaneously of the authorizing but invisible presence of the omnipotent puppet master playwright, creator of all meaning" (1995, 9). Such a situation certainly existed with the Abbey Theatre, where everyone who could buy a ticket was welcome to the "dance," but it was the fiddler who called the tune. And it was utterly counter to the aesthetic strategies of both popular melodramas and amateur nationalist theaters. In those spaces, the audience could perform their complicity or discontent in audible and visible ways without fear of arrest.

Although an intriguing forum for resolving conflicts regarding the theater, the debate regarding *The Playboy of the Western World* was ultimately long and long-winded, and did not resolve any points concerning the freedom of the theater or Synge's play. Records of the debate reflect how complicated the fight was, however, and how varied the opinions and motives of those who attended. Some clearly felt moral outrage; some were intellectually debating the role of the theater. The critic W. G. Lawrence saw the debate as a chance for his moment in the

---

11. The Abbey's expectation of polite and approving response from their audience showed itself in an anecdote regarding the trial of the "rioters." The judge asked the nonplussed Abbey prosecutor why none of the people who disrupted the performance by shouting down the dissenters or cheering the play were brought into court even though they, too, were making a public disturbance. See "The Abbey Theatre," *Daily Express*, 4 February 1907, 2, qtd. in Hogan, Burnham, and Poteet 1978, 140.

limelight. Many were defending art over propaganda. Others were looking for a fight or a show. The debate may not have resolved opinion regarding *The Playboy of the Western World*, but it did confirm that the Abbey, for better or worse, would insist on upholding its own artistic principles over the popular nationalist sensibilities within the movement. The Abbey's artistic principles, furthermore, assumed codes of behavior for the Abbey audience that they were expected to obey.

In early 1908, the Abbey Theatre lost W. G. Fay, along with his wife Bridget O'Dempsey and his brother Frank. Fay had been invaluable to the company as founder, educator, director, leading actor, stage manager, set designer, set builder, and business manager, but he was also temperamental and not well suited for directing productions outside the company's peasant fare. He felt he was losing control over the actors, and when in 1907 Annie Horniman arranged for Ben Iden Payne to direct all nonpeasant plays at the Abbey, Yeats found himself dancing around the egos of the two managers and his benefactor. Payne left later that year and went on to head up Horniman's other theatrical project, the Gaiety in Manchester. The insult to Fay contributed to his decision to leave as well.

The Fays decided to make their mark in the United States. Their departure was friendly until controversy over fees for playing Yeats's dramas and the Fays' being billed mistakenly as the Abbey Theatre Company caused the directors brusquely to expel the Fays from membership in the society. Rumors scattered throughout Dublin that the Fays had been pushed out of the company, but although the directors had been encouraging W. G. Fay to change his role in the society, he did leave of his own accord. Still, the rough treatment the Fays received after a misunderstanding while they were on the other side of the Atlantic confirmed for many the assumption that Yeats ran the Abbey with an iron fist.

While the Abbey experienced these internal conflicts over the establishment of its artistic identity and cultural mission, old and new groups challenged its authority to call itself the national house—building or no building. Dramatic groups made out of members of branches of the Gaelic League continued to perform throughout Dublin and the rest of

Ireland. Although the acting and the structure of their plays were generally considered poor, they did provide opportunities for the Irish language to be heard in a dramatic milieu. The National Players Society, made up of Gaelic Leaguers and members of Cumann na nGaedheal, also performed nationalist propaganda plays regularly around Dublin. The National Players generally received favorable comments on their existence but poor reviews of their productions. The Ulster Literary Theatre usually performed in Belfast but occasionally toured its innovative dramas around other parts of Ireland and generated much excitement in Dublin. In 1908, Count Markiewicz began writing plays for the Independent Theatre Company, which usually starred his wife, the revolutionary Constance Markiewicz. His dramas were really more society events than socially relevant theater. And outside of Dublin, the Cork Dramatic Society was formed, providing the first stage for future playwrights such as Daniel Corkery, Lennox Robinson, and T. C. Murray.

The strongest competitor for the title "national theater" in Dublin was made up of individuals who had once been intimately involved in establishing the Abbey. In early 1906, the Irish National Theatre Society members who had resigned in protest of the new rules formed a new company, Cluithcheoiri na hEireann, or the Theatre of Ireland. Along with the recent defectors, the new organization included other noted supporters of Irish nationalist theater, such as Edward Martyn, James H. Cousins, Constance Markiewicz, and Padraic Pearse.[12] Nic Shiubhlaigh fulfilled her obligation to the Abbey until the end of the year, then worked only with amateur theater groups until 1910. She comments in her memoirs: "Although for most of us who took the course of secession, the action meant the finish of any progress we might have been making individually towards international distinction as Irish players. . . . I doubt if many of us had regrets at the time. For myself, I can only say that at that period I had no desire to act, professionally or otherwise,

---

12. Theatre of Ireland members included Edward Martyn, president; Padraic Colum, secretary; George Nesbitt, stage manager; T. M. Kettle, P. H. Pearse, Seamas Sullivan, Helen Laird, J. H. Cousins, and T. G. Koehler, officers; and Maire Nic Shiubhlaigh, Proinsias Nic Shiubhlaigh, George Nesbitt, Vera Esposito, and Joseph Goggins.

with any theatrical project unlike the one I helped launch in 1902" (1955, 73).

The Theatre of Ireland gave its first presentation at the Gaelic League Oireacthas, presenting a Gaelic translation of Padraic Colum's play *The Land*. In a flyer distributed at the event, the new company announced that it had "been founded to produce plays in Irish and English. Believing that drama can be of inestimable value in moulding and giving expression to the thought of the people, the Theatre aims at giving free and full dramatic utterance to everything that makes for the up-building of an enlightened and vigorous humanity in Ireland" (*Cluithceoiri na h'Eireann* 1906, 3). Whereas Yeats espoused "first, does it please us, and then, does it please you," the Theatre of Ireland strove to create more communal events with the people. Whereas the Abbey performed exclusively in English, the Theatre of Ireland high-lighted its facility in plays in Irish.[13]

Although it is not clear when she wrote it, a motherly (or matroniz-ing) Lady Gregory wrote on the back of a Theatre of Ireland flyer in-cluded in the Abbey Theatre Scrapbook, "Distributed at the Oireachtas August '06—Bless Them!" But the separation created a huge rift in Irish nationalist circles, as the nationalist amateur actor of the Theatre of Ireland offered a vision for the construction of national drama sepa-rate from the vision offered by the professional theater workers at the Abbey.

On 6 December 1906, the Theatre of Ireland performed Hyde's *Casadh an Tsugain,* Cousins's *The Racing Lug,* and act 4 of Ibsen's *Brand* in the Molesworth Hall. In the *Sinn Fein* review, "The Drama in

---

13. In the 1904 *Samhain,* Yeats responded to criticism that the Irish National The-atre Society played only in English: "If one says a National literature must be in the lan-guage of the country, there are many difficulties. Should it be written in the language that one's country does speak or the language that it ought to speak?" (3). It was an ex-cellent answer to an important philosophical problem within the nationalist movement, but even now Ireland is struggling to maintain the Irish language and funds the work of Irish-language writers, dramatists, and theater companies. The ability of the Theatre of Ireland to perform in Irish gave it a distinct advantage over the Abbey in the eyes of the Gaelic League community.

Dublin," "Sinn Dicat" praised the work of the Theatre of Ireland but scoffed at the Abbey Theatre's choice to produce Yeats's *The Shadowy Waters* and Lady Gregory's *The Canavans*:

> Certainly very strange notions seem to have crept into the National Theatre Society since they became a limited company. There is no doubt that the adoption of commercial principles has seriously affected their artistic judgment. . . . Cluithcheoiri na h-Eireann has come apparently just at the right time. . . . And there is an audience not only willing but eager to listen to and appreciate good plays, and beginning to get a little weary of the vagaries of the National Theatre Society, Limited. (15 December 1906, 3)

The playlists for some of the Theatre of Ireland productions make it seem that the clock had been reversed on the previous four years of the Irish National Theatre Society, for they included many old names from the original group. Yet they also named people who had become celebrities of sorts in other areas of the nationalist movement. In its first two events, the Theatre of Ireland performed classics of the Irish National Theatre Society in its pre-Horniman period. When the company performed Alice Milligan's *The Last Feast of the Fianna*, they reached back into the repertoire of their days performing under the auspices of Inghinidhe na hEireann and the Irish Literary Theatre. Their production of *Deirdre* included Russell as the Druid, Maire Nic Shiubhlaigh as Deirdre, and Con Markiewicz as Lavarcam. They conscientiously kept ticket prices low—sometimes only one penny—and performed benefits for national causes.

As early as its performances at the 1906 *Oireachtas,* it was clear that the Theatre of Ireland would not be able to reproduce the artistic standard found on the stage of the Abbey Theatre, but in some circles it threatened the Abbey's status as national house on ideological rather than aesthetic grounds. Company members retained their nationalist principles; had good, popular playwrights such as Colum and Seamas O'Kelly (author of *The Shuiler's Child*) writing for them, and after training with the Fays for so many years and playing on stage so often before so many discerning audiences, some of them were excellent actors. The Theatre of Ireland also received the directorial guidance of Fred and Jack Morrow, the brothers who were involved in founding the Ulster Literary Theatre.

Yeats apparently was aware of the threat the dissenting actors' company posed to the Abbey, and he began a skillful marketing campaign to control the damage. Throughout the busy first years of the Abbey, Yeats faithfully published *Samhain,* the journal of the Irish National Theatre Society, and from 1906 published a second journal, *The Arrow.* The 1903 *Samhain,* written two years after the dissolution of the Irish Literary Theatre and during the development of the new Irish National Theatre Society, spoke about the dramatic movement in Ireland generally. Yeats did, however, mention particular interest in the work of the Irish National Theatre Society and acknowledged that it had performed his plays. But he did not link himself exclusively with that group: "Though one welcomes every kind of vigorous life [in the theater] I am, myself, most interested in 'The Irish National Theatre Society,' which has no propaganda but that of good art" *(Samhain,* September 1903, 4). But the 1906 edition of *Samhain* rewrote the history of Yeats's involvement in the Irish National Theatre Society:

> Our main business is to create an Irish dramatic literature, and a list of plays from the outset of our movement. . . . The movement was begun by the Irish Literary Theatre, which produced or promoted the performance of Irish Plays with English Players, there being no others to be had at the time, for one week a year, for three years. . . . After that, a company of Irish players, with Mr. William Fay to stage manage them, and Mr. Frank Fay to teach them elocution, took up the work, and Lady Gregory, Mr. Synge and myself have been responsible or mainly responsible for the choice of plays and the general policy of the National Theatre Society, as this Company is now called, from the opening of the Abbey Theatre, the Company's first permanent home in 1904. (December 1906, 3)

Yeats did not mention Inghinidhe na hEireann, the Gaelic League, or any of the organizations integral to developing the Irish National Theatre Society. Except for Frank Benson (a professional, English actor), the only persons mentioned by name are those still working for the National Theatre Society. Finally, Yeats included a list of plays at the end of the journal entitled, "Dates and Places of the First Performance of Plays produced by the National Theatre Society and its Predecessors." The list starts with the performances of the Irish Literary Theatre, then on to *Kathleen ni Houlihan* and *Deirdre* by the Irish National Dramatic Company in 1902, then exclusively the Irish National Theatre Society. With a few strokes of a pen, Yeats blotted the complex web of collaborations that built up the Abbey Theatre, and he designed a linear narrative of the Irish dramatic movement with himself at the center of all activity.

Lady Gregory creates the same elision in the appendix to her history of the Abbey, *Our Irish Theatre*. She begins her list of "Plays produced by the Abbey Theatre Company and Its Predecessors" with the Irish Literary Theatre, but when she gets to the first productions of the Irish National Theatre Society in 1903, she adds the note: "The first prospectus of this Society, dated March, 1903, and signed by Mr. Fred Ryan began as follows: 'The Irish National Theatre Society was formed to continue on a more permanent basis the work of the Irish Literary Theatre' " (Gregory 1913, 262). As discussed above, Gregory takes this point out of context and ignores the actual makeup of that diverse, idealistic group.

While the Abbey directors were solidifying their version of the history of the Irish dramatic movement and the dominant position of the National Theatre Society, Ltd., in the dramatic movement, they also kept aware of (and supported) other nationalist theatrical activity and rented their space to other performance groups, including branches of the Gaelic League, the National Players Society, the Ulster Literary Theatre, and, later, the Theatre of Ireland. In the coming years, all of these groups would perform on the stage of the Abbey Theatre—not as members of the National Theatre Society, Ltd., but as nationalist organizations renting the national theater space.

The various groups one could observe on the Abbey stage made it a collaborative site for Dublin theater, but the National Theatre Society,

Ltd., maintained its hierarchical authority in allotting use of the theater. In 1908, the Theatre of Ireland was mistakenly listed as the Abbey Theatre Company in a newspaper advertisement and, although the Theatre of Ireland corrected the error the same day, Horniman banished the company from the building (Nic Shiubhlaigh 1955, 96).[14]

In the 1908 *Samhain*, Yeats criticized the other Dublin theater companies, claiming that "the Ulster Players are the only dramatic society, apart from [the Abbey,] which is doing serious artistic work." He attacked the Independent Theatre Society for "show[ing] little sign of work or purpose." Of the Theatre of Ireland, he said, "it made me indignant because . . . there was even less evidence of work and purpose. . . . I have a right to speak, for I asked our own company to give up two of our Saturday performances that we might give the Independent Theatre and the Theatre of Ireland the most popular days" (November 1908, 5).

When a company performed in the Abbey, Yeats felt that it gave him, as head the Abbey's resident company, authority to critique the relevance of that production in the context of the nationalist theater movement. But simply by allowing a group to perform in the Abbey Theatre, Ireland's national stage, Yeats and the directors of the Irish National Theatre Society effectively legitimated that organization's theatrical work as relevant to nationalism and the dramatic movement. In other words, Yeats contributed to the discourse surrounding groups outside the National Theatre Society, Ltd., by virtue of his being the landlord of the national house.

As different companies performed in the Abbey space, the Abbey Theatre became a site of nationalist discourse on both the physical and

14. In the seven years described in this chapter, there were two other instances when a company of former Irish National Theatre Society members got in trouble for "appropriating" the name of the National Theatre Society. In 1904, Yeats sent John Quinn to investigate Dudley Digges's company playing at the St. Louis Exhibition as "the Irish National Theatre Company." When the Fays toured the United States, Frohman's booking agency billed them as the "Abbey Theatre Company," and the directors snatched away their membership in the National Theatre Society.

ideological landscapes of Dublin. As the holder of the Abbey patent, the Abbey Theatre Company (the National Theatre Society, Ltd.) was guaranteed dominance—or at least high visibility—in nationalist and theater circles. They now had the economic freedom to present longer seasons on their own schedule, to encourage new, promising playwrights, and to produce these plays with well-trained, professional actors. Horniman's subsidy gave them the comfort to develop their work regardless of the public's response. Yeats wrote, "we will give you nothing that does not please ourselves, and if you do not like it, and we are still confident that it is good, we will set it before you again, and trust to changing taste. . . . All true arts . . . are a festival where it is the fiddler who calls the tune" *(Samhain,* September 1903, 3).

The subsidy also allowed them to make nationalist statements through the theater that would have gone unnoticed or been impossible in smaller performance groups. In 1909, for example, the Abbey defied the British censor by producing George Bernard Shaw's *The Shewing-Up of Blanco Posnet,* although it had been banned in Britain. This act was nationalist in that it foregrounded nationalist Ireland's disdain for English legislation (see Foster 1996, 409–11). And by 1910, when Horniman abandoned the theater in anger that it remained open after the death of King Edward VII, the company had developed enough of a following to continue to pursue high artistic standards without her money.

The National Theatre Society, Ltd., performed vital work in establishing the Irish dramatic movement. It was the artistic home of Yeats, Synge, Gregory, Colum, Boyle, Fitzmaurice, and many other important playwrights. It trained dozens of actors and created through its performances its own style of acting, which would go on to influence the Little Theatre movement and other artistic developments. But although the directors may have been the "fiddlers who called the tune" in the National Theatre Society, Ltd., they were not the only fiddlers in Dublin or even the only company. Amid the intense excitement of the Irish cultural revival, the Irish National Theatre Society, Ltd., did not serve as a monument to Irish culture, but as a creator of it, a site of resistance against English domination and a forum for debating identity and culture within the movement. It grew out of the collaboration of several nationalist aesthetics and ideologies, and throughout the first decades of the twentieth century, it continued to change and be changed by the array of nationalisms and theatricalities that pervaded the Irish dramatic movement.

5

The Boys of St. Enda's

The Rhetoric of Redemption in Padraic Pearse's Social and Aesthetic Theaters

> The Last Scene: Padraig Pearse walked from his cell to the execution ground with an easy step, and without betraying any emotion; with the same calmness and deliberation he was wont to show when mounting a public platform. . . . Death would be important only after the volley which would ensure him the twofold immortality: that of the Christian entering the eternal communion of God, that of the patriot taking premier rank among the heroes of his nation.
>
> —Margaret Pearse, *The Home-Life of Padraig Pearse*

IN 1911, FIVE YEARS BEFORE the real-life execution described in the epigraph, a group of students and faculty from Padraic Pearse's two Irish nationalist schools rented the stage of the Abbey Theatre and performed a Passion Play in Irish. The schools, St. Enda's School for Boys and St. Ita's School for Girls, had already acquired a reputation for providing their students with both a strong, modern education and a solid background in Irish language, culture, and history. Children of the nationalist elite—Kuno Mayer's son, William Bulfin's daughter, George Moore's nephew, to name a few—attended the school, and leaders of the nationalist movement such as Standish O'Grady, John MacBride, and Douglas Hyde, as well as younger idealists such as Mary Maguire and Padraic Colum, lent their support as lecturers or full-time faculty.

The professionalism of the actors and the elegance of the staging surprised many members of the audience. Maire Nic Shiubhlaigh called the play "probably the most outstanding Gaelic production seen in Dublin before 1916" (Nic Shiubhlaigh 1955, 148). Joseph Holloway, who could not understand Irish, was also moved: "I was greatly impressed with by what simple means great effects can be produced and illusion intensified on the stage" (qtd. in Edwards 1977, 141). Even the *Irish Times,* a comparatively conservative paper, was impressed: "We confess that we had not been prepared for so touching a performance" ("Passion Play at the Abbey Theatre," 7 April 1911, 5). One of the actors in the play, Desmond Ryan, remembered that for many of those involved, the event carried political as well as spiritual weight:

> The audience which, slowly and without applauding, passed out of the Abbey on the two nights of the performance had much to think of. The Irish medium, strange to most of it, had not veiled but intensified the meaning and pathos of the story. Some of us, too, thought, though to many it may seem an irreverence, that our national and individual struggle was in ways a faint reflection of the Great One just enacted. It is not so? The Man is crucified as the Nation, and the Soul moves slowly, falteringly, towards the redemption. (Ryan 1918, 108)

Ryan's description of the performance elides the redemption of the Irish state through insurrection with the redemption of the world through Christ's crucifixion, thus turning the drama into a violent metaphor: a call for the Irish nationalist to accept his/her own cross and be prepared to die for Ireland. Such an understanding of the play echoes the teachings of its author: the founder and headmaster of St. Enda's and St. Ita's, Padraic Henry Pearse.

Padraic Pearse was arguably the greatest actor of the early Irish dramatic movement, but not for his performance as one of the thieves in the Passion Play. Rather, he is remembered for the real-life drama he created through the Easter Rising of 1916. After the rebels' surrender, Pearse's arrest and execution was framed in a way that would make Pearse appear to be an Irish martyr. The deaths of Irish nationalist soldiers and civilians during the five days of the rebellion were ultimately regarded as blood sacrifices to renew Ireland and the nation.

Since childhood, Pearse had been enthralled by the cultural movement in Ireland. Although he passed the bar, he took only one case in his career, instead devoting his efforts to being a writer and politician in the nationalist movement. He edited *An Claidheamh Soluis* (The Sword of Light), the Gaelic League paper, for several years. His grand visions of expansion for the paper nearly ran it into financial ruin. Pearse's poems and short stories in Irish and English earned him a modest reputation as an artist, but he gained real visibility in the movement with the establishment of his nationalist school, St. Enda's, in 1908. When he joined the Irish Republican Brotherhood in 1910, Pearse's political philosophy moved from cultural nationalism and support of parliamentary action to an increasingly militant strategy. He convinced his fellow nationalists that revolution was necessary, and he became the president of the Provisional Republic of Ireland when that revolutionary "state" was declared from the steps of the General Post Office on Easter Monday 1916.

At first, many Dubliners greeted the news of their "revolution" with disbelief. Later, when civilian death tolls began to climb, they began to express anger at Pearse and his comrades. Many Dubliners took advantage of the chaos to loot shops on Grafton Street and other areas (an aspect of the rising recounted in Sean O'Casey's controversial play *The Plough and the Stars*). The rebellion was squelched five days later, and the British began methodically to execute almost all the leaders of the rebellion, including Pearse. When Pearse stood before the firing squad, he did exactly what he had been telling the movement for years he was going to do: he offered his Irish blood as a sacrifice to renew the land and its people. Eventually, enough people believed in that sacrifice to create an independent state on the foundation of his sacrificial act.

Several scholars have recounted the way that the idea of sacrifice, redemption, and violence came to pervade the political ideals of Pearse and other leaders of the Easter Rising. Ruth Dudley Edwards's excellent biography, *Padraic Pearse: The Triumph of Failure* (1977), traces this development in Pearse's political life, personal life, and writing.

The classic analysis of the ways the ideology of sacrifice informed the writings of those involved in the Easter Rising, including Pearse, is William Irwin Thompson's *The Imagination of an Insurrection* (1967). Both works claim that Pearse's sense of personal failure led to his desire to die gloriously for Ireland, so that his name would live on in triumph.

More recently, Sean Moran has created a psycholinguistic analysis of Pearse's life and work in his book *Patrick Pearse and the Politics of Redemption* (1994). Moran's thesis is in a way more terrifying, for he concludes that key aspects of Pearse's life caused him to believe the choice of a suicidal insurrection was ultimately a life-affirming act. "Life springs from death," Pearse declared in his famous graveside panegyric for O'Donovan Rossa, "and from the graves of patriot men and women spring living nations" (qtd. in Edwards 1977, 236). But Pearse's performance of sacrifice in the Easter Rising was not his only conscious performance of nationalism, but the climax of a highly theatrical political career.

Pearse approached all his nationalist activities with the self-conscious intensity of a trained actor. The low, even tones with which he delivered the fiery rhetoric of his speeches; the camaraderie, devotion, and patriotism he cultivated among his students; and his almost unwavering insistence during the rebellion on the glory of his outrageous attempt to free the nation point to Pearse's calculated performance of himself as Irish hero in almost every private and public situation. And his ultimate success lay in his ability to impose his vision of an ideal Irish community—of a society infused with his own interpretations of the values found in Celtic myth and Roman Catholicism—on his own and his circle's everyday activities. To be a student at St. Enda's, a member of the audience at one of the school's performances, a fighter in the rebellion, or a citizen expressing outrage at Pearse's execution was to be a participant in Pearse's political drama.

The passage that begins this chapter points to the ways the performed and the real became elided in the historical memory of Pearse's political acts. Margaret Pearse's description of her brother's death by firing squad portrays it as a calculated performance of religious and nationalist martyrdom. She aligns the immortality of the faithful Christian who will be remembered in heaven with the immortality of the faithful nationalist who will be remembered on Earth.

She further theatricalizes her description of her brother's death by writing of it in the practical format of a stage direction, framing it as a performance informed by the same calculation he used in performing a speech at a nationalist rally. The only audience for the actual execution was a group of English soldiers, but the way in which Pearse confronted death was already formed in Margaret's and the nationalist movement's imagination by Pearse's writing, speeches, and acts. Calls for Ireland's redemption through blood sacrifice rang through both the social work of his speeches and journalistic writing and the aesthetic work of his plays and their legendary martyr-heroes. And out of this dialectic between the social and the aesthetic emerged a synthesis: the idealized image of the executed Pearse as the martyr on whose blood modern Ireland would build its state.

Richard Schechner, Victor Turner, and others have observed a reciprocal relationship between actions in everyday life and actions on a stage, or "social drama" and "aesthetic drama" in the perception of art and life. Schechner imagines this relationship as an "infinity loop" in which the social and political actions of the "social drama" affect the theatrical techniques of "aesthetic drama," which in turn affect the ways in which the "social dramas" are "staged":

> The politician, activist, militant, terrorist all use techniques of the theater (staging) to support social action—events that are consequential, that is, designed to change the social order or to maintain it. The theater artist uses the consequential actions of social life as the underlying themes, frames and/or rhythms of her/his art. . . . There is a flowing back and forth, up and down, characterizing the relationship between social and aesthetic dramas; specific elements (shows) may "travel" from one hemisphere to the other. (1988, 190)

Although this "infinity loop" was clearly at work throughout the self-conscious performance of national identity in turn-of-the-century

Ireland, it was especially pronounced in the case of Padraic Pearse, who transformed his aesthetic ideals into social acts in the Easter Rising. And it was constantly at work in the social and aesthetic dramas "enacted" every day by the students at St. Enda's and St. Ita's schools. These schools were training grounds not merely for the intellectual development of young nationalist children, but also for the development of the aesthetic, cultural, and ideological ideas throughout the nationalist community that led to the violent acts of Easter 1916. The vision of nationhood embodied in performance by the children and staff of St. Enda's and St. Ita's was vital to the development and promulgation of the schools'—and Pearse's—ideological vision.

But although critics and historians invariably assume an inherent theatricality in Pearse's political work, there has been very little discussion surrounding Pearse the dramatist. Yet these dramas—moments when Pearse's conception of an ideal Ireland was embodied before the nationalist community—were integral to the material and ideological development of Pearse's political goals. Nationalist dramas and pageants were common aspects of life at St. Enda's from its founding in 1908. Further, they were an effective, recognized mode of nationalist performance in Dublin's fecund theatrical milieu in the early twentieth century—another model for an Irish national theater. Public performances of Pearse's plays galvanized support for the school in the Dublin nationalist community and deeply affected many of the youth involved in the productions. Pearse's experiences as a theater practitioner helped him formulate his political ideals and share them effectively with the larger nationalist community.

In order to develop a context for understanding the performance ideology of St. Enda's School, my discussion begins with an overview of Pearse's work as a nationalist educator and playwright, and of the philosophies that drove it. Pearse's ideals for Ireland and his journalism, plays, and speeches for the nationalist cause influenced profoundly the lives of his students and staff, turning St. Enda's and St. Ita's into nationalist laboratories, where idealists "performed" their idea of Ireland on stage and in everyday life. The students' performances of plays by

Pearse and others helped mold the theoretical and practical nationalist commitment of Pearse, his actors, and their audiences. Analyzing performance and the performative surrounding St. Enda's and St. Ita's creates a basis for an examination of the reciprocal relationship between the ideology of Pearse's aesthetic dramas and the social drama enacted Easter week 1916.

Pearse's performance rhetoric, like his political ideology, emerged from a blending of contemporaneous nationalist discourses. His work translated, reflected, and emulated Irish myth and folk culture to prove Ireland's cultural depth. And by tracing the history of the Irish struggle through a series of past, generally unrelated insurrections, he made his battles appear part of a unified, centuries-old struggle for Irish freedom. Pearse's most significant rhetorical power, however, lay in his ability to co-opt for his own political ends the symbols of the pervasive Irish Catholic sensibility within the nationalist movement.

The Catholic Church's increased political involvement in the late nineteenth century had effectively politicized Irish religious practice. As the church's stand on nationalist issues was preached from the pulpit, these political positions became church positions and, for the parishioners, church doctrine. The blurring of distinctions between the religious and the political in public perception—especially for Irish-Irelanders in the Gaelic League—was inevitable.[1] And for Irish who had been educated in Catholic schools, with the church as the social and, to an increasing extent, political center of everyday life, political struggle could easily begin to describe itself within the rhetoric of church doctrine and ritual. When political events became framed in the narratives

1. *Irish-Ireland* was the term used in Gaelic League circles and later during the formation of the Irish state to define the group of Irish who believed their connection to the Catholic Church and often to Irish language reflected their allegiance to Ireland and its heritage. Anglo-Irish nationalists such as Yeats and Lady Gregory belonged to a ruling class that Irish-Ireland leaders chose to tolerate but not revere. The Northern Irish response to Irish-Ireland, despite the incredible diplomatic progress of the late 1990s, continues to be all too clear.

of religious rhetoric, they too attained a quasi-religious status: secularized religious rituals that could be read through church practice, thus gaining enormous symbolic power.

The Catholic Church's concern for the nation, however, lay in maintaining the strength of Catholicism in Ireland, not necessarily in creating a free Irish state. Nationalism needed the church, but the church did not need nationalism, and the two often worked at cross-purposes. During the 1890s, the church announced that any member of the Irish Republican Brotherhood would face excommunication.[2] The venomous condemnations of Yeats's nationalist play *The Countess Cathleen* were spurred on by a Catholic bishop who had neither read nor seen the play. For any popular nationalist vision to succeed, it needed at least tacit approval from the church.

Pearse's deeply religious background and use of Christian rhetoric and symbols make him seem at first glance to be in perfect harmony with the church. Because he usually dressed in black, did not drink, smoke, or use profane language, and was never known to be involved in a sexual relationship, he was often compared to a priest. Yet despite his deep religious convictions, he held the church hierarchy in some contempt, and his commitment to religious rhetoric and ritual became increasingly connected to his passion for Irish nationalism. Pearse actually appropriated the symbols of Irish Catholicism for nationalist ends, making what Daniel J. O'Neil calls a "secularized" religious rhetoric, which evoked religious symbols to incite energetic—and even violent—responses among the people (1987, 17–19).

In the revolutionary essay *Peace and the Gael,* for example, Pearse gave religious status to the call to insurrection:

2. One of the most poignant examples of conflicts between the Catholic Church and the nationalist movement occurred during the Dublin lockout of 1911–12. As members of the Irish General Workers and Transport Union struggled to keep their fight for fair working conditions going, English persons sympathetic to the cause offered to look after the children of striking families. The church, concerned that living in non-Catholic homes would shake the children's faith, insisted that they stay in Dublin with their families, although that meant going hungry for most of them.

Ireland will not find Christ's peace until she has taken Christ's sword. What peace she has known in these latter days has been the devil's peace, peace with sin, peace with dishonour. . . . Christ's peace is lovely in its coming . . . But it is heralded by terrific messengers; seraphim and cherubim blow trumpets of war before it. We must not flinch when we are passing through that uproar. . . . Winning through it, we (or those of us who survive) shall come unto great joy. (qtd. in O'Neil 1987, 14)

Written in 1915, *Peace and the Gael* reflects the impatience shared by most of Pearse's circle, as the tensions of World War I and the rise of Irish militant nationalism raised the levels of excitement and tension within the movement. For Pearse, the militant revolutionary transcended being a political soldier to become in fact a religious prophet. In his poem "The Rebel," for example, the revolutionary claims:

> I am flesh of the flesh of these lowly, I am bone of their bone,
> I that have never submitted;
> I that have a soul greater than the souls of my people's masters,
> I that have vision and prophecy and the gift of fiery speech,
> I that have spoken with God on the top of His holy hill . . .
> And I say to my people's masters: Beware, . . .
> Beware of the thing that is coming, beware of the risen people . . .
>   (Pearse 1967, 102–3)

The secularized religious rhetoric of this poem turns the outlaw "rebel" into an apostle of Irish nationalism. He has spoken with God, has been imbued with divine power, and proclaims an immanent "rising." But Pearse implies that for the people to be "risen" spiritually into a new nation, they must physically "rise," taking arms against the oppressive "master," England.

Such appropriation of Christian symbols in the deeply religious environment of the Irish-Ireland movement for militant nationalist ends was indeed striking. But it was even more powerful when inflected in Pearse's adaptations of ancient Irish myth. In almost all nationalist figures' translations and adaptations of Irish literature, there is a heavy emphasis on the assumed nobility, honor, and, most importantly, strength of ancient Irish culture. Pearse, like many nationalist writers, chose Cuchulain, the noble and militant boy warrior of the Red Branch saga, as the role model for modern Ireland's nationalist men. In Yeats's plays *The Green Helmet* and *On Baile's Strand,* the author created his "anti-mask" in his characterization of Cuchulain, the "man of action" whose deep sense of honor leads to actions that transcend the petty squabbles of those around him (a reflection of Yeats's frustration with particular nationalist factions). Like Yeats, Pearse "translated" the Red Branch hero to fulfill his own vision for Ireland, and perhaps his ideal for himself, by distorting both the Cuchulain myth and Roman Catholic ideology in order to interpret Cuchulain as "a harbinger of Christ," "[f]or the story of Cuchulain symbolises the redemption of man by a sinless God. The curse of primal sin lies upon a people; new and personal sin brings doom to their doors; they are powerless to save themselves; a youth free from the curse, akin with them through his mother but through his father divine, redeems them by his valour; and his own death comes from it. . . . And it is like a retelling (or is it a foretelling?) of the story of Calvary" (Pearse 1967, 13). Pearse's philosophies for his nationalist schools reflect his sense of Cuchulain as an ideal hero for modern Ireland.

As an Irish-language teacher for the Gaelic League, Pearse grew fascinated by the possibilities of politicizing the Irish people through cultural study, and in 1908 he got the chance to pursue this dream when he opened St. Enda's School for Boys. Pearse took an enormous risk opening this school, relying on the financial and personal help of his family and friends. Yet the school soon evolved into a politically potent training ground for Irish nationalist youth.

St. Ita's School for Girls opened a year later, but Pearse was never involved with it to the degree he was with St. Enda's. He respected the need for nationalist education for girls as well as for boys and occasionally stopped into the girls' school for lectures or informal conversation, but the bulk of his time and energy remained with the boys' school. Although there simply were not enough hours in the day for Pearse to run St. Ita's with the same passionate devotion he poured into St. Enda's, his comparatively passive attitude toward St. Ita's may also reflect his opinion of the role of women in the nationalist movement. He respected women in the nationalist movement and supported women's suffrage. What really shaped his ideas about women, however, was the devoted support of his mother, aunt, and sisters, who adored the oldest son of the family. In the few Pearse plays in which women do appear or are even mentioned, they are invariably patient mothers or pure young girls, variations on the symbol of the Virgin Mary. Pearse's idea of the most important role for women in the movement may be best summed up in his comment, " 'tis women who keep all the great vigils" (qtd. in Ryan 1919, 95).

In the *Prospectus for 1911–1912,* St. Enda's claimed that its objective was "[to provide] for Irish boys a secondary education distinctively Irish in complexion, bilingual in method, and of a high modern type generally" ([Pearse] n.d., 3) and the curriculum was indeed modern. Pearse and his brother had experienced the typical Irish education for middle-class children that entailed rote learning and ceaseless preparation for the civil-service exams, with no attention paid to the special needs or talents of the students. Pearse combined both what he claimed to be the elements of the old Irish educational system and modern pedagogical techniques to create what was actually an extremely progressive educational institution.

A supporter of the Montessori system of education, Pearse planned his curriculum "with a view to capturing [the students'] imaginations, quickening their powers of observation and reasoning, and giving them a pleasant interest in the world of life round about them" ([Pearse] n.d., 5). Classes were often taught outside (students with an interest in natural science were even given their own garden plots), and field trips and guest lecturers were common. The curriculum was shaped to fit the particular interest of each boy, and unlike the impersonal, even cruel atmosphere of most Edwardian boarding schools, St. Enda's prided itself on a "private and homelike character," going so far as to point out that the students' "domestic welfare is in charge of ladies, a fact suited for the education of sensitive or delicate boys" (ibid., 7).

The children at St. Enda's and St. Ita's developed a vigorous Irish patriotism. The boys at St. Enda's were expected to participate in Irish games such as hurling, Gaelic football, handball, and Irish dancing. They were "taught to prize bodily vigour, grace, and cleanliness, and the advantage of an active life [was] constantly insisted on" (ibid., 6). St. Enda's had its own branch of the Gaelic League, and all classes were taught in Gaelic as much as possible. The children of the Celtic Revival elite attended the school. But even if the children were not from famous families, they were from nationalist ones and were thus already politicized and supportive of the Irish cause.

So were the faculty. Mary Maguire Colum, one of Dublin University's first women graduates, a supporter of the Abbey Theatre in its earliest days, and a faculty member at St. Enda's, recounted the nationalist commitment of the staffs at both schools; they were "knit into all the causes. . . . [I]t seems incredible that so many young people were eager to devote their lives to the service of causes and ideals other than to the normal things of youth. That they should take on themselves the arduous task of running a school . . . seems unbelievable. But then it seemed equally incredible to some that parents would want to entrust their children to a group of young people whose chief recommendation was their ideals, their scholarship, their sense of art, and in other ways their lack of experience" (Maguire Colum 1966, 134). Other staff members included Louise Gavan-Duffy, daughter of Sir Charles Gavan-Duffy, and Thomas MacDonagh, scholar, playwright (his drama *When the Dawn Is Come* was performed by the Abbey Theatre in 1909), and signer of the Proclamation declaring an Irish Republic in 1916. All the faculty developed close relationships with the students.

But Pearse could not have run the schools without the aid of his family. By 1914, all the family's funds were invested in the schools—even the family furniture was used at St. Enda's. His mother and sisters were, for all intents and purposes, the support staff of the school. Along with teaching and providing administrative support, Padraic's brother William (Willie) arranged all the plays and pageants at St. Enda's and "designed the scenery and discussed every detail with Padraic in the course of long nightly talks" (Ryan 1918, 95).

Pearse and his brother were inseparable; the two men often conversed in a kind of baby talk that made those in earshot slightly uneasy. Yet Padraic was clearly the leader of the two. Since the death of Pearse's father, the entire family had been utterly committed to supporting the goals of the oldest son, Padraic. His mother and aunt doted on him, and except for some bullying from his big sister Margaret when he was very young, the whole family threw their wholehearted support into any of Pearse's projects. Sean Moran (1994), however, claims that this familial devotion led to a kind of megalomania in Pearse, preventing him from properly separating from his family to develop independent, adult relationships. Out of such psychological issues, Moran argues, emerged the singleness of purpose and determination in Pearse necessary for his leadership in the Easter Rising.

In his essays in *An Macaomh* (The Young Boy or The Youth), the St. Enda's journal, Pearse claimed that the school's educational system came not only from Montessori but also from "the old Irish plan of education, as idealised for boys in the story of the Macradh of Eamhain and for girls in that of Grianan of Lusga, [which] was the wisest and most generous that the world has ever known. . . . Such was the education of Cuchulain, the most perfect hero of the Gael" (Pearse 1967, 55–56). St. Enda's students were put under the "fosterage" of a wise and great man (Pearse), who would bring them up in a beautiful environment (the school campus in the Dublin suburb of Rathfarnham). They would be allowed "free government within certain limits" and were provided with a "scrupulous correlation of moral, intellectual and physical training." Helping Pearse foster the students were "the captains, the poets, the prophets of the people"—speakers such as John MacBride and Padraic Colum, and idealistic teachers such as Thomas MacDonagh and Mary Maguire Colum (Pearse 1967, 55).

Pearse engineered St. Enda's mission to be the production of not just learned Irish men, but Irish heroes: "Cuchulainn may never have lived and there may never have been a Boy-Corps at Emhain; but the picture endures as the Gael's idealization of the kind of environment and the kind of fostering which go to the making of a perfect hero"

(Pearse 1967, 56). The militant assumptions of this "heroism" became poignantly clear in another edition of *An Macaomh,* in which Pearse listed the kinds of heroes St. Enda's boys were to emulate:

> We must be worthy of the tradition we seek to recreate and perpetuate in Eire, the knightly tradition of the macradh of Eamhain Macha, dead at the Ford "in the beauty of their boyhood," the high tradition of Cuchulainn, "better is short life with honour than long life with dishonour," "though I were to live but one day and one night, if only my fame and my deeds live after me;" the noble tradition of the Fianna, "we, the Fianna, never told a lie, falsehood was never imputed to us," "strength in our hands, truth on our lips, and cleanness in our hearts;" the Christlike tradition of Colm Cille, "if I die, it shall be from the excess of the love I bear the Gael." It seems to me that with this appeal it will be an easy thing to teach Irish boys to be brave and unselfish, truthful and pure; I am certain that no other appeal will so stir their hearts or kindle their imaginations to heroic things. (Pearse 1967, 57)

This list of nationalist sentiments, culled from volumes of Celtic writings, formed the moral and social code for St. Enda's students and was affirmed by every facet of life at the school. At the first site of the school, each day the students passed by a mural of Cuchulain in the main hall, with the caption, "I care not though I were to live but one day and one night, if only my fame and deeds live after me." The boys were constantly reminded that their duty as Irish nationalists included a readiness for personal sacrifice, and students and faculty embraced that challenge, living the social drama of Ireland's national school.

John Hutchinson has noted that "the aim of cultural nationalists is the moral regeneration of the historical community" (1994, 124). The microsociety of St. Enda's seemed to have succeeded in actually embodying such a community, for although St. Enda's was in many ways a modern European school, it was also a kind of Irish nationalist utopia— Pearse's vision of an ideal Irish community. Students remember St. Enda's as such an Edenic place (Desmond Ryan called his memoirs *Re-*

membering Sion). Pearse knew all the boys personally and wrote the progress reports for the parents himself.

The code of honor was strictly enforced among the boys, who showed a terrific degree of self-discipline. "Pearse's very presence . . . was a discipline in itself," one former student remembered. "The most noisy dormitory or study-hall became hushed and silent as he entered with his peremptory *'Ceard e seo? Ceard e seo?'* ('What is this? What is this?'). A silence due to respect and not fear" (qtd. in Edwards 1977, 85). He often joked with the boys, and he made storytelling *(sgealaid-heacht)* from the ancient Irish cycles "an essential part of education" (Ryan 1919, 83). Often a *sgealaidheacht* was held outside on the beautiful grounds of the Hermitage—the St. Enda's campus. The romance of the school was compounded by the beauty of the estate and by the story that Robert Emmet had wooed his love, Sarah Curran, on the grounds.

Every day for the St. Enda's student entailed a self-conscious performance of his participation in this Irish community. He would dress in the traditional kilt of Irish nationalists. He would speak Irish at least as much as English throughout the day, to the delight of his young and idealistic instructors. He would play Irish games, learn Irish crafts, and listen to lectures on his culture and history from the most important figures in the nationalist movement. To be a student or staff member at St. Enda's was to "take Ireland for granted," to pretend that this ideal world was possible beyond the walls of the school.[3] In other words, the "social drama" of attending the school was informed by the ideological aesthetics of Pearse's interpretation of the rhetoric of the Irish cultural revival.

Recollections of St. Enda's are filled with descriptions of the use of performance in school activity. A *ceili* was held fortnightly, and half-day

3. This argument is similar to the one espoused by Sinn Fein after the rebellion. Although Ireland was officially part of the United Kingdom, Sinn Fein "took Ireland for granted" by setting up its own government and courts of law, encouraging Ireland's citizens to turn to them—not England—for their civic needs.

holidays with special speakers were commonplace. William Pearse regularly arranged dramatic readings and other kinds of performances as part of school events.[4] Performance and pageant, for the public and for themselves, were integral aspects of life at St. Enda's. For example, when Pearse returned from his tour in the United States to raise funds in 1915, the boys "welcomed him back with a magnificent demonstration from the roof of the square, grey imposing building, which is the Hermitage. Some of us lined the roof, waving the school banner and making the air resound with trumpet calls and the music of pipes. The rest of the school lined the avenue to greet him with the traditional Sgoil Eanna three shouts of welcome" (Ryan 1918, 109–10). Such a moment moves the boys' performance into the realm of ritual. The event becomes a celebration both *by* St. Enda's students and faculty and *for* themselves—a moment of confirmation of and identification with the ideological system they were enacting in performance.

St. Enda's nationalist intensity in performance was also contagious outside the school walls. In 1909, Pearse wrote a pageant for the boys—aptly called *The Boy Deeds of Cuchulain.* He explained that he chose this subject because "we were anxious to crown our first year's [dramatic] work with something worthy and symbolic; anxious to send our boys home with the knightly image of Cuchulainn in their hearts and his knightly words ringing in their ears" *(An Macaomh,* Christmas 1909, 16) These "knightly words" were often violent and foretold the rhetoric of violence and sacrifice that Pearse increasingly pronounced as he trudged closer to 1916.

Pearse nurtured a sense of community in the production, writing the parts in what he jokingly called his "masterpieces to order" (Ryan 1919, 94) with the traits of particular boys in mind. Although casting

---

4. Willie Pearse was also involved in theater groups outside St. Enda's, including the Irish Theatre at Hardwicke Street and the Leinster Stage Society. Margaret Pearse wrote several plays for the latter company. William Pearse was an intelligent, eager, cooperative, but not very talented actor. In fact, when the Leinster Stage Society went on tour to raise money for St. Enda's in 1914, they were received so poorly that Padraic had to juggle the school finances to garner enough money for Willie to return to Dublin.

parts according to "type" is the usual practice in most school dramas, the casting of Pearse's "masterpieces to order" seems to have done ideological work as well. Pearse's *An Macaomh* description of preparing the play points to the reciprocal relationship between the real and the performed in his thinking about the play—how closely he equated the actual personalities of the boys at St. Enda's with their heroic counterparts from Irish myth. "I feel sure," he wrote, that "Eamon Bulfin will be very beautiful and very awful as Cathbach the Druid; that Denis Gwynn will be singularly noble as Conchobar mac Neasa . . . and that Frank Dowling will realise, in face and figure and manner, my own high ideal of the child Cuchulainn . . . a boy merely to all who looked upon him, and unsuspected for a hero save in the strange moments of exaltation, when the sevenfold splendours blazed in his eyes and the herolight shone about his head" (Christmas 1909, 16).

The aesthetic drama clearly reflects the social drama of the school, as pronounced traits among the boys in their social interactions at St. Enda's become equated with their performance as heroic Irish figures in the pageant. And if the aesthetic world of Cuchulain can be so easily realized by the social world of St. Enda's, this event implies that the reverse may be possible as well. Could these boys in ancient costumes become modern Irish heroes?

After performing the pageant at St. Enda's, the company was invited to perform it at the Castle Bellingham Feis, in the very area where Cuchulain was said to have been raised as a boy. Student Desmond Ryan remembered that after performing the play, as the actors marched away from the *feis* behind their school banner, still dressed as Cuchulainesque warriors, their "performance" continued, for "a crowd gathered round, wondering at our strange weapons and our dusty faces. They followed us, and soon they were singing 'Who Fears to Speak of '98' [a popular ballad about the United Irishman Rebellion of 1798] as they tramped and surged round us. MacDonagh was delighted at the commotion we had raised. 'Egad!' he said, as the crowd swelled to the dimensions of a riot, 'they expect us to lead them against [Dublin] castle' " (qtd. in Edwards 1977, 133). This spontaneous outpouring of nationalist fervor by the children's "audience" caused the pageant to break out of both the outline of the text and the boundaries of the *feis*. It even broke down the distinctions between actor and audience, creating, however vaguely, a moment when the aesthetic action (rallying in support of the St. Enda's children and singing patriotic songs) might turn into social action (storming the seat of British rule in Ireland or performing some other political act).

The carnivalesque atmosphere of the *feis* and the abstract symbols of the pageant must have contributed to the ease and spontaneity with which the crowd playfully, then more urgently joined in the performance by the St. Enda's boys that day. Yet the student actors were also successful at drawing in more jaded Dublin audiences.

In March 1909, St. Enda's presented its first production of nationalist dramas for the public—a play by Douglas Hyde and Standish O'-Grady called *The Coming of the Fionn*—in the school gymnasium. The field of Irish national theater in Dublin by this time was crowded with performance groups, each with its own aesthetic, organizational, and political points of view. The Abbey Theatre had its own space, internationally famous playwrights, and professional status for its actors. Yet the controversies surrounding *The Playboy of the Western World* continued to keep many nationalists from its doors. Its benefactor, Annie Horniman, was about to abandon the project—a further challenge to the economics of the company.

The Abbey often rented its space to other nationalist performance groups, such as Casimir Markiewicz's Independent Dramatic Company or the National Players. The Theatre of Ireland, made up of former Abbey actors who wanted to maintain their amateur status, were not allowed on the Abbey stage after 1908, however, and usually performed in Molesworth Hall, although they occasionally performed in larger venues, such as the Rotunda. The Gaelic League continued to garner support for Irish nationalism with *feisianna*. P. J. Bourke's melodramas were put on by his No. 1 Company at the Queen's Royal. Outside Dublin, groups such as the Ulster Literary Theatre and the Cork Dramatic Society were developing stagings of national representations of Ireland in their own communities.

What made St. Enda's nationalist theater unique, however, was its connection to the social and ideological work of the school. Performances by St. Enda's were often read as aesthetic outpourings of the social drama the students and staff members enacted daily in the nationalist school. Thus, the nationalist community rallied around those performances, perhaps more eager to express support for nationalist education than for St. Enda's stab at nationalist theater. In a review of the March 1909 production, for example, Stephen MacKenna saluted its aesthetic elegance (using the same standards for costume and diction W. B. Yeats was espousing in his own plays), its ease with the Irish language (one of the goals of Gaelic League theatrical activity), and its relation to the daily work of the school. MacKenna wrote, "with all the beauty of the costumes, exquisite by the art of colour-blending as they are of themselves graceful in line and flow, there was the Irish itself, perfectly enunciated and modulated, or delightfully changed, by fresh Irish children, who, ninety-four already, are growing up to be Irish, and to talk Irish and to think Irish, the new generation Gaelic in the grain" (*An Macaomh*, Christmas 1909, 37).

To attend a performance by the students at St. Enda's—to be awed by the naturalness and authority of the young actors—was to support the possibility that the imagined Irish community of the school not only might foster the "new generation" of Ireland, but also might be the founders of a new nation "Gaelic in the grain."

Pearse wrote of the production in *An Macaomh*, "We had an audience of over a hundred each evening . . . including Sir John Rhys, Mr. Eoin MacNeill, Mr. W. B. Yeats, Mr. Stephen Gwynn, Mr. Edward Martyn, Mr. Standish O'Grady, and Mr. Padraic Colum. All these, especially Mr. Yeats, were very generous in their praise of our lads, who, I hope will not be spoiled by the tributes they received from such distinguished men" (Christmas 1909, 13). This is an impressive list of patrons for a school play, but it was also one that saw itself as an "integral" audience—leaders of the Irish Literary Renaissance witnessing Pearse's work in Irish nationalist education. Equally impressive is the attention the production received in the press. The *London Sphere* and the *Irish Independent* actually printed photographs, and every Dublin newspaper was there.

All were pleasantly surprised by the technical strength of the production. Like MacKenna, most reviewers delighted in the simplicity and elegance with which the boys performed. W. P. Ryan wrote in the *Nation:* "The boys in the Sgoil Eanna plays for the most part were serenely and royally at home. *An Craoibhin*'s delicate and tender little drama was delicately and tenderly interpreted; it had a religious sense and atmosphere about it, and the miracle seemed fitting and natural" (qtd. in *An Macaomh,* Christmas 1909, 13). In an article in *Sinn Fein,* Padraic Colum inferred that the performance stood as an example of the triumph of the committed nationalist amateur actor: "In the production there was no professionalism, no elaborate illusion. It was one with all noble art, because it came out of a comradeship of interest and aspiration; the art was here not rootless, it came out of belief, work, and aspiration" (qtd. in *An Macaomh,* Christmas 1909, 15). For almost a decade, Irish nationalist actors had worked to create a "naturalness" in Irish acting, to present either a true to life portrayal of Irish culture or, in the case of nonrealistic plays such as Yeats's poetic dramas and the plays presented at St. Enda's, an elemental aspect of Irish emotional or spiritual life. The students at St. Enda's seem to have been weirdly successful at establishing this sense of naturalness in performance.

Perhaps what the reviewers responded to, besides the actors' technical skill, was the sincerity with which the actors approached their roles, the "belief, work, and aspiration" of which Colum wrote. Just as in a Gaelic League or Inghinidhe na hEireann performance, the body of the St. Enda's student took on multiple significations on the stage—as group member, as nationalist actor, as character portrayed. The audience's awareness that the figures before them were both characters and students, playing on a ground that was both set and school, increased the sense that these productions were spontaneous outpourings of St. Enda's life, further blurring the semiotic boundaries between the real and performed, between the social work and the aesthetic work enacted on stage or even at St. Enda's.

As the school's theatrical activities expanded during the next five years, St. Enda's produced three plays on the stage of the Abbey Theatre, and members of the Theatre of Ireland were known to help out with productions at St. Enda's (Nic Shiubhlaigh 1955, 148). The school continually drew individuals and organizations into its performances as playwrights, producers, and audience members, and these persons added to the political significance of the school's dramatic work.

St. Enda's production of the Passion Play discussed earlier in this chapter reflects how the organizational aesthetic of all St. Enda's productions also elided the work of the theater with the work of the school. Padraic Pearse played one of the thieves and his brother Willie played Pontius Pilate. Mary Maguire, a teacher at St. Ita's, played Mary Magdelen, and Thomas MacDonagh stage managed the event. The head gardener, Michael Mac Ruagh, played Barabas. Mary Bulfin, St. Ita's student and the daughter of the nationalist writer William Bulfin, played the Blessed Virgin. What the audience witnessed in this production was the presentation of a story deeply important to the Catholic faith being performed by members of the St. Enda's community—from groundskeepers to the elite of the nationalist movement and their children—in impeccable Irish. By blurring the distinctions between character and actor and between the aesthetic act of the play and the social act of the school, the production could evoke profound nationalist resonances.

From 1910 onward, as Pearse's political ideals became increasingly violent, the rhetoric of sacrifice began to pervade his thought, shadowing the themes of the plays he wrote for his students at St. Enda's. His 1912 play *The King* makes this philosophy startlingly clear. In the play, a young boy, Giolla na Naomh ("the Servant of the Saints"), sacrifices himself to absolve his country of its evil king and free the people. Ruth Dudley Edwards has summed up just how closely the play aligns with Pearse's thought: "First, it showed his growing preoccupation with the sacrifice of Calvary, for Giolla is the embodiment of the Christ-child who must die to save his people. Second, it was a reaffirmation of his belief in the essential purity of childhood. Third, it stated the necessity of sacrificing the young and sinless to save a decadent nation" (1977, 142).

Pearse gave the play a four-part structure. In the first section, a group of boys, students at a monastery, discuss the king and the ongoing war. The king is losing the war because of "the thousands he has slain" and "the churches he has plundered" (Pearse 1968, 50). Then they argue among themselves who should be king, but when Giolla is asked if he would like to be king, he replies: "I would not. I would rather be a monk that I might pray for the King" (Pearse 1967, 50). In the second section, the abbot and the monks enter, discussing the king's losses in battle. The abbot proclaims: "The nation is guilty of the sins of its princes. I say to you that this nation shall not be freed until it chooses for itself a righteous King" (52–53). Where can such a king be found? Among the purest of the boys. Giolla, who would rather serve the king than attain the glory of the title, is the obvious choice. In the third section, the king appears, having lost again in battle, and relinquishes his sword to the abbot, who bestows it on Giolla. Pearse includes an elaborate scene in which Giolla is ritually dressed in the trappings and armor of the king, then Giolla receives the abbot's blessing and rides off into battle. The king, abbot, and monks on stage describe the offstage battle. Giolla leads the army to victory but dies in battle. In the final section, his body is carried on stage, followed by keening women (the first appearance by St. Ita's students in this play). The king kneels at the funeral bier, saying: "I do homage to thee, O dead King, O victorious child! I kiss thee, O white body, since it is thy Purity that hath redeemed my people" (67). The scene closes as the keening women sing a *Te Deum*.

The King reflects both life at St. Enda's and Pearse's political philosophy in several important ways. First, the play begins with young students of a monastery playing and talking on the grounds. Thus, the actors (St. Enda's students performing on the school grounds) are performing a scene directly parallel to one they presumably enacted every day at St. Enda's. The adult conflict is between a corrupt king, unable to expel his enemy because of his own inherent evil, and the abbot of the monastery, who takes the king's sword away from him and gives it to the purest of the young boys. This conflict becomes a metaphor for Pearse's understanding of the corruption in Irish government. To Pearse, the fading idealism of Ireland's increasingly anglicized population was the real reason for the nation's inability to gain independence. He calls for a moral upholder of tradition (the abbot) to pass the power on to an innocent soul who ultimately becomes the nation's champion. Only a pure sacrifice can redeem the nation against the evils performed by the king and return peace and freedom to the community. Such a reading also implies that Pearse saw the boys of his school as modern Giollas, raised with the purity of heart necessary for Irish heroism/martyrdom.

Pearse uses a similar plot in his 1915 play *The Master*. That production, also, is set in an early monastery, with a master teaching a group of boys the "new" religion, Christianity. The Christianity reflected in the play, however, is a violent one. At the beginning of the play, in a discussion among the boys about the disciples, little Iollan, the most beautiful and pure of the boys, comments that Peter was right to strike out against the guards in the Garden of Gethsemane to defend Christ. When the master corrects him that Jesus rebuked Peter, Iollan responds, "The Lord did wrong to rebuke him. He was always down on Peter. . . . But when He wanted a rock to build His church on He had to go to Peter" (Pearse 1918, 79–80).

In the climax of the play, little Iollan literally has a sword put to his throat by the evil king, who wishes for proof of the power of Christ. The king demands that the master call down an angel to save the boy. The master is afraid to tempt God in that way, preferring to let God's will determine what should happen to the boy without his intercession. Iollan, however, is not afraid, but calls on the angel Michael, who appears dressed as a warrior, "clothed in light" (79). The king, converted, descends to his knees. The master, overcome by the splendor, falls over dead.

In a way, *The Master* reflects Yeats's *The Hour-Glass,* in which an intellectual who has turned his students away from faith in God must repent in his final hour of life by converting someone back to faith. *The Hour-Glass* is ultimately an intellectual exploration of the mystery of faith against atheistic empiricism. Pearse's *The Master,* however, demands that action—even violence—be an integral part of faith. If the Irish people wish to be redeemed—want to become a spiritual and political nation—they must not wait for divine intervention, but call down the warrior angels and even be the warrior angels themselves. But just as Pearse's interpretation of Irish nationalism was not the only one in the movement, so was there potential for different interpretations of his nationalist plays.

St. Enda's School originally produced *The King* at the school in 1911, but its most famous performance occurred two years later at the Abbey Theatre. The school was facing bankruptcy that year, and Pearse, accompanied by Mrs. Reddin, "the wife of his solicitor and a well-known figure in Dublin theatrical circles, who had two sons at St. Enda's" (Edwards 1977, 171), visited Yeats at the Abbey to ask for help. Yeats eagerly agreed to have the Abbey produce Rabindranath Tagore's *The Post Office* with the St. Enda production of *The King* and to give St. Enda's two-thirds of the profits. The plays were well attended and served as a very successful fund-raiser for the school.

Both Tagore and Pearse were involved in creating nationalist schools to maintain the language and culture of the youth of their respective colonized nations; Yeats called Tagore's school "the Indian St. Enda's." Tagore's play, about a young, dying boy who teaches the people of his village of the power of imagination and the importance of the spiritual over the material, seemed to Yeats to fit well with Pearse's drama about the sacrifice of an innocent child for the redemption of a corrupt state. But although this production was a moment of material collaboration between the anticolonial, nationalist theaters of St. Enda's, the Abbey, and, to a lesser extent, Tagore, there remained tension between the ideological goals of the plays and their producers.

Pearse wrote that both he and Tagore "had in our minds the same image of a humble boy and the pomp of death" and that "in our respective languages, he speaking in terms of Indian village life, and I in terms of Irish saga, we have both expressed the same truth that the highest thing anyone can do is to serve" (qtd. in Ryan 1918, 85). According to Yeats in his preface to Tagore's play, however, Tagore believed that his play captured the moment when "the 'I,' seeking no longer for gains that cannot be 'assimilated with its spirit,' is able to say, 'All my work is thine' (Sadhana, pp. 162, 163)" (1914, n.p.). The child in *The Post Office* does not sacrifice his life in violence, but transcends the pain of his dying body as he gives up his soul to the eternal. Yeats wrote, "On the stage the little play . . . conveys to the *right* audience an emotion of gentleness and peace" (1914, n.p.). Giolla's sacrifice in *The King* is a violent one, designed to imply the need for sacrifice and insurrection. For Pearse, the "right audience" responds not with "gentleness and peace" but a willingness—even an eagerness—for violent action.

"The politics of political theater," William B. Worthen notes, "emerge not only in the themes of the drama but more searchingly in the disclosure of the working of ideology in the making of meaning in the theater, in the formation of the audience's experience and so, in a manner of speaking, in the formation of the audience itself" (1992, 146). In Pearse's nationalist theater at St. Enda's, the "making of meaning" worked on its participants in several important ways. For members of the community of St. Enda's, to perform in these productions was to participate in the aesthetic reflection of the social drama they enacted daily at the school. The audience of a St. Enda's production witnessed, in a sense, the "staging" of two worlds: the mythic, heroic world generally presented in the actual drama and the idealized nationalist community at St. Enda's out of which the production emerged.

The "naturalness" and general enthusiasm with which the students performed reflect that these productions were doing real ideological work: they served to confirm the philosophy of the school and the patriotism of its students. They helped make more real the students' sense of themselves as potential Irish heroes. The spectators of a St. Enda's performance ultimately became what Schechner terms "integral" audience members, performing their support of the school and its ideals by attending the event. Performances on the St. Enda's school grounds also highlighted the relationship between the social work of the school and the aesthetic work of the drama.

This kind of response was relatively easy to garner at performances on the St. Enda's grounds or in a romantic historical setting such as the Bellingham Feis. At play performances within conventional, commercial theater spaces, such as Hardwicke Street and the Abbey, the potential for the production to transcend traditional audience/actor relationships was restrained by the limits of the liminoid theater space. Yet accounts of audience response to productions such as the Passion

Play point out that even in venues unrelated to the school, audiences often felt themselves participating in a larger nationalist project. The Abbey Theatre's identification with nationalist performance practice in 1912 also served to promote the political resonances of Pearse's play there. The tensions among the ideologies of diverse plays, players, and audiences are indicative of the creative energy of the Irish dramatic movement and of the nationalist movement in general during this period. But in terms of Pearse's political goals outside the theater, these tensions reflect the need for an even more urgent political rhetoric—a clearer implication of the audience in the aesthetic drama of his theater and the social drama of his political goals.

From 1913, when Pearse was admitted into the Irish Republican Brotherhood, until his death by an English firing squad in 1916, Pearse's rhetoric of redemption moved from a theoretical idea to a call for very real action in his work, as he foregrounded the need for sacrifice in his own generation through the examples of previous "glorious failures" in the history of the Irish struggle. When Pearse transferred his rhetoric of redemption from the stages of St. Enda's to the streets of Dublin in the Easter Rising, he was aware of the need to implicate his "audience"—the people of Ireland—in the drama. They needed to recognize the sacrifice and thus participate with him in Ireland's spiritual and political redemption. In the months preceding the rebellion, Pearse tried to galvanize nationalist groups—such as the Irish Republican Brotherhood, the Irish Volunteers, and the Irish Citizen Army—by representing his mission as aligned with that of previous heroes. For example, in his 1915 graveside panegyric for O'Donovan Rossa, a Young Ireland leader, Pearse successfully linked the work of the current militant nationalists with the efforts of the United Irishmen in 1798 and of the Young Irelanders in 1867, stating, "we know only one definition of freedom: it is Tone's definition, it is Mitchel's definition, it is Rossa's definition. Let no man blaspheme the cause that the dead generations of Ireland served by giving it any other name and definition than their name and their definition" (qtd. in Deane 1991, 293). Of course, the twentieth-century Pearse is speaking of his own definition of a free Ireland. Yet his rhetoric represents the current movement as a "rebirth" of the energies of previous heroes.

Pearse's most famous and influential use of this trope is found in the Proclamation of the Irish Republic—the document that announced the Easter Rebellion. In the first sentence, the Proclamation aligns itself with past rebellions: "IRISHMEN AND IRISHWOMEN: In the name of God and of the dead generations from which she receives her old tradition of nationhood, Ireland, through us, summons her children to her flag and strikes for her freedom" (qtd. in Edwards 1977, 280).

Most of the Irish people responded apathetically when Pearse first read this document on the steps of the General Post Office. As the fighting ensued, instead of rallying around the opportunity to join the historic pattern of struggle, many chose to loot city shops or cheered British soldiers bringing "order" to the city. Only after five days of fighting and the arrest of its signers did the rebellion develop real significance, as the signers' social acts fulfilled the promises of sacrifice and insurrection made in the document.

In his speech from the dock before his conviction, Pearse again claimed a place for the rebellion among other glorious failures: "The time [for the rebellion], as it seemed to me, did come, and we went into the fight. I am glad we did. We seem to have lost. We have not lost. To refuse to fight would have been to lose; to fight is to win. We have kept faith with the past, and handed on a tradition to the future. . . . If you [English] strike us down now, we shall rise again and renew the fight" (qtd. in Edwards 1977, 318). With this statement, Pearse evoked the historical (Robert Emmet's speech from the dock in 1803), cultural (Cuchulain's oath for a short, honorable life rather than an anonymous long one), and religious (Christian rhetoric of resurrection) sensibilities of Irish nationalism. The English judges' sentence of death merely affirmed Pearse's rhetorical claims. By recognizing Pearse as an English traitor, the judges inadvertently made him an Irish hero. Irish nationalists, who had been raised not only on Pearse's rhetoric of redemption but on centuries of stories about martyred Irish heroes, ultimately rallied toward Pearse's fashioning of the event.

Pearse did not get the opportunity granted Robert Emmet to proclaim his speech before a gallery of fellow nationalists as well as his accusers. Like the other signers, he was tried in a room with three judges and only a few officials. But the speech was recorded and retold, joining the long lineage of such oratorical performances in the Irish nationalist canon.

After Pearse's death, his reputation as an Irish hero (encouraged by the representation of his deeds given by his mourning mother and sisters, other nationalist leaders, and Pearse's own writings) ultimately claimed for him the heroic, "martyred" status he had struggled for years to attain. It also affected the way Pearse's work came to be read, as his writings began to be interpreted to reflect the events surrounding the Easter Rebellion. This reading of the relationship between Pearse's life and writing is especially true of his last, unfinished play, *The Singer* (1915).

The Singer is much less fanciful than Pearse's earlier plays and reflects a more intimate connection for Pearse between his own acts and the ones he was portraying in his writing. Instead of an innocent little boy, the hero is an older, more experienced character, which makes his relationship to the nation for which he will die more mature and more complex (though not more tragic) than the simple offerings of a young child. The play opens with a woman, Maire, and her adopted daughter waiting by the hearth, while the men of the community prepare for an uprising against the British. MacDara, the son of the house, has already left the home for the national cause. The mother and her foster daughter (who is deeply in love with MacDara) wait for him to return. Meanwhile, members of the community gather in Maire's home to await the arrival of "the Singer" to lead them in the insurrection. From the beginning of the play, the Singer is described in Christ-like terms: "Diarmaid said that in the Joyce country they think it is some great hero that has come back again to lead the people against the Gall, or maybe an angel, or the Son of Mary Himself that has come down on the earth" (Pearse 1918, 111). "The Singer"—teacher, war hero, and Christ figure—turns out to be MacDara.

MacDara has been away from the house for years, working as an insurgent poet, a teacher, and now a military leader. The comparison to Pearse's own resumé is obvious. The people in his home village remember him as a scholar who was also adept at Irish sports: "I'd say that he'd wild a caman or a pike with any boy on the mountain" (111), one of his comrades remarks. But although he was an ideal Irish hero even as a boy, he obviously underwent a transformation while he was away from home. Now that he has returned, like Christ returning to Jerusalem, he realizes that his martyrdom is immanent. As he comments to his old teacher, "I meant this to be a home-coming, but it seems only like a meeting on the way. . . . When my mother stood up to meet me with her arms stretched out to me, I thought of Mary meeting her son on the Dolorous Way" (115).

When his identity as the Singer is revealed, all the men kiss his hand as if he were a religious leader. He speaks to them in parables. When the news comes that his comrade, Colm, and his fifteen men have been killed, these soldiers seem to represent John the Baptist and other prophets who came before Christ. They have already set an example that has been unheeded by the people. Thus, MacDara decides to face the Gall alone. He tells the men, "the fifteen were too many. Old men, you did not do your work well enough. You should have kept all back but one. One man can free a people as one Man redeemed the world. I will take no pike, I will go into the battle with bare hands. I will stand up before the Gall as Christ hung naked before men on the tree! *(He moves through them, pulling off his clothes as he goes)*" (125). MacDara's Christ-like moral strength and faith in the national cause were designed to develop a sense of nationalist faith in modern Irish. But although *The Singer* may be good nationalism, it is bad theater. The dialogue is cliché; the stage business is sloppy. In fact, the text is not even finished. But the hero is clearly Pearse.

Before the rebellion, Joseph Plunkett said of the play, "If Pearse were dead, this would cause a sensation" (qtd. in Ryan 1919, 94), and he was exactly right. *The Singer* was never performed during Pearse's lifetime, but when he became a martyr in the Easter Rebellion, readers of the play linked Pearse to the character MacDara, and the play developed a biographical resonance for its readers. In the 1930s, the Board of Education recommended that the play be taught in Ireland's schools. With its heady dose of misconstrued but recognizably patriotic Christian symbolism (Edwards 1977, 340), *The Singer* epitomized the rhetoric of sacrifice and devotion to the nation present in the conservative political climate of the first years of the free state.

The theater of St. Enda's, like the school itself, provided a stage on which young Irish nationalists could embody an idealized image of a heroic Ireland. The boys of the school did so with a naturalness, eagerness, passion, and beauty that touched, aesthetically and politically, many of the political and artistic leaders of the nationalist movement. These performances garnered significant nationalist interest and helped smooth the way for Pearse's rise in the nationalist movement. But Pearse's plays were sermons to the converted; on 24 April 1916, Pearse and his fellow actors performed before a captive audience in the Dublin town center. More than any of Pearse's social or aesthetic dramas, the rebellion managed to implicate the entire Irish community, forcing everyone to respond in some way to Pearse's bloody ideology. Dim reflections of Pearse's tragic vision for the Easter Rising can be seen in the rhetoric of sacrifice in his school plays. Travesties of it flicker in the flames of Ireland's continuing troubles.

Afterword

Did that play of mine send out,
Certain men the English shot?
> —W. B. Yeats, "The Man and the Echo"

THE EASTER RISING points to the theatricality of political life in Ireland in the first decades of the twentieth century—the self-conscious performance of the nation in an attempt to direct its national destiny. That is not to say that the devastation of Dublin in the rebellion was not a real event that damaged, ruined, and took away people's lives. But the ultimate efficacy of the rebellion—as in any moment of theater— stemmed from its audience's response to the rebels' performance of martyrdom. The people had been prepared for this moment by other political theaters of the nineteenth century: Robert Emmet's speech from the dock in 1803, O'Connell's "monster meetings" in the 1830s, Land League protests at the sites of tenant evictions of the 1870s and 1880s, the small and large gestures of Irish resistance on individual and institutional levels by the Gaelic League, and the wealth of theatrical performance on nationalist themes in many venues throughout Ireland.

The theatricality of 1916 was visible even to its contemporaries. John Redmond warned the British not to execute the leaders of the rebellion, knowing that their deaths would place them in the pantheon of Tone and Emmet. Margaret Pearse used the convention of the stage direction to describe her brother's execution. Histories of the events were given titles such as Desmond Shaw's *The Drama of Sinn Fein*. The theatricality of the Easter Rising—the way it played into particular tropes of nationalist myth, tradition, and performance practice—transformed the event from a doomed insurrection to a heroic tragedy. And in the decades of violent and nonviolent revolutions to come, the Irish people were invited to take a role.

This level of theatricality can be effective, however, only in a community that has established recognizable tropes for the performance of Irish nationhood. Other elements of Irish life—such as religious practice, economics, and Irish nationalist literature—also contributed to the readability and effectiveness of the rebellion. Yeats overstated his case in "The Man and the Echo" when he wrote, "Did that play of mine send out / Certain men the English shot?" (Yeats 1983, 345). But the theater in turn-of-the-century Dublin was an undeniably essential element in the cultural formation of nationalist Ireland, an active contributor to Irish nationalist discourse.

Although the theatricality of Irish politics is declared an integral aspect of Irish nationalism, the politics of Irish theater—the way theater became a recognized avenue for nation building as debates about identity were literally "played out" on stage—has not been deeply examined. This book asserts that the Irish dramatic movement did not merely reflect nationalist debate, but was an instrument of it.

In 1913, Con Markiewicz—Inghinidhe member, Fianna Fail founder, actress, suffragist, labor leader, and future Easter Rebellion soldier and Irish senator—declared that there were three great political movements in Ireland: the nationalist movement, the women's movement, and the workers' movement, "all fighting the same fight, for the extension of human liberty" (qtd. in Owens 1984, 74). But the fight for women's and labor rights took a back seat in the first, conservative decades of the Irish Republic, as well as in Northern Ireland's history. Historical scholarship has worked to debunk some of the myths of Irish national and cultural history by pointing out the true diversity of identity and experience in twentieth-century Ireland. This book was designed to expand that debate into the realm of theater history.

In the energetic years of the Irish literary renaissance, the theater was an essential vehicle for embodying a version of national identity, thus registering resistance against colonial oppression and debating strident cultural and political issues by performing them on stage. The Abbey and its directors were essential to the formation of the Irish dramatic movement as we know it. Yeats, Gregory, and Synge were three of the great dramatists of this century. But they did not act alone. Like every other of the numerous Dublin theaters of the Celtic Revival, the Abbey was built up from the talents and efforts of many individuals and groups.

For almost every idea of a nation in Ireland at the turn of the century, there was an idea of a theater. To recover the diversity of ideologies and practices during the early years of the Irish dramatic movement is to discover new potencies within it, for these dramas were not merely nationalist assertions of a unified idea of Irish culture, but intranational debates about culture and identity being invented and enacted on Ireland's nationalist stages.

APPENDIX

REFERENCES

INDEX

A Timeline of Political and Theatrical Events in Ireland

1861   Dion Boucicault's Irish melodrama *The Colleen Bawn* performed in Dublin. Begins a trend of "alternative" stage Irishmen performed on the Irish popular stage.

1883   J. W. Whitbread becomes manager of Queen's Royal Theatre. Nationalist melodramas with titles such as *The Famine, Wolfe Tone,* and *For the Land She Loved* performed at Queen's for decades to come.

1884   Gaelic Athletic Association formed in County Tipperary. The group promotes the playing of Irish games—i.e., Irish football and hurling—and forbids its members to play English games. Branches spring up across Ireland and are closely watched by British officials.

1890   W. G. Fay—the "father" of the Abbey style of acting, a method promoting naturalness on the stage that would influence the Little Theatre movement in the United States—travels across Ireland with Lacy's Theatrical Company and learns the basics of scene design and marketing.

Douglas Hyde publishes *Beside the Fire*, a collection of Irish folktales.

Fall of Charles S. Parnell from his position as leader of the Home Rule Party, after he is named in the divorce proceedings of Katherine O'Shea.

1891   Irish Literary Society formed in London.

Parnell dies.

1892   W. B. Yeats and Douglas Hyde form Dublin's National Irish Literary Society, one of the most significant intellectual organizations surrounding the Irish revival.

Hyde's speech "The Necessity for De-Anglicising Ireland" creates wellspring of support for Gaelic revival.

1893   Hyde publishes *Love Songs of Connacht;* Yeats publishes *The Celtic Twilight.*

Second Home Rule Bill passes House of Commons, fails in House of Lords.

Douglas Hyde, Eugene O'Growney, and John (Eoin) MacNeill form the Gaelic League to promote the proliferation of Irish language and culture, and it soon spreads across Ireland. Significant part of Gaelic League activity includes nationwide festivals where Irish songs, dances, and recitations are performed. Tableaux and one-act plays also in Gaelic League festival repertoire.

Gaelic League sponsors *oireachtas* in Dublin every August—a week-long event of concerts, speeches, dances, contests, and dramatic performances. Smaller events, festivals, concerts, and performances occur at other times of the year throughout Ireland.

1894   Yeats's play *The Land of Heart's Desire* produced at the Avenue Theatre, London, along with G. B. Shaw's *Arms and the Man.* The production funded in part by an anonymous patron, Annie Horniman, who later funds the Abbey Theatre.

Irish Agricultural Organizational Society founded by Horace Plunkett.

1895   Tories take power in English Parliament.

1897   United Irish League founded by William O'Brien.

W. B. Yeats, Lady Gregory, George Moore, and Edward Martyn send out letter asking for subscriptions to support founding the Irish Literary Theatre.

1898   In protest of English imperial presence in Ireland during Queen Victoria's jubilee, W. B. Yeats, Maud Gonne, Arthur Griffith, James Connolly, and others carry a coffin labeled "The British Empire" through the streets of Dublin. When police confront them on a bridge, they throw the coffin into the River Liffey.

The Passing of Conall produced at Aonach Tir Conaill, Letterkenny. The drama includes one scene in Irish.

J. W. Whitbread produces his play *Wolfe Tone* at the Queen's Royal Theatre.

Douglas Hyde and Norma Borthwick perform a Punch and Judy show in Irish at a party for local children at Lady Gregory's Coole Park.

Local Government Act puts municipal and county power in hands of elective county councils—a limited form of home rule.

British prime minister William Gladstone dies.

1899   The Irish Literary Theatre gives its first season. One of the first productions, *The Countess Cathleen,* inspires vitriolic attacks on what many nationalists see as an anti-Catholic bias in the work.

Arthur Griffith and William Rooney found the Irish nationalist newspaper the *United Irishman.*

Frank J. Fay, W. G. Fay's brother, is the theater critic for the *United Irishman.* Among his aesthetic pronouncements for the national theater, Fay calls for (1) a natural acting style and (2) the use of Irish actors in national drama.

Queen's Royal performs benefit performance of *Wolfe Tone* to raise money for William Rooney memorial fund.

Somerville and Ross (Edith Somerville and Violet Martin) publish *Some Experiences of an Irish RM.*

Irish Transvaal Committee forms, supporting the Boers in the Boer War.

1900   A group of women organize a nationalist Children's Treat. Twenty thousand children attend, along with six marching bands, noted nationalist speakers, and dozens of nationalist volunteers. The success of the event leads the women to form a permanent organization, Inghinidhe na hEireann (Daughters of Erin).

Inghinidhe na hEireann hires W. G. Fay to teach its members elocution and acting and to help direct some of their plays.

The Irish Literary Theatre produces Alice Milligan's *Last Feast of the Fianna,* along with Moore's *The Bending of the Bough* and Edward Martyn's *Maeve.*

Gaelic League forms a campaign to force the British postal service to accept and deliver any piece of postage addressed in the Irish language.

Cumann na nGaedheal is founded, a nationalist organization designed to promote political and cultural unity in Ireland.

Douglas Hyde and the Gaelic League take on Trinity College, Dublin, dons who denigrate the study of Irish language and literature in the schools and universities.

1901   George Moore of the Irish Literary Theatre hires W. G. Fay to direct the Irish Literary Theatre production of Douglas Hyde's play in Irish *The Twisting of the Rope*. Play performed by members of the Keating Branch of the Gaelic League. They also produced Moore and Yeats's *Diarmuid and Grania*. After these productions, the Irish Literary Theatre disbands.

The Fays, Inghinidhe na hEireann, Russell, and Yeats decide to collaborate on a production in the spring of 1902.

J. W. Whitbread announces a play contest at the Queen's Royal Theatre for a drama on an Irish theme by an Irish playwright.

1902   The Irish National Dramatic Company performs *Deirdre* and *Kathleen ni Houlihan*. The production is such a success that they produce the plays again, along with others, at the Cumann na nGaedheal festival in October.

The Post-Bag: A Lesson in Irish, a one-act operetta by Alfred Graves and Michele Esposito, performed.

Lady Gregory publishes *Cuchulain of Muirthemne*.

John Eglinton's essay "The De-Davisisation of Irish Literature" appears.

1903   Irish National Theatre Society formed; Yeats is elected president, although he is not present at the discussion regarding the group's formation. Among its first plays are Synge's *The Shadow of the Glen* and Colum's *Broken Soil*.

Inghinidhe na hEireann members perform Padraic Colum's *The Saxon Shillin'*.

1904   Land Purchase Act passes, allowing tenants an opportunity to buy their farms.

Ulster Literary Theatre formed in Belfast on Irish National Theatre Society model. They produce Bulmer Hobson's *Brian of Banba* and Lewis Purcell's *The Reformers* in Belfast.

Annie Horniman gives subsidy for Irish National Theatre Society to move into the Abbey Theatre. Patent taken out in Lady Gregory's name. Arguments arise within the democratically structured company over the ways in which plays are chosen. Maud Gonne resigns from society when it refuses to produce *The Saxon Shillin'*. Gonne likes the politics of the play, but Yeats insists that it is "bad art." The actor Dudley Digges and his wife leave the company when it insists on producing Synge's *Shadow of the Glen*. Among plays produced this year are Yeats's *The Shadowy Waters* and Synge's *Riders to the Sea*.

Dudley Digges and Maire Quinn leave the Irish National Theatre Society and go to the United States to perform at the St. Louis Exhibition. They raise Yeats's furor when they are billed as being from the Irish National Theatre Society.

Lady Gregory publishes *Gods and Fighting Men*.

Trinity College, Dublin, matriculates women.

1905   Yeats stages a "coup" that shifts administrative authority into the hands of the directors (Yeats, Gregory, and Synge), effectively making the (still nationalist) actors hired workers. In protest, a coterie of the actors, including Maire Nic Shiubhlaigh, leaves the now-named National Theatre Society, Ltd.

D. P. Moran publishes *The Philosophy of Irish Ireland*.

Arthur Griffith founds the separatist National Council; Edward Martyn made president.

Dungannon Clubs, Irish separatist groups, founded by Irish Republican Brotherhood members Denis McCullough and Bulmer Hobson.

1906   Theatre of Ireland formed from dissident Irish National Theatre Society actors. Edward Martyn becomes their president. Their first performance occurs in August at the Gaelic League festival in Dublin.

Seamas MacManus's *Orange and Green* performed by the National Players.

Abbey stages William Boyle's first-produced play, *The Eloquent Dempsey*.

The liberals regain the English Parliament, but home rule remains at the bottom of the agenda.

1907   The Abbey Theatre production of *The Playboy of the Western World* causes a riot. Yeats calls in the police to clear protestors from the theater. Other significant Abbey dramas that year include Lady Gregory's *The Rising of the Moon* and George Fitzmaurice's *The Country Dressmaker*.

J. W. Whitbread retires from Queen's Royal after twenty-four years as manager.

1908   The Fays leave the Abbey. Significant Abbey productions include W. F. Casey's *The Man Who Missed the Tide,* Lady Gregory's adaptation of Molière's *The Rogueries of Scapin,* and Thomas MacDonagh's *When the Dawn Is Come.*

Sinn Fein is formed through a merger of such nationalist groups as the Dungannon Clubs, Cumann na nGaedheal, and the National Council.

Cork Dramatic Society founded.

Independent Dramatic Company founded.

Ulster Literary Theatre performs for the first time on the Abbey stage.

Jim Larkin founds the Irish Transport and General Workers Union.

Francis Sheehy-Skeffington and Margaret Cousins found the Irish Women's Franchise League.

Padraic Pearse founds St. Enda's School for Boys.

1909   P. J. Bourke takes over management of the Queen's Royal Theatre.

J. M. Synge dies; Cork dramatist Lennox Robinson replaces him as an Abbey director.

The Theatre of Ireland performs perhaps its most famous production, Seamas O'Kelly's *The Shuiler's Child.* Also that year, the theater produces Rev. Thomas O'Kelly's Irish-language version of *Deirdre.*

Abbey Theatre produces G. B. Shaw's *The Shewing-Up of Blanco Posnet,* a play banned by the British censor.

St. Enda's students perform plays by Standish O'Grady and Douglas Hyde before a distinguished nationalist audience on the school grounds.

Cork Dramatic Society produces T. C. Murray's *Wheel of Fortune* and Lennox Robinson's *The Lesson of Life.*

National University of Ireland founded. This university and the Queen's University, Belfast, agree to matriculate women.

Bulmer Hobson and Con Markiewicz found the Fianna Fail, an Irish equivalent of the Boy Scouts, only with a strong streak of Irish nationalism.

1910   Edward VII dies. When the Abbey stays open the day of his death, Annie Horniman withdraws her involvement with the theater.

Casimir Markiewicz's play *The Memory of the Dead: A Romantic Drama of '98* performed by the Independent Dramatic Company.

Padraic Pearse's *Iosagan* and Colum's *The Destruction of the Hostel* performed at St. Enda's School.

Theatre of Ireland produces first productions of Gerald MacNamara's *The Spurious Sovereign* and Seamus O'Kelly's *The Homecoming*.

Important Abbey productions include Synge's *Deirdre of the Sorrows* and Yeats's *The Green Helmet*.

Sir Edward Carson elected president of the Ulster Unionists.

1911   Padraic Pearse's Passion Play performed by St. Enda's students at Abbey Theatre.

George Moore publishes *Hail and Farewell*.

Jim Larkin founds the newspaper the *Irish Worker*.

Irish Women's Suffrage Federation formed.

British Parliament abolishes the House of Lords veto, increasing the power of the House of Commons and making more likely the chance of Ireland gaining independence through Parliament.

1912   St. Enda's students perform Tagore's *The Post Office* and Pearse's *The King* at the Abbey Theatre.

St. John Ervine's *The Magnanimous Lover* produced by the Abbey.

Thomas Macdonagh's *Metempsychosis* and Lewis Purcell's *The Reformers* produced by Theatre of Ireland.

Solemn League and Covenant Oath signed by 250,000 Protestants in Ulster, announcing their opposition to Irish home rule.

Ulster demonstration at Balmoral, a suburb of Belfast, includes 100,000 men saluting a giant British flag.

The Home Rule Bill once again appears before the British Parliament. With the House of Lords veto abolished, it seems probable that it will pass.

1913   P. J. Bourke's *When Wexford Rose* at the Queen's Royal Theatre.

G. B. Shaw's *John Bull's Other Island* produced by the Dublin Repertory Theatre.

Abbey Theatre produces St. John Ervine's *The Magnanimous Lover,* R. J. Ray's *The Gombeen Man,* and George Fitzmaurice's *The Magic Glasses,* among other plays.

Ulster Volunteers founded—100,000 men.

Irish Volunteers founded in response to Ulster Volunteers activity.

Larkin calls a strike of the Irish Transport and General Workers Union. The Dublin lockout begins.

A warrant out for his arrest, Larkin hides out at Con Markiewicz's home and leaks out word that he will appear on O'Connell Street to give a speech. He does manage to say a few words on a balcony at the Imperial Hotel before police drag him away. The crowd present to hear him begin to riot. Four hundred injured, one killed.

Irish Citizen Army formed by James Connolly to protect workers from police.

Con Markiewicz and other women start feeding the families of striking workers from the kitchen of the basement at Liberty Hall.

Carson moves an amendment to the Home Rule Bill that would exclude all nine counties of Ulster.

1914   The Irish Women's Franchise League produces Francis Sheehy-Skeffington's *The Prodigal Daughter.*

St. John Ervine's *The Orangeman* produced at the Abbey Theatre.

The Irish Theatre Company produces Edward Martyn's *The Dream Physician.*

Cumann na mBan (the Women's Association) formed.

Guns landed for Ulster Volunteers at Larne.

Guns landed for Irish Volunteers at Howth. Following the landing, ecstatic nationalists celebrate at Bachelor's Walk, taunting police. Three persons killed by soldiers.

Home Rule Bill finally passes, but law suspended until the end of World War I. Home rule soon becomes lost in the confusion and horror of the Great War, creating nervousness and itchy trigger fingers among militant Irish nationalists.

1915   St. John Ervine becomes Abbey Theatre manager. Company produces his play *John Ferguson.*

Irish Theatre Company produces Thomas MacDonagh's *Pagans,* Anton Chekov's *Uncle Vanya,* and John MacDonagh's spoof on Irish peasant plays *Author! Author!* among other plays.

Irish Theatre Company produces *Fe Bhrig na Mionn* (The Troth) by Rutherford Mayne, translated by Liam O Domhnaill.

Dail Eireann founded—alternative municipal government for Irish nationalists.

Padraic Pearse's graveside panegyric for O'Donovan Rossa enflames the spirit of the Irish Republican Brotherhood and other militant nationalist groups.

Roger Casement in Germany, trying to recruit for the Irish rebellion any Irish soldiers who had been imprisoned in German POW camps while fighting for England.

1916   Yeats's *At the Hawk's Well* performed in Lady Cunard's London home.

Abbey Theatre produces Lennox Robinson's *The Whiteheaded Boy* and a series of Shaw plays, among other works.

Irish Theatre Company produces August Strindberg's *Easter* one month before the Easter Rebellion.

The Easter Rebellion begins Easter Monday. Padraic Pearse, the president of the Provisional Irish Republic, reads the Proclamation from the steps of Dublin's General Post Office. Members of the Irish Volunteers, the Irish Citizen Army, and Cumann na mBan take over several positions in Dublin. The first person killed fighting, Sean Connolly, was an actor for the Abbey Theatre. Five days later, the rebels surrender. Much Dublin property looted and destroyed, and civilian and military lives lost. The British methodically retaliate after the surrender by executing almost all the leaders. Con Markiewicz's death sentence is commuted because she is a woman.

References

Archival Sources

Harvard Theatre Collection, Harvard University, Cambridge, Massachusetts
  George Roberts Papers Relating to the Abbey Theatre and the Irish National Theatre Society.

SUNY Stony Brook, Stony Brook, New York
  The William Butler Yeats Collection at SUNY Stony Brook.

National Library of Ireland, Dublin, Ireland
  Abbey Theatre Papers, mss. 19,844–19,845.
  The Fay Papers, ms. 10,950.
  The Holloway Papers, ms. 22,404.
  Minutes of the Theatre of Ireland, ms. 7,388.

Pearse Museum, Dublin, Ireland
  Documents, journals, books, and photographs from the collection of the museum.

Microfilm and Microfiche Sources

The Annie Horniman Collection in the John Rylands Library of the University of Manchester. Theatre History Series, no. 1. Fiche 1–77. Manchester: Emmett, 1989.
Irish Political and Radical Newspapers of the Twentieth Century. Dublin: Irish Microforms, 1987.

J. M. Synge Manuscripts from the Library of Trinity College, Dublin. Brighton, Sussex: Harvestor Microform, 1987.

Scrapbooks of W. A. Henderson, 1899–1911, from the National Library of Ireland, Dublin. *The Abbey Theatre and Cultural Life*. Reading, Berkshire, England: Research Publications (microform), 1989.

Newspapers and Journals Contemporary to the Period

The Arrow (London)

Beltaine (Dublin)

Daily Express (Dublin)

Irish Figaro (Dublin)

Freeman's Journal (Dublin)

Irish People (Dublin)

Irish Playgoer (Dublin)

Irish Times (Dublin)

Leader (Dublin)

Leprechaun (Dublin)

An Macaomh (Dublin)

The Nation (London)

Punch (London)

Samhain (Dublin)

Sinn Fein (Dublin)

Shan Van Vocht (Belfast)

Times (London and Dublin)

United Irishman (Dublin)

Published Sources

Allen, Michael, and Angela Wilcox, ed. 1989. *Critical Approaches to Anglo-Irish Literature*. Totowa, N.J.: Barnes and Noble.

Alloula, Malek. 1986. *The Colonial Harem*. Translated by Myrna Godzich and Wlad Godzich. Minneapolis: Univ. of Minnesota Press.

Anderson, Benedict. 1992. *Imagined Communities: Reflections on the Origin and Spread of Nationalism*. Rev. ed. London: Verso.

Anonymous. 1996. *Primary Colors*. New York: Norton.

Arnold, Matthew. 1867. *On the Study of Celtic Literature*. London: Smith, Elder.

Beckett, J. C. 1981. *The Making of Modern Ireland: 1603–1923*. London: Faber and Faber.

Bell, Sam Hanna. 1972. *The Theatre in Ulster: A Survey of the Dramatic Movement in Ulster from 1902 until the Present Day*. Dublin: Gill and MacMillan.

Bennett, Susan. 1990. *Theatre Audiences: A Theory of Production and Reception*. New York: Routledge.

Benson, F. R. 1933. *My Memoirs*. London: Sir Isaac Pitman and Sons.

Bhabha, Homi K. 1986. "Signs Taken for Wonders: Questions of Ambivalence and Authority under a Tree Outside Delhi, May 1817." In *"Race," Writing, and Difference,* edited by Henry Louis Gates Jr. Chicago: Univ. of Chicago Press.

———. 1990. *Nation and Narration*. New York: Routledge.

Booth, Michael. 1991. *Theatre in the Victorian Age*. Cambridge: Cambridge Univ. Press.

Boucicault, Dion. 1984. *Plays by Dion Boucicault*. Edited by Peter Thomson. Cambridge: Cambridge Univ. Press.

———. n.d. *The Colleen Bawn or the Brides of Garryowen*. French's Standard Drama, Acting Edition, no. 366. New York: French.

Bourke, P. J. 1959. *Kathleen Mavourneen*. Adapted by Seamas de Burca. Dublin: P. J. Bourke.

———. 1991. *For the Land She Loved*. In *For the Land They Loved: Irish Political Melodrama, 1890–1925,* edited by Cheryl Herr. Syracuse, N.Y.: Syracuse Univ. Press.

Boyce, D. George. 1982. *Nationalism in Ireland*. London: Croom Helma.

Boyle, William. n.d.a. *The Building Fund*. A Playscript, Fay Collection, ms. 10,950, National Library of Ireland, Dublin.

———. n.d.b. *The Eloquent Dempsy: A Comedy in Three Acts*. Dublin: M. H. Gill and Son.

Cairns, David, and Shaun Richards. 1988. *Writing Ireland: Colonialism, Nationalism, and Culture*. New York: St. Martin's.

Cardozo, Nancy. 1978. *Lucky Eyes and a High Heart: The Life of Maud Gonne*. New York: Bobbs-Merrill.

Chaudhuri, Una. 1995. *Staging Place: The Geography of Modern Drama*. Ann Arbor: Univ. of Michigan Press.

Cluithceoiri na h'Eireann. 1906. Dublin: n.p.

Colum, Padraic. 1902. "The Saxon Shillin'." *United Ireland,* 15 November, 3.

———. 1972. "Life in a World of Writers." In *A Paler Shade of Green,* edited by Des Hickey and Gus Smith. London: Leslie Frewin.

———. 1986. *Selected Plays.* Edited by Sanford Sternlicht. Syracuse, N.Y.: Syracuse Univ. Press.

———. 1988. "Early Days of the Irish Theatre." In *The Abbey Theatre: Interviews and Recollections,* edited by E. H. Mikhail. London: MacMillan.

Connolly, Sean. 1987. *Religion and Society in Nineteenth-Century Ireland.* West Tempest: Dandalgan.

Corish, Patrick. 1986. *The Irish Catholic Experience.* Dublin: Gill and MacMillan.

Courtney, Sister Marie-Therese. 1952. *Edward Martyn and the Irish Theatre.* New York: Vintage.

Cousins, J. H., and Margaret Cousins. 1950. *We Two Together.* Madras: Ganesh.

Cullingford, Elizabeth. 1981. *Yeats, Ireland, and Fascism.* London: MacMillan.

Curtis, L. Perry. 1971. *Apes and Angels: The Irishman in Victorian Caricature.* Washington, D.C.: Smithsonian Institution Press.

Dalsimer, Adele M. 1981. "Players in the Western World: The Abbey Theatre's American Tours." *Eire-Ireland: A Journal of Irish Studies* 16, no. 4: 75–93.

Davis, Tracy C. 1991. *Actresses as Working Women.* New York: Routledge.

Deane, Seamus. 1977. "The Literary Myths of the Revival: A Case for Their Abandonment." In *Myth and Reality in Irish Literature,* edited by Joseph Ronsley. Waterloo: Laurier Univ. Press.

———, ed. 1990. *Nationalism, Colonialism, and Literature.* Minneapolis: Univ. of Minnesota Press.

———, ed. 1991. *The Field Day Anthology of Irish Writing.* Vol. 2. Derry: Field Day.

de Burca, Seamus. 1983. *The Queen's Royal Theatre Dublin, 1829–1969.* Dublin: S. de Burca.

Delaney, Barry. 1896. "Maud Gonne." *Shan Van Vocht,* 7 February, 33.

Dieltjens, Louis. 1988. "The Abbey Theatre as Cultural Formation." In *History and Violence in Anglo-Irish Literature,* edited by Joris Duytschaever and Geert Lernout. Amsterdam: Rodopi.

Digges, Dudley. 1988. "A Theatre Was Made." In *The Abbey Theatre: Interviews and Recollections,* edited by E. H. Mikhail. London: MacMillan.

Dorn, Karen. 1984. *Players and Painted Stage: The Theatre of W. B. Yeats*. Totowa, N.J.: Barnes and Noble.

Duggan, G. C. 1968. *The Stage Irishman*. New York: Benjamin Blom.

Dunleavy, Janet Egleson, and Gareth W. Dunleavy. 1991. *Douglas Hyde: A Maker of Modern Ireland*. Berkeley: Univ. of California Press.

Eagleton, Terry. 1990. *The Ideology of the Aesthetic*. Cambridge: Basil Blackwell.

Edwards, Ruth Dudley. 1977. *Patrick Pearse: The Triumph of Failure*. London: Victor Gollancz.

Ellmann, Richard. 1979. *Yeats: The Man and the Masks*. New York: Norton.

Enloe, Cynthia. 1990. *Bananas, Beaches, and Bases: Making Feminist Sense of International Politics*. Berkeley: Univ. of California Press.

Etherton, Michael. 1989. *Contemporary Irish Dramatists*. New York: St. Martin's.

Fanon, Franz. 1963. *The Wretched of the Earth*. New York: Grove.

Fawkes, Richard. 1979. *Dion Boucicault: A Biography*. London: Quartet.

Fay, Frank J. 1899. "Irish Drama at the Queen's Theatre." *United Irishman*, 30 December, 7.

———. 1970. *Towards a National Theatre: The Dramatic Criticism of Frank J. Fay*. Edited by Robert Hogan. Dublin: Dolmen.

Fay, William G., and Catherine Carswell. 1935. *The Fays of the Abbey Theatre: An Autobiographical Record*. New York: Harcourt Brace.

Field Day Theatre Company. 1985. *Ireland's Field Day*. London: Hutchinson.

Fitzgerald, Mary Margaret. 1973. "The Dominant Partnership: W. B. Yeats and Lady Gregory in the Early Irish Theatre." Ph.D. diss., Princeton Univ.

Fitz-Simon, Christopher. 1983. *The Irish Theatre*. London: Thames and Hudson.

Flannery, James W. 1976. *W. B. Yeats and the Idea of a Theatre*. New Haven: Yale.

———. 1982. "High Ideals and the Reality of the Marketplace: A Financial Record of the Early Abbey Theatre." *Studies: An Irish Quarterly Review* 71: 246–69.

Foster, R. F. 1988. *Modern Ireland*. New York: Penguin.

———. 1998. *W. B. Yeats: A Life*. Oxford: Oxford Univ. Press.

Frazier, Adrian. 1987. "The Making of Meaning: Yeats and *The Countess Cathleen*." *Sewanee Review* 95, no. 3: 451–69.

———. 1990. *Behind the Scenes: Yeats, Horniman, and the Struggle for the Abbey Theatre*. Berkeley: Univ. of California Press.

Garvin, Tom. 1987. *Nationalist Revolutionaries in Ireland: 1858–1928.* Oxford: Clarendon.

Gates, Henry Louis, Jr., ed. 1986. *"Race," Writing, and Difference.* Chicago: Univ. of Chicago Press.

Genet, Jacqueline, and Richard Allen Cave, eds. 1991. *Perspectives of Irish Drama and Theatre.* Gerrards Cross, Ireland: Colin Smythe.

Goldring, Maurice. 1993. *Pleasant the Scholar's Life: Irish Intellectuals and the Construction of the Nation State.* London: Serif.

Gonne MacBride, Maud. 1974. *A Servant of the Queen.* London: Victor Gollancz.

Gregory, Lady Augusta. 1913. *Our Irish Theatre.* New York: G. P. Putnam's Sons.

———. 1970. *Cuchulain of Muirthemne.* New York: Oxford Univ. Press.

———. 1983. *Selected Plays.* Edited by Mary FitzGerald. Washington, D.C.: Catholic Univ. of America Press.

———. 1996. *Selected Writings.* Edited by Lucy McDiarmid and Maureen Waters. London: Penguin.

Gwynn, Denis. 1930. *Edward Martyn and the Irish Revival.* London: Jonathan Cape.

Gwynn, Steven. 1903. *To-day and To-morrow in Ireland.* Dublin: Hodges, Figgis.

Harrington, John P. 1997. *The Irishman on the New York Stage.* Lexington: Univ. of Kentucky Press.

Harris, Claudia W. 1988. "The Martyr-Wish in Contemporary Irish Dramatic Literature." In *Cultural Contexts and Literary Idioms in Contemporary Irish Literature,* edited by Michael Kenneally. Totowa, N.J.: Barnes and Noble.

Herr, Cheryl. 1990. "The Erotics of Irishness." *Critical Inquiry* 17 (autumn): 1–34.

———, ed. 1991. *For the Land They Loved: Irish Political Melodrama, 1890–1925.* Syracuse, N.Y.: Syracuse Univ. Press.

Hickey, Des, and Gus Smith, eds. 1972. *A Paler Shade of Green.* London: Leslie Frewin.

Hobsbawm, E. J. 1991. *Nations and Nationalism Since 1780: Programme, Myth, Reality.* New York: Cambridge Univ. Press.

Hobsbawm, Eric, and Terence Ranger, eds. 1983. *The Invention of Tradition.* New York: Cambridge Univ. Press.

Hogan, Robert, Richard Burnham, and Daniel P. Poteet. 1978. *The Abbey The-*

atre: The Years of Synge, 1905–1909. Atlantic Highlands, Monmouth: Dolmen.

———. 1984. *The Rise of the Realists: 1910–1915*. Atlantic Highlands, Monmouth: Dolmen.

Hogan, Robert, and James Kilroy. 1975. *The Irish Literary Theatre: 1898–1901*. Atlantic Highlands, Monmouth: Dolmen.

———. 1976. *Laying the Foundations: 1902–1904*. Atlantic Highlands, Monmouth: Dolmen.

Holloway, Joseph. 1967. *Joseph Holloway's Abbey Theatre*. Edited by Robert Hogan and Michael J. O'Neill. Carbondale: Southern Illinois Univ. Press.

Horniman, Annie. 1904. "Miss Horniman's Offer of Theatre and Society's Acceptance." *Samhain* (December): 53.

Hunt, Hugh. 1979. *The Abbey: Ireland's National Theatre: 1904–1978*. New York: Columbia Univ. Press.

Hutchinson, John. 1987. *The Dynamics of Cultural Nationalism*. London: Allen and Unwin.

———. 1994. "The Dynamics of Cultural Nationalism." In *Nationalism*, edited by John Hutchinson and Anthony D. Smith. Oxford: Oxford Univ. Press.

Hyde, Douglas. 1991. *The Twisting of the Rope*. In *Selected Plays of Douglas Hyde, with Translations by Lady Gregory*, edited by Gareth W. Dunleavy and Janet Egleson Dunleavy. Washington, D.C.: Catholic Univ. of America Press.

Inghinidhe na h'Eireann. 1901. *Inghinidhe na h'Eireann First Annual Report*. Dublin: O'Brien and Ards.

Innes, C. L. 1993. *Woman and Nation in Irish Literature and Society: 1880–1935*. Athens: Univ. of Georgia Press.

"Irial" [Fred Ryan]. 1901. "Has the Irish Literary Theatre Failed?" *United Irishman*, 9 November, 3.

[Irish National Theatre Society]. 1903. *Irish National Theatre Society [Statement of Aims]*. N.p.: n.p.

JanMohamed, Abdul R. 1983. *Manichean Aesthetics: The Politics of Literature in Colonial Africa*. Amherst: Univ. of Massachusetts Press.

Jeffares, A. Norman. 1989. *Yeats: A New Biography*. New York: Farrar, Straus, Giroux.

Joy, Maurice. 1904. "The Irish National Theatre." *Speaker*, 24 December.

Kee, Robert. 1972. *The Green Flag: The Bold Fenian Men*. New York: Penguin.

Keeler, Chester William. 1973. "The Abbey Theatre and the Brothers Fay: An

Examination and Assessment of the Influence of the Theatrical Practice of the Irish National Theatre Society and the National Theatre Society, Limited, upon the Irish Dramatic Movement, 1902–1903." Ph.D. diss. Univ. of California, Santa Barbara.

Kenneally, Michael. 1989. "The Autobiographical Imagination in the Irish Literary Autobiographies." In *Critical Approaches to Anglo-Irish Literature,* edited by Michael Allen and Angela Wilcox. Totowa, N.J.: Barnes and Noble.

Kiberd, Declan. 1995. *Inventing Ireland: The Literature of the Modern Nation.* Cambridge, Mass.: Harvard Univ. Press.

Kinsella, Thomas. 1989. *Myth, History, and Literary Tradition.* Dundalk, Ireland: Dundalk Arts.

Kosok, Heinz. 1988. "John Bull's Other Ego: Reactions to the Stage Irishman in Anglo-Irish Drama." In *Medieval and Modern Ireland,* edited by Richard Wall. Totowa, N.J.: Barnes and Noble.

———. 1991. "The Image of Ireland in Nineteenth-Century Drama." In *Perspectives of Irish Drama and Theatre,* edited by Jacqueline Genet and Richard Allen Cave. Gerrards Cross, Ireland: Colin Smythe.

Krause, David. 1982. *The Profane Book of Irish Comedy: An Irreverent Look at Fourteen Irish Dramatists.* Ithaca: Cornell Univ. Press.

Kruger, Loren. 1992. *The National Stage: Theatre and Cultural Legitimation in England, France, and America.* Chicago: Univ. of Chicago Press.

Laity, Cassandra. 1985. "W. B. Yeats and Florence Farr: The Influence of the 'New Woman' Actress on Yeats's Changing Images of Women." *Modern Drama* 28, no. 4: 620–37.

Larkin, Emmett. 1984. *The Historical Dimensions of Irish Catholicism.* Washington, D.C.: Catholic Univ. of America Press.

Lee, Joseph. 1973. *The Modernisation of Irish Society: 1848–1918.* Dublin: Gill and MacMillan.

Lloyd, David. 1993. *Anomolous States: Irish Writing and the Post-Colonial Moment.* Durham, N.C.: Duke Univ. Press.

Lyons, F. S. L. 1971. *Ireland Since the Famine.* London: Weidenfeld and Nicolson.

———. 1979. *Culture and Anarchy in Ireland: 1890–1939.* New York: Oxford Univ. Press.

MacDonagh, Oliver, W. F. Mandle, and Paudric Travers, eds. 1983. *Irish Culture and Nationalism: 1750–1950.* New York: St. Martin's.

Maguire Colum, Mary. 1966. *Life and the Dream.* Dublin: Dolmen.

Martyn, Edward. 1899. *The Heather Field and Maeve.* Introduction by George Moore. London: Duckworth.

———. 1969. *A Tale of the Town.* In Irish Drama Series, vol. 3, edited by William J. Feeney. Chicago: DePaul Univ. Press.

Mason, Jeffrey D. 1993. *Melodrama and the Myth of America.* Bloomington: Indiana Univ. Press.

Maxwell, D. E. S. 1984. *A Critical History of Modern Irish Drama: 1891–1980.* Cambridge: Cambridge Univ. Press.

McConachie, Bruce A. 1989. "Using the Concept of Cultural Hegemony to Write Theatre History." In *Interpreting the Theatrical Past: Essays in the Historiography of Performance,* edited by Thomas Postlewaite and Bruce A. McConachie. Iowa City: Univ. of Iowa Press.

———. 1992. *Melodramatic Formations: American Theatre and Society, 1820–1870.* Iowa City: Univ. of Iowa Press.

Miller, Liam. 1977. *The Noble Drama of W. B. Yeats.* Atlantic Highlands, Monmouth: Humanities.

Milligan, Alice. 1900. *The Last Feast of the Fianna: A Dramatic Legend.* London: D. Nutt.

———. 1967. *The Last Feast of the Fianna.* In *"Maeve" and "The Last Feast of the Fianna."* Irish Drama Series, vol. 2, edited by William J. Feeney. Chicago: De Paul Univ. Press.

Moonan, George A. 1900. "The Movement in Dublin: Annual Report of the Central Branch." *An Claidheam Soluis* (16 June): 215.

Moore, George. 1900. *The Bending of the Bough.* Chicago: Herbert Stone.

———. 1985. *Hail and Farewell.* Edited by Richard Allen Cave. Washington, D.C.: Catholic Univ. of America Press.

Moran, Sean Farrell. 1994. *Patrick Pearse and the Politics of Redemption: The Mind of the Easter Rising, 1916.* Washington, D.C.: Catholic Univ. of America Press.

Murphy, Cliona. 1989. *The Women's Suffrage Movement and Irish Society in the Early Twentieth Century.* Philadelphia: Temple Univ. Press.

Murphy, John A. 1975. *Ireland in the Twentieth Century.* Dublin: Gill and MacMillan.

Nandy, Asish. 1983. *The Intimate Enemy: Loss and Recovery of Self under Colonialism.* Delhi: Oxford Univ. Press.

[National Theatre Society, Ltd.]. n.d. *Rules of the National Theatre Society, Ltd.* Dublin: Cahill.

Nelson, James Malcolm. 1978. "From Rory and Paddy to Boucicault's Myles,

Shaun, and Conn: The Irishman on the London Stage, 1830–1860." *Eire-Ireland* 13, no. 3 (fall): 79–105.

Nic Shiubhlaigh, Maire, with Edward Kenny. 1955. *The Splendid Years.* Dublin: James Duffy.

O'Casey, Sean. 1949. *Inishfallen Fare Thee Well.* New York: MacMillan.

O'Connor, Ulick. 1984. *Celtic Dawn.* London: Hamish Hamilton.

O'Donnell, F. Hugh. 1899. *Souls for Gold.* London: Nassau.

O'Driscoll, Robert, ed. 1971. *Theatre and Nationalism in Twentieth-Century Ireland.* Toronto: Univ. of Toronto Press.

O'Grady, Hubert. 1985. *Emigration.* Edited by Stephen Watt. *Journal of Irish Literature* 14 (January): 14–25.

O hAoidha, Michael. 1974. *Theatre in Ireland.* Oxford: Basil Blackwell.

O'Neil, Daniel. 1987. "The Secularization of Religious Symbolism: The Irish Case." *International Journal of Social Economics* 14: 3–24.

Owens, Rosemary Cullen. 1984. *Smashing Times: A History of the Irish Women's Suffrage Movement, 1899–1922.* Dublin: Attic.

Pearse, Margaret, ed. 1934. *The Home-Life of Padraig Pearse.* Dublin: Browne and Nolan.

Pearse, Padraic. 1918. *The Singer and Other Plays.* Dublin: Maunsel.

———. 1967. *The Best of Pearse.* Edited by Proinsas Mac Aonghusa and Liam O Reagain. Cork: Mercier.

———. 1980. *The Letters of P. H. Pearse.* Edited by Seamas O'Buachalla. Gerrards Cross, Ireland: Colin Smythe.

[Pearse, Padraic]. n.d. *Prospectus for 1911–1912: Sgoil Eanna, St. Enda's College, Rathfarnham.* N.p.: n.p.

Pick, John. 1983. *The West End: Mismanagement and Snobbery.* Eastbourne, East Sussex: J. Offord.

Programme for Deirdre and Kathleen ni Houlihan. 1902. Dublin: n.p.

Rahill, Frank. 1967. *The World of Melodrama.* University Park: Pennsylvania State Univ. Press.

Renan, Ernest. 1897. *The Poetry of the Celtic Races.* Translated by W. G. Hutchinson. London: Walter Scott.

Reynolds, John J. 1902. "The Daughters of Erin." *Gael* (August): 258.

Robinson, Lennox. 1951. *Ireland's Abbey Theatre: A History, 1899–1951.* London: Sidgwick and Jackson.

———. 1995. "Women on the Threshold: J. M. Synge's *The Shadow of the Glen,* Teresa Deevy's *Katie Roche,* and Marina Carr's *The Mai.*" *Irish University Review* (spring-summer): 143–62.

Roche, Anthony. 1994. "Woman on the Threshold: J. M. Synge's *The Shadow of the Glen,* Teresa Deevy's *Katie Roche,* and Marina Carr's *The Mai.*" *Irish University Review* (winter): 142–62.

Rules of the National Theatre Society, Ltd. [1905]. Dublin: Cahill.

Russell, George. 1929. *Deirdre.* In *Plays of the Irish Renaissance: 1880–1930,* edited by Curtis Canfield. New York: Ives Washburn.

Ryan, Desmond. 1918. *The Story of a Success.* Dublin: Maunsel.

———. 1919. *The Man Called Pearse.* Dublin: Maunsel.

———. 1934. *Remembering Sion.* London: Arthur Barker.

Ryan, Mary P. 1990. *Women in Public: Between Banners and Ballots, 1825–1880.* Baltimore: Johns Hopkins Univ. Press.

Saddlemeyer, Ann, ed. 1982. *Theatre Business: The Correspondence of the First Abbey Theatre Directors: William Butler Yeats, Lady Gregory, and J. M. Synge.* Gerrards Cross, Ireland: Colin Smythe.

Saddlemeyer, Ann, and Colin Smythe, eds. 1987. *Lady Gregory: Fifty Years After.* Gerrards Cross, Ireland: Colin Smythe.

Schechner, Richard. 1988. *Performance Theory.* Rev. ed. New York: Routledge.

Sommer, Doris. 1990. "Irresistible Romance: the Foundational Fictions of Latin America." In *Nation and Narration,* edited by Homi Bhabha. New York: Routledge, 71–98.

Spain, Daphne. 1992. *Gendered Spaces.* Chapel Hill: Univ. of North Carolina Press.

Spurr, David. 1993. *The Rhetoric of Empire: Colonial Discourse in Journalism, Travel Writing, and Imperial Administration.* Durham, N.C.: Duke Univ. Press.

Synge, J. M. 1968. *The Playboy of the Western World.* In *The Plays and Poems of J. M. Synge,* edited by T. R. Henn. London: Methuen.

———. 1986. *The Playboy of the Western World and Riders to the Sea.* London: Unwin.

Tagore, Rabindranath. 1914. *The Post Office: A Play.* Translated by Devabrata Mukerjea. Dublin: Cuala.

Taussig, Michael. 1993. *Mimesis and Alterity.* New York: Routledge.

[Theatre of Ireland]. [1906]. *Cluithceoiri na h'Eireann.* N.p.: n.p.

Thompson, William Irwin. 1967. *The Imagination of an Insurrection: Dublin, Easter 1916.* West Stockbridge, Mass.: Lindisfarne.

Tickner, Lisa. 1988. *The Spectacle of Women: Imagery of the Suffrage Campaign, 1907–1914.* Chicago: Univ. of Chicago Press.

Ward, Margaret. 1983. *Unmanageable Revolutionaries: Women and Irish Nationalism*. London: Pluto.

———, ed. 1995. *In Their Own Voice: Women and Irish Nationalism*. Dublin: Attic.

Watt, Stephen. 1983. "Boucicault and Whitbread: The Dublin Stage at the End of the Nineteenth Century." *Eire-Ireland* 18, no. 3: 23–53.

———. 1985. "The Plays of Hubert O'Grady." *Journal of Irish Literature* 14 (January): 3–13.

———. 1991. *Joyce, O'Casey, and the Irish Popular Theatre*. Syracuse, N.Y.: Syracuse Univ. Press.

Whitbread, J. W. 1991. *Wolfe Tone*. In *For the Land They Loved: Irish Political Melodrama, 1890–1925*, edited by Cheryl Herr. Syracuse, N.Y.: Syracuse Univ. Press.

White, Terence Vere. 1988. "The Stage Irishman." In *Essays by Divers Hands: Being the Transactions of the Royal Society of Literature*, edited by Richard Faber. Wolfeboro, N.H.: Boydell.

Wilmer, Steve. 1991. "Women's Theatre in Ireland." *New Theatre Quarterly* 7, no. 28: 353–60.

Witoszek, Walentina, and Patrick F. Sheeran. 1988. "Irish Culture: The Desire for Transcendence." In *Cultural Contexts and Literary Idioms in Contemporary Irish Literature*, edited by Michael Kenneally. Totowa, N.J.: Barnes and Noble.

Worth, Katherine. 1986. *The Irish Drama of Europe from Yeats to Beckett*. London: Athlone.

Worthen, William B. 1987. "The Discipline of the Theatrical Sense: At the Hawk's Well and the Rhetoric of the Stage." *Modern Drama* 30: 90–103.

———. 1992. *Modern Drama and the Rhetoric of the Theatre*. Berkeley: Univ. of California Press.

Yeats, William Butler. 1914. Preface to *The Post Office: A Play*, by Rabindranath Tagore and translated by Devabrata Mukerjea. Dublin: Cuala.

———. 1923. *Plays and Controversies*. London: MacMillan.

———. 1936. *Dramatis Personae*. New York: MacMillan.

———. 1953. *The Collected Plays of W. B. Yeats*. New York: MacMillan.

———. 1961. *Essays and Introductions*. New York: MacMillan.

———. 1962. *Explorations*. New York: MacMillan.

———. 1966. *The Variorum Edition of the Plays of W.B. Yeats*. Edited by Russell K. Allspach. New York: MacMillan.

——. 1975. *Uncollected Prose by W. B. Yeats.* Vol. 2. Edited by J. P. Frayne and C. Johnson. New York: Columbia Univ. Press.

——. 1983. *The Collected Poems of William Butler Yeats.* Edited by Richard J. Finneran. New York: MacMillan.

"Yeats's Speech on Opening Night of Abbey." 1904. *Irish Daily Independent,* 28 December. Annie Horniman Collection, Press Cuttings, vol. 1, John Rylands Library, Univ. of Manchester.

Young, Ella. 1995. "Flowering Dusk." In *In Their Own Voice: Women and Irish Nationalism,* edited by Margaret Ward. Dublin: Attic.

Zach, Wolfgang, and Heinz Kosok, eds. 1987. *Literary Interrelations: Ireland, England, and the World.* 3 vols. Tübingen, Germany: Narr.

Index